The Hidden Truths to Spiritual Adulting

Published by Mindstir Media, LLC

45 Lafayette Rd | Suite 181| North Hampton, NH 03862 | USA

1.800.767.0531 | www.mindstirmedia.com

Printed in the United States of America

ISBN-13: 979-8-9856733-4-0

The Hidden Truths to Spiritual Adulting

How You're Guided by the Universe to Achieve Wholeness

Dr. Frances Yahia

MINDSTIR MEDIA

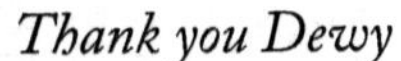

Thank you Dewy

Contents

Appendices/Images

Spiritual Adulting

INTRODUCTION

When my children were small, I was deathly afraid of sending them to middle school. I had heard that middle school is a wasteland where your children can easily end up in the wrong crowd. As a therapist, I understood developmental phases, adolescent storms, and Erikson's Stages of Psychosocial Development (especially regarding identity versus role confusion), but as a spiritual aspirant, I wasn't yet clear on what was in store for my kids. I am often perplexed that people think we only have a blueprint for physical growth, and that the Universe failed to provide us one for our spiritual and mental growth. There are obvious unknowns in what that blueprint contains, but we are more spiritually guided than we believe. We have not been dropped on this planet without guidance, cycles of growth, and a roadmap. Unfortunately, traditional Abrahamic religions have hidden universal laws and Hermetic philosophy and instead created a mythology (e.g., the Virgin Mary) that has left us confused and stuck in a particular story.

This book is written to clear up this confusion. It's for anyone interested in how the spiritual process, from birth to death, unfolds. It is also for anyone who is starting out on a spiritual path and needs some guidance. The principles in this book can also be integrated into an existing spiritual practice to fill in any gaps. Anyone seeking spiritual growth will benefit from this book.

What You Will Discover in this Book

The first few chapters discuss the first 14 years of life, which set the foundation for the years that follow and on which I focus the bulk of this book. Spiritual literature asserts that our karmic baggage is handed to us at 14. Prior to this, we are under our parental umbrella. At 14, we assume our own karma whether we address it or not. Often called "the adolescent storm," this is actually a karmic cycle that starts our spiritual adulting. Biologically, we grow into *physical* adults. However, most of us never grow into *spiritual* adults (Appendix I), mainly because we don't know how.

I will focus on two main universal laws: the Principle of Cause and Effect and the Principle of Rhythm. The first one is also known as *karma*. I will discuss the types of karma and how we create and burn karma in both this lifetime and others. These cycles travel from womb-to-tomb; you don't need to believe in "past lives" to gain insight from this principle. The Principle of Rhythm rules the spiritual cycles in our lifetime. Just as the seasons have set timeframes, so, too, do our cycles of karma and spiritual growth. I will address each key age range, how to identify the patterns in your life so you can more easily track them, and how to approach each age for attaining maximum spiritual growth. Many of the metaphors and examples I use are feminine or of women, but the process of spiritual adulting in the book applies to everyone.

I will use Greek mythology and other religious texts to demonstrate that all traditions and philosophies teach the same principles. At the same time, we have become so literal in how we translate these teachings that we lost sight of the language of the universe, which speaks to us through symbol, myth, and metaphor. I will also use the myth of Zeus and Themis ("goddess of justice") as the foundation of these teachings and discuss their relationship to other philosophies. I will discuss their philosophical "children," *The Horai*: Eunomia, Eirene and Dike, whose names mean "good order," "peace," and "justice," respectively. They are also known as Auxo, Carpo and Thallo, goddesses of the order or nature. They are in charge of the cycles of nature and the revolutions of the constellations. We are bound to these cycles, but we can use them to find peace, balance, and stability. *The Horai* are also proof that we are all divinely guided and that there is a spiritual timeclock, not just a biological one.

Jesus often spoke in parables related to seeds when referring to us and our spiritual lives. Similarly, *The Horai* relate to the conditions required at each age and stage for our "spiritual adulting." In my previous book, *The Seven Gates: Seven Steps Beyond Self-Awareness*, I focused on how to get out of the vicious cycle of "child," which is about trying to get your needs met by anyone other than yourself. In that book, I take you from child to teenager to adult, exposing that process and providing a process where you meet your own needs and develop self-accountability. In this book, I go beyond "adult" and into "spiritual adult." A spiritual adult is not only aware of what they create in their life to meet their needs; a spiritual adult (and the process of "spiritually adulting") brings you into individuation and prepares you for the spiritual journey you are here to take. Here, you begin to integrate your parents and transmute the influence of their shadow—the negative aspects and limiting beliefs you have suppressed in your own psyche, dethrone your parents by becoming the ruler of your own life, and simply keeping them on as subconscious advisors, creating your own value system (based on theirs), and then "doing it differently" by living your own authentic life.

Throughout the book, I will often refer to my "Twelve Truths to Spiritual Adulting"– you can also think of them as steps—that are fundamental to successfully moving through the process of spiritual adulting. I share these truths with my clients to help guide their journey back to spiritual wholeness. Those truths are as follows:

Truth One: Truth of Thought

Truth Two: Truth of Desire

Truth Three: Truth of Emotion & Breath

Truth Four: Truth of Instinct, Intellect & Intuition

Truth Five: Truth of Ego, Personality & Soul

Truth Six: Truth of Purification & Health

Truth Seven: Truth of Balance & Fun

Truth Eight: Truth of the Shadow

Truth Nine: Truth of Wisdom & Mentorship

Truth Ten: Truth of Simplicity & Silence

Truth Eleven: Truth of Service

Truth Twelve: Truth of Unity

I've devised these twelve truths according to my understanding of how our spiritual growth gradually unfolds at each age. They are further organized into my three-stage Band-AID model of spiritually adulting: Awareness, Integration, and Doing it differently (*aka. dethroning your parents*). The first stage refers to becoming aware of what you've created in your life and owning your child script. This is usually linked to the first four truths: *The truth of your thoughts. Truth of your desires. The truth of your emotions and breath. The truth of your intuition.* This is linked to your unchangeable nature inherited at conception. The second stage, integration, refers to a realization that you are your parents—the good, the bad, and the ugly, that we willingly stay in child to get our needs met, and that while we aren't yet transmuting that pattern, we understand what we are doing and why. This stage includes mental awareness and knowledge, but not necessarily wisdom or heart awareness. The truths associated with integration include the following: *The truth of the ego, personality and self-love. The truth of purification. The truth of balance and fun. The truth of the shadow.* The third stage relates to dethroning your parents. These truths are directly related to wisdom, the intelligence of love, and transmutation, and include the following: *The truth of wisdom. The truth of silence. The truth of service. The truth of unity and universal consciousness.*

I will give you clear instructions on what happens at each cycle of your karmic and spiritual growth—corresponding to specific ages—and how to identify the primary themes in your soul so you can shift energetic patterns and maximize your spiritual development. By "soul," I mean the divine spark of God that resides within each of us and holds our divine will and divine purpose. The personality, which includes the masks we wear, bogs down the work of the soul and is why we often feel lost. I equate the soul to a diamond and our personality to honey covering the diamond. The personality includes impure thoughts, emotions, and desires that we inherit at conception—judgments from our parents that we internalize and link to our values. During the spiritual adulting process, you start to analyze these Thoughts, Emotions, and Desires—what I call a "personal TED talk"—and burn off the honey or masks so the soul can shine through. The soul then knows exactly what to do and where to go.

Lastly, I will provide a step-by-step instruction manual from womb-to-tomb to help you identify the karmic pattern you are obligated to follow in this lifetime. Only one karmic thread is woven through your life. That thread shows up in every story and situation and does not change until your next incarnation.

Spiritual Adulting Archetypes

Throughout the book I reference **The Archetypal Spiritual Adulting Brain Map** in Appendix H. The image below reflects the twelve archetypes that exist in the Universe, existing in our psyche at conception. These twelve archetypes are projections from our psyche and show up as people, places, things or situations in our life. The twelve archetypes have light and shadow aspects and they are linked to certain stages of the spiritual adulting process. The image below lists the shadow and light aspects for each archetype. Although all twelve exist in our lives, we have preferred archetypes at certain ages, that drive the stages, some that we struggle to integrate throughout life. During *skinny cow* years, *neutralizer* years and *valor* years, all being led by the sage archetype, those difficult to integrate archetypes tend to show up as nemeses to help with the integration process. The unintegrated archetypes, or shadow aspects, tend to show up as inner or outer conflict and judgements about others. I call these the competitive voices, while easily integrated archetypes are collaborative voices in the psyche. Each archetype is in a pair. If you struggle with one half of the pair, as most people do, these 0 to 100 swings, will rule your life. These tend to represent the extremes of your parents behavior. For instance, if one was overt, and the other covert, you may misinterpret this as different, when in reality all of our parents, at the moment of our conception, were the same coin; however, different sides. As we swing from 0 to 100, attempting to neutralize the swings and integrate both parents, we cannot. It is only with the 48 to 52 balance; we can neutralize swings and achieve self-mastery. Any swings of the archetypes, often in one light side will show up as a nemeses as the shadow side of that archetypal pair. The rebel is linked to freedom and no constrictions, the opposite archetype in the sage (see the map below), which will feel as restrictive and limiting in its shadow aspect. It will appear as a nemeses, in the shadow side of the sage (viewed as restrictive); however, it is the wisdom of your psyche, that is creating that person, place, thing or situation for you to learn to integrate both parents, both sides of the coin. In the Odyssey, Odysseus said to Penelope "you cannot separate the olive branch from the marital bed". You are the olive branch! You're the peacemaker and mediator, in your psyche, the midpoint of your parents, the 48 to 52. The only way to become a spiritual adult is to find the 48 to 52 to the 0 to 100 swings. Much about this is discussed in Chapter 11.

Planetary Archetype	Shadow	Light	Planetary Archetype	Shadow	Light
Chiron	Orphan/Wounded Child	Everyday Man	Lilith	Prostitute	Ruler
Neptune	Victim/Savior	Innocent	Pluto	Devil	Magician
Saturn	Scrooge/Limitations	Sage/Senex	Uranus	Chaos	Rebel
Venus	Eros Lover	Agape Lover	Jupiter	Escapism	Seeker
Mercury	Trickster (Dual Consciousness)	Trickster (Unified Consciousness)	Mars	Ego	Creator
Moon	Dark Mother	Good Mother	Sun	Narcissus	Hero

The shadow & light aspect of the twelve archetypes to spiritual adulting

Each phase of our spiritual development tends to be guided by a set (or two) of archetypes. I discuss the prevalent planets or archetypes most common during each stage. Astrological planetary glyphs are what I call psychological organs or the archetypes I use in my model. The everyday man (Chiron glyph) or ruler (Lilith glyph) archetypes, are asteroids, not true planets, but no less relevant.

We tend to have 0 to 100 swing in between pairs of archetypes on the Spiritual Adulting Archetypal Map and as we get closer to spiritual adulting, ruled by the everyday man and the ruler archetypes, at the top of the map, they balance out to what I call the "wounded ruler" archetype. Here we learn self-mastery by living the gray area called the 48-52 and the 0 to 100 swings slow. Once we fully become spiritual adults, we need to return to the lover archetype and show up in the world with our heart open for others. There are two lover archetypes I discuss in Chapter Six, *Aphrodite Pandemos* and *Aphrodite Urania*. Aphrodite Pandemos is desirous and erotic love that gives us the drive at 21 to seek love and financial stability; however, after honoring our desires and accomplishing our goals, both materially, romantically and as a spiritual adult (ruled by Aphrodite Pandemos), our humanity kicks in with a heart-opening and Aphrodite Urania, agape love, becomes the order of the day. This cannot occur until we integrate all archetypes and spiritually adult, if not it is false selfless-ness. Selfless does not exist, only Self and selfish. Once you integrate all archetypes and achieve Self and individuation, then you can drop into the heart space and love another, what I call service as self, not service instead of self.

The child years are dictated by the moon and sun which resemble the feminine and masculine energies. Each archetype is typically cat-egorized as masculine or feminine. The trickster in reality is non-bi-nary, but for this book, we will categorize the right-side column as masculine and the left side column as feminine. These are energies and have nothing to do with sexuality or gender roles. We come from a universal consciousness which is intact, and houses all archetypes as one consciousness; however, upon conception, because an egg and a sperm are involved, the metaphorical cosmic egg is cracked and the first division in the psyche is linked to the masculine and feminine. This corresponds to a metaphysical called the *Principle of Gender*. Again, this is energy, and the law indicates that masculine and feminine are not separate, but rather intertwined within each other. There is no true distinction; however, because of the human mind and our compartmentalization and sorting tendencies, the first crack is to categorize things as masculine and feminine. In Spiritual Adulting, slowing the swings, in the gray area of the 48 to 52, confirms that all masculine and feminine divisions are indeed obsolete, and the unification of the energies is the only way towards balance and indeed becoming a spiritual adult.

We commonly identify the first split as mother and father in our life. The spiritual adulting process begins at the bottom of the map, noted by the glyph of the moon and the sun. The archetypes are caretaker and hero and their shadow aspects are the unintegrated aspects of the masculine and feminine. Rarely do we leave this space in our psyche, keeping us in child script for most of our lives, child psyche's living in adult bodies, nowhere near a spiritual adult! A shadow caretaker cares for others and neglects themselves often in a guise of the "great mother" or "good mother", denying her dark side or womanhood in the name of caretaking. It is a manipulative way to get your needs met and an attempt at getting others to love you unconditionally, when that is solely your job with the Spiritually Adulting process. The hero archetype can become narcissistic if they're not aware of their shadow aspects. The shadow aspects remind us we are human and flawed. Extremes of the hero shadow archetype may be inferiority or superiority complex, playing small or apparent fearlessness.

The image below represents the myth of the *Birth of Athena*. Zeus births Athena from his head with the help of Hephaestus. Athena is the goddess of wisdom; however, she rules the rational mind. Hephaestus helping her indicates we need (and have) something beyond the rational mind to understand the depths of our psyche. Hephaestus is the god of the forge and metals. The seven metals in alchemy, corresponding to the primary seven planets are the primary archetypes and used to stop at Saturn or the sage. That is why so much of our spiritual adulting process is ruled by Saturn cycles, the skinny cows. As additional planets and asteroids were discovered, they were integrated into our psyche, but the initial archetypes indicate the metals of alchemy, that turn us into gold, the ruler or our lives.

The Birth of Athena with the help of the god Hephaestus. With her are born the planetary archetypes that are the psychological organs that dictate our spiritual adulting process. Integration of the archetypes, through each stage of life, leads to spiritual adulting and happiness.

The teenage years are ruled by the trickster and creator archetypes. The shadow aspects are low-level trickster ruled by lying, cheating and stealing and wearing veils of self-deceit. Here we believe we are dual and do not understand that we are all unified. The creator archetype shadow is allowing the ego and personality to believe that is our true self, and forgetting the divine will is really the one who runs the show and the ego and personality are simply along for the ride! The separateness we feel due to the trickster, fuels the ego, in hopes of covering the wound that we really feel lost and insignificant in the world. Both of these archetypes are necessary to pave our own path forward and enter the forbidden doors of the psyche at 18 and to begin individuation from the parents. There is some overlap between the trickster and creator and lover and seeker ruling both teenage years and adult years as I mention in Chapter Three.

I bounce back and forth between the planetary names; Greek and Roman gods and the branding archetype names throughout the book. In Appendix J I provide a chart of all of the names that I use interchangeably. Some of the Greek & Roman gods are not exact; however, these are the archetypes, linked to myth and astrology and depth psychology I use at *Hidden Truths College of Metaphysics* where I teach these topics, so for continuity these are the gods I am using throughout the text.

The lover, seeker, sage, rebel, innocent and magician archetypes rule the adulting years. The lover shadow aspects are desirous love overshadowing the light aspects of self-love or agape love; however, we need all three. The seeker is an escape artist and can remain seeking and never settle down, always in the name of searching for something more or better. The lover and seeker rule ages 21 -24 while we are establishing our romantic and financial relationships. Together they can keep us pining for desires of the flesh and gluttony and greed, never getting enough. The seeker archetype is also Jupiter, which I write about in Chapter 6, linked to spiritual growth cycles, if he plays well with the sage archetype, or Saturn, during the skinny cow years. This infrastructure can help us work with or against or sage and rebel archetypes that rule 28- 49 years old. The sage or senex shadow can be bitter, set-in dogmatic thinking or judgements while his counterpart the rebel seeks chaos and cannot handle any constrictions, freedom at all cost is the name of the game. The sage is a wise man or crone (see Triple Goddess archetype on page 123) and is linked to the skinny cow years. Albeit a strict teacher, he is the consistent spiritual teacher throughout our lives, beginning at ages 14-16. The rebel as a light aspect can allow us to create new beginnings, leaving behind outdated scripts, but when the extreme is freedom, we have forgotten that freedom is found in the psyche and is freedom of limited thinking not from a boss, a mortgage or a marriage. The rebel shows up at 42 to help us seek deeper meaning in life. Becareful not to blow up your life here as I explain in Chapter Ten.

The innocent archetype's shadow shows up as victim, martyr, rescuer or savior. If you need a savior, the magician shows up as the devil to complete the story! The magician is truly the magic in our lives, but often comes with pain, death, divorce, loss, no closure and we deem him the criminal or perpetrator in our story. We fail to see that we are that unintegrated aspect and we created the criminal to help us get out of our own way. This can happen at 33 when we live out the Jesus story, metaphorically or later in life when we have failed to return home and integrate our parents between 48 to 52 years old and we need a stronger push than the skinny cows. The *skinny cows, neutralizers* and *valor* years, that appear on schedule every seven years are linked to the sage or senex archetype. These are minor nudges compared to the magician's way of transforming us, a forced death-rebirth cycle. In mythology, Saturn was the father of Pluto. Saturn is the sage and ruled for thirty years, so he is patient and consistent with his message; however, when he cannot accomplish the task with his nudges, neutralizers and skinny cows he send his son Pluto, the magician, who infamously abducted Persephone into the Underworld, so both she and her mother Demeter could grow up and break the enmeshment and delusion in the relationship. The delusion we live in, what I call the snowglobe, needs to be shattered and represents the innocent or victim, and nothing but a devil or a sudden crisis will do the job.

Once Pluto has finished his transformation and you leave the abyss, you're ready to spiritually adult by integrating the everyday man and ruler archetypes. Together they are the *wounded ruler*, because we have owned our divinity and our humanity, and we have assumed our rightful throne and own our kingdom, this life. The shadow aspects are the orphan or wounded child and the prostitute. If we live out the shadow aspects, we will engage in what Carolyn Myss calls woundology and rather than rule through our wound, we will use our flawed human self and vices against ourselves, inflicting pain and suffering through the prostitute archetype. The prostitute collects her due in the psyche, which is self-betrayal, self-hatred and constant crisis. At 48 to 52 years old, Chiron or the everyday man makes a full revolution around the astrology chart and brings us back home, to Self. If we failed to integrate our parents up until now, we will remain wounded children, blaming our parents and playing victim to any representatives of our parents in the system. In my book *The Seven Gates: Seven Steps Beyond Self Awareness*, I establish that every person, place, thing and situation represents our parents and situations, creating conflict and opportunities to integrate these aspects of our psyche. Many people stay in the child step of spiritual adulting (caretaker and hero), simply trying to integrate mother and father, masculine and feminine energies, and never really "leaving home", retraumatizing themselves with their childhood story and blaming their parents. Constantly seeking a caretaker and or a hero, leaves you as the orphan or child of the story, every time. The ruler archetype reminds you that you are a child of no one because the Universe is cyclical, not hierarchical. Bert Hellinger, the creator of the therapeutic model *Family Constellations* said, 'your parents gave you life and that's enough'. In the subconscious models I write, your parents gave you the vehicle to do your soul's work. Attached to that vehicle, the body, you have a limiting thought, negative emotional response, desire or deadly sin and a low-level of consciousness. At your first breath, you have everything you need to become a spiritual adult. Holding on to the child story, keeps you in orphan and licking the wound, never seeking true solutions. The spiritual adult seeks a vocation where he opens the wound daily and the mess of the wound becomes the medicine for himself, and as he returns to Aphrodite Urania, the medicine for others if they choose to accept it. The prostitute becomes the ruler of the kingdom. Rather than self-hatred and self-betrayal for the rejection and abandonment traumas in the psyche, since conception, she learns to rule, despite the wound. No matter which archetype, phase of life or your age you can begin to spiritually adult right now!

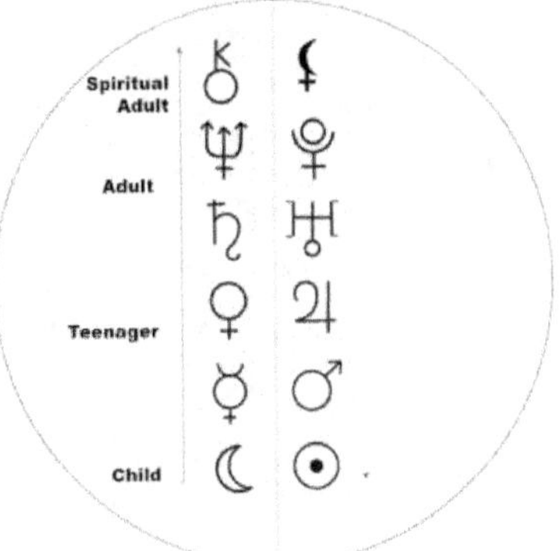

Everyday Man; Ruler

Innocent; Magician

Sage; Rebel

Lover; Seeker

Trickster; Creator

Caregiver; Hero

The Archetypal Spiritual Adulting Brain Map and the names of the light aspects of each archetype.

CHAPTER ONE:
Mythology

Uranus (Father Sky) and Gaia (Mother Earth) had a daughter named Themis. She was from a class of gods called the Titans, whose enemies were the Olympians. The Olympians, ruled by Zeus, dethroned the Titans and started a rivalry in the heavens. Themis emerged as a lover of Zeus, creating a bridge between the Titans and the Olympians. Themis, also known as "Lady Justice," is the bridge between our animal tendencies (Titans) and our spiritual tendencies (Olympian) during our time on Earth. Themis means "to put into place." We are put into a place while on Earth—pre-determined from previous lifetimes—and are held to that place throughout our life. However, there is another predetermined place that has been allotted to us that I call our kingdom, our throne. Yet most never choose to take that place, choosing instead to stay in the same place they started at birth. Due to limiting thoughts and staying attached to family traditions and the beehive from childhood, we avoid the destination we are entitled to and waste our spiritual potential.

At the moment of conception, we emerge in a state of low-level consciousness, predetermined by our previous karma. Before incarnating, we choose our parents based on their vibrational level, which becomes our vibration at conception. If we stay at this level of consciousness during our lifetime—which is directly related to impure thoughts, emotions, desires—we never leave the manger. Our *real* objective is to attain Christ consciousness, which requires us to transmute our low-level consciousness into a higher state. The constellation of Cancer, linked to family, has a cluster of stars known as the beehive cluster or Presepe, which in Italian means "manger." We must leave the manger—the animal or low-level consciousness inherited at conception—and seek our individual journey. This is determined by developing our own set of values in order to put our soul in its rightful place.

Step one of any spiritual tradition is the observation of thoughts. On my podcast, "The Mistress of the Subconscious," I have an episode about *"mind your pleck." Mind your Pleck* was on a sign I saw at the Amsterdam airport many years ago. It was translated as, "mind your place." I learned that when we mind our place, we can "own our price" linked to our self-worth, whether it's managing our time, money, or resources. However, when we don't mind our pleck, we don't know our price (self-worth). We misuse our resources to meet unmet needs through cunning and manipulation because we know of no other way to get love. For example, we may not honor our own time, allowing ourselves to get distracted from our path or rescuing others while we sink to the bottom of the sea. We may charge too little because we don't value our services or feel fraudulent if we raise the price.

For example, many spiritual counselors struggle with how much to charge for their services. I grew up in a cult where the leader was a thief, robbing us blind for her own vices, and I later struggled with my rates as I built my practice and was never sure how or when to end a session. Fortunately, my spirit guides would determine when to raise my prices, always commensurate with my experience and where I was on my spiritual path. As I learned the connections between these struggles and self-worth, I began to *mind my pleck*. I am clear about my rates, and a minute before a session ends, I say with confidence, "Anything else before we go?", and end on time. This is self-love, self-respect, and honoring boundaries and I model for clients what I wish for them. In the cult I grew up understanding balance was when spirit and matter were unified; therefore, not valuing your time, money or resources isn't more spiritual, it's imbalance.

There is a myth behind *Mind Your Pleck* involving Hestia, goddess of the hearth. She is responsible for manning the fires in the agora— the open space where the people in ancient Greece would meet. She cannot leave the fires unattended and cannot participate in any other ceremonies; she has to stay put. This is symbolic of our third chakra—

the Manipura chakra which means "crown of jewels"— representing our fire, our self-worth, and our "throne." We cannot leave our place to tend to someone else or pursue selfish aims. Manning our fires, minding our place, is about the Self. You don't take anyone's power and don't let anyone take yours. Only when we integrate our shadow and learn self-love can we begin to truly love another. Only by keeping our fires strong can we live an authentic life and dethrone our parents.

Answering the Call

In addition to representing justice, Themis is also the goddess of "divine law." Divine law is even beyond the gods. In my book, *Dethroning Olympus*, I explain that the gods have been internalized in our subconscious as our parents, and that our (symbolic) mother and father sit on our subconscious throne in the sixth chakra: the seat of consciousness. Unless we dethrone them, we'll be stuck honoring *their* values in this lifetime and not ours. Abraham, the first patriarch of the Jewish people, was the first to teach the idea that there was only one God; before that, people believed in many gods. Abraham dethroned his father Terach, who made a living selling idols of various gods. In the Jewish tradition called Midrash, there are a number of stories about Abraham smashing his father's idols when he realized there can be only one God, and thus monotheism was born. In the same way, we need to smash our own parental and family snowglobes to honor the divine spark within and, like Abraham, carve our own divinely guided path.

It's important to point out here that we have both a material family and a spiritual family and that there is room for both, but most of us fail to honor the spiritual family and remain stuck in the earthly family beehive. Carolyn Myss, in her book *Sacred Contracts*, views our spiritual family as a series of sacred contracts that were in place before we were born, guiding us to certain people and places to fulfill those contracts. She writes,

"[T]hat contract contains a wide range of agreements regarding all that we are intended to learn in this life. It comprises not merely what kind of work we do but also our key relationships with the people who are to help us learn the lessons we have agreed to work on. Each of those relationships represents an individual contract that is part of your overall sacred contract and may require you to be in a certain place at a certain time to be with that person."

Many of the cycles I speak about in this book are about finding a way to honor and integrate both the spiritual and the material, creating a true union. This is divine law, and the marriage of Themis and Zeus (low-level and high-level consciousness) is the only way to honor it.

The Horai, the three children of Zeus and Themis, are Auxo the grower, *Carpo* the fruit-bringer, and *Thallo* the plant-raiser. These three goddesses are responsible for the seasons and the cycles of plants; however, they also dictate the rhythm of our spiritual and material lives. Auxo is responsible for the ages of 14—28 when we are growing into adulthood, finding our own spiritual path, and questioning our parents' values. This phase is related to "leaving home." Carpo is responsible for ages 28—59 when we bear children, produce materially in the world, and build our life. Thallo is responsible for 60 and beyond. We are no longer raising children or a bank account but are dedicated to our spiritual lives. In a parable, Jesus spoke about seeds, and how by landing on grass, they grow. This is the stage where we plant our spiritual seeds and watch them grow until we die. In the Vedas, this fourth stage of life is called *moksha*—liberation.

For one of Hercules's many "labors," he is asked to catch a Cretan bull and bring it to the temple. Hercules rides the bull in, which indicates equal effort toward balancing both an earthly life (matter is the bull) and our spiritual life (spirit riding matter). Many of my students are on a spiritual path, and the first two first truths—or steps—of that path are to observe one's thoughts and then to honor earthly *and* spiritual life. It perplexes me when I see people going on retreats and pilgrimages who have never analyzed their thoughts or where those thoughts are coming from. You won't make any real progress until you understand the path that has brought you to where you are, which is by looking deeply at your thoughts and desires and what they are saying about you and your life and the needs you are trying to fill.

Jesus said, "Give Caesar what is Caesar's, and give God what is God's"—a recognition of earthly and spiritual aspirations. This doesn't usually start until around 60 years old, when Thallo rules your life. However, you can start younger if you are so called. There's a great scene in the movie *The Devil Wears Prada* where Nate says to Andie, "Tell me the phone calls you take, and I'll tell you who your priorities are." If most of your life is dedicated to earthly things, you are taking calls from Carpo. When your spiritual life becomes your focus, you are taking calls from Thallo. My spirit guides often say "we are either spiritual looking for a material life, or material seeking a more spiritual life.". Divine law tells us that we should honor both our earthly adulting and our spiritual adulting.

Unfortunately, spiritual values have often come last on the lists of priorities in the Western world, second to material wealth and academic success. Seen through the lens of the Vedas, *kama*, the second stage (desire), and *atharva*, the third stage (adult responsibilities), have taken precedence over *dharma* (the first stage—morals and righteousness) and *moksha* (the fourth stage—liberation and spiritual values). However, as more and more younger people seek spirituality, it's more and more important to provide tools and literature early on to support a strong spiritual foundation.

In this *Age of Aquarius*, many people are turning to astrology, the Akashic records, and the development of their intuition as tools for connecting to their inner guidance and spiritual selves. I teach all of these techniques, but this is not spirituality, this is intuition development, truth four on the spiritual path. Spirituality is more about "spiritual adulting": leaving home, following your own path, raising your level of consciousness, returning home, dethroning your parents and doing it differently while honoring them, and, finally, owning your spiritual kingdom and knowing your spiritual family. Intuition development is Truth Four (the fourth step) in the spiritual adulting process, and many aspirants skip to this stage without first doing the spiritual work of examining their thoughts, desires, and emotions. **Your intuition and guidance are only as clear as your subconscious thoughts,** and this is where the work begins. If you don't engage with step one of the spiritual path—understanding and controlling the quality of your thoughts—you will be unable to move forward and your "guidance" will keep leading you back to that original impure thought.

Spiritual adulting, like biological adulting, has a flow, an order. Luckily, many developmental theorists like Erickson have written about psychosocial development while spiritual philosophers such as, Jean Gebser, Ken Wilbur, and James Fowler have written about consciousness and spiritual development. Piggybacking on these theorists, this book provides a step-by-step, *age-by-age* breakdown of what occurs spiritually from womb to tomb. This book does that so you can earn the kingdom on Earth owed to you by Themis, the divine law. To get there, though, distinct and orderly laws will need to be followed.

I often say, "Consider the crime, not the criminal." The crime is a lack of awareness of universal laws that dictate everything, and therefore we are all criminals in the eyes of divine law. Being ignorant of such laws does not keep us from being held accountable. This is how the justice system works in the spiritual realm: The biggest crime is a failure to know the laws and how and when they work. We feel victimized when we are fired from a job or our child doesn't call or we go bankrupt. However, all of these outcomes are predetermined by you according to how these laws work. You are the orchestrator—and the sole perpetrator—of your life. You are not a victim. Calling the boss, the child, the court system, or the bank "the criminal" keeps you in child mode, but the criminal is you, and the sentencing is your life. We call that *karma* and say "Karma is a bitch," but it's *your* karma, the criminal result of not knowing the law and why something happened the way it did.

Themis had a sister named Nemesis, *the goddess of retribution.*

Nemesis is a term we use for an enemy, someone who's against us. However, in our spiritual family, our nemesis is our sister. Like Themis always being followed by her sister, we are always being followed by our nemesis, in whatever moment we are living. Our spiritual family helps us to adult spiritually, to earn and assume our throne; our earthly family helps us stay in the family beehive, in the status quo, like a crab in a pot. In Alice Bailey's *The Labours of Hercules: An Astrological Interpretation*, she explains how Cancer is the sign of the masses. Crabs notoriously walk side-to-side. The constellation of Cancer has no bright lights; all the stars are equally dim. The adage, "crabs in a pot," refers to how crabs pull down other crabs that are trying to get out. Our earthly family isn't evil, and members of our spiritual family are often incarnated as our earthly family. However, at the moment when your mother and father conceive you, your level of consciousness is low. It's extremely hard to raise this vibration, which is the purpose of spiritual adulting. And when other family members are birthed at that same level of consciousness, the challenge is even greater and, subconsciously, your growth is discouraged.

As Joseph Campbell noted, in every mythology, the hero must answer a call. I believe that the call of the hero's journey is the call to spiritual adulting—to leave home, follow your own path, raise your level of consciousness, and then return home. Like the story of the Prodigal Son, we must leave home in order to achieve this mission. Leaving home doesn't necessarily mean physically, although this is often the only way we know how to transmute those energies. A spiritual pilgrimage can be taken on the couch, in your pajamas. Gurdjieff, an Armenian philosopher, founded a series of principles and instructions he called the Fourth Way. He didn't believe in retiring from the world in the way of the fakir, the monk, or the yogi; rather, he believed we should do the work of spiritual adulting in the earthly realm. There, we meet our spiritual family—our nemeses—who will push us forward. If you enjoy spiritual retreats and the ashram life, then by all means do them, but these are simply escapes from real life in the guise of spirituality.

In many myths, like that of Persephone, the child is abducted by a villain. In this story, it was Hades. However, the abduction is more psychological in that it is necessary for the child to leave the beehive to discover their brightness. Unless some outside force, a nemesis—a spiritual family member often disguised as a perpetrator—abducts us from the comforts of our snowglobe world, we would rarely leave voluntarily. Many of the children we call "late-bloomers" are afraid to leave the comfort of a nice home with seemingly loving parents. The term boomerang generation is used for adults 18-24 who move out and boomerang right back. In my opinion, they are the hardest to crack and the hardest to sprout. As Jesus noted in "The Parable of the Sower," spiritual seeds (our spiritual potential) often fall on rocky ground not because there is no desire to grow, but because they are lulled into complacency in the comfort of their parents' kingdom. Jesus also tells of a farmer who sows seeds indiscriminately. Some seeds fall on the path (wayside) with no soil, some on rocky ground with little soil, some on thorny soil, and some on good soil. Each of us has the same opportunities to grow and sprout our seeds.

The Trauma of Conception

There are spiritual cycles of the universe dictated by the *Principle of Rhythm* available to everyone. Free will is how you choose to use these cycles for your growth. Each of us will experience a metaphorical abduction—several, actually, throughout our lives—to force us to leave home, both physically and subconsciously. Some may leave home subconsciously but not physically; others will leave home physically but not subconsciously—they will stay stuck in a cycle of child and victim, never owning their kingdom or their potential in this lifetime.

When we are conceived in the womb, we will have left the original snowglobe of universal consciousness and entered a lower-level snowglobe of consciousness—which is now cracked because by incarnating in physical life, we automatically feel abandoned. This is also the first step of subconscious programming. We then enter the womb, which is another false snowglobe, thinking that our needs are being met when it's really a parasitic, not a symbiotic, relationship. This is the second step in subconscious development. The third step in the subconscious development is our birth story, how we enter the world. This is another subconscious crack in a seemingly intact snowglobe. From ages 0 and 7, the fourth stage of the subconscious development, our snowglobe will crack again as we become aware that we are separate from our parents and others in the world. This state of consciousness, when you realize that you are in a separate body, is called the waking state and is ego-centered. During this time, we start living out the false story (subconsciously) that our family is perfect and our parents are gods. The depth of the cracks in your snowglobe will depend on the severity with which you came to believe—based on your parents' disapproval and judgements—the story that you are "not enough" and/or not loved unconditionally. Ultimately, the size of the cracks and the reasons behind them don't matter—being reprimanded for spilling your milk or kicking the neighbor's dog are treated equally by the subconscious. It concludes, "I am different" or "I don't belong," your inner child gets stuck, and your crisis in the world begins. Once we leave the intact snowglobe of universal consciousness at the moment of conception, we inherit a flawed existence and then build a story and a life that tries to honor it.

In the twelfth truth of spiritual adulting, *the truth of unity*, we return to that original snowglobe although we are still in the body. At this point, we understand that we are not separate from anything or anyone. The universe is one and consciousness is everything. Prior to this, we will have woven a story confirming that we deserved to be kicked out of Olympus—the universal womb, the intact snowglobe—because we were unworthy. But when we return, we stop being a child, even a "child of God," because the universe is perfection, connected and One. There is no hierarchy, and therefore parents and children can't exist.

If you never grow up and face the shadow of your parents' influence, you will continue to think—erroneously—that mother and father, either human or godly, will come and save you. The story associated with that first crack in the snowglobe keeps you repeating that same story. But they aren't coming. Whether dead or alive, if you yell and scream and beg them to do it differently, they can't. That moment has passed. Your snowglobe has cracked and they will never meet your true needs. You aren't three years old anymore. It is time for you to show up and rewrite the script for yourself.

The first of the Buddha's Four Noble Truths is *the truth of suffering*. All of us are spiritual sojourners in the world, on a pilgrimage for wholeness. Often mistaken for happiness, which is simply fleeting moments of elation, what we truly seek is balance and stability. This is Themis' domain. Truth Seven in a spiritual practice, the truth of balance and fun, is to identify the 0 to 100 swings in our behavior that represent doing the same or the opposite of what our parents did—an attempt to do things differently but is still linked to our original trauma—and seek balance: the 48 to 52. (*This is the balance of the 0-100 swings not to be confused with ages 48-52 when we return home to dethrone our parents.) In the spiritual realm, we call this justice, when everything feels in order. The chaos has calmed, the storm has passed. We can breathe easily. This can only happen when we balance the forces of Themis and Zeus, the earthly and the spiritual realms. No matter how cracked your snowglobe, whatever your feelings of being misplaced, insufficient, or imperfect, your story is no different than anyone else, only in degrees of intricacy. We are all here doing the same work.

When I realized that I had created a story about myself that seemed complicated and "out of this world," it was just another way to be "different" and "special." Some people need more characters, story lines, and plots; others are fine with a simpler narrative. Regardless of what you create, it boils down to what I call being thrown out of Olympus—the land of the gods in Greek mythology. One particular god, Hephaestus, was born club-footed and kicked out of Olympus by his mother, Hera, who threw him to the bottom of the ocean where he was raised by the nymphs. Once we realize our snowglobe is cracked, each of us feels like Hephaestus. Abandoned, imperfect, and physically, emotionally, or mentally club-footed, we enter the world seeking others—the nymphs—to raise us. But this responsibility is ours alone; no one else can raise us.

Bert Hellinger, creator of the therapeutic method Family Constellations, said, "Your parents gave you life, and that's enough." Your earthly parents were assigned one task: to give you an earthly vehicle—a body—packaged with a limiting thought, desires and low-level consciousness, so you could do your spiritual work, your spiritual adulting. Nothing more. When one or both our parents become our nemesis, you know they did their job correctly. Even if you think your snowglobe is intact, somewhere in your psyche, your inner child was stunted and your snowglobe cracked—maybe even shattered—when you realized you weren't perfect. It could have been when your brother was born, or you saw your mother crying, or your father left, or your grandfather died, or you were shamed when touching yourself to explore your body, or embarrassed by your mother in a restaurant. Your child psyche got the message loud and clear: You aren't perfect. You aren't okay as you are.

It's important to remember that your snowglobe first cracked at the moment of conception, when Uranus told Gaia, "Let's birth a child." You are the child of both Father Sky and Mother Earth. You are both divine, like the sky (renamed "the Heavenly Father" by Christians), and earthly (flawed), like the physical body, which grows old and dies. Themis, the goddess of justice, offers divine law: the opportunity to find your place, *mind your pleck*, in this world. But there are many who look in the wrong places or never look at all. Our spiritual family members often work overtime to help us down our true path, and yet we scoff and scowl and don't heed their warnings. When we decided as souls to leave cosmic consciousness and enter the womb, we also entered what the Greeks called Lethe, the "river of forgetfulness"—the waters of the womb—so we wouldn't remember the size of our souls while experiencing the limitations of a body.

In *The Republic*, Plato writes that all were obliged to drink a certain amount of water from the river Lethe in order to forget their life before incarnating on Earth. It was believed that only when the memories of the dead have been erased by Lethe—who is also a goddess—can a soul be reincarnated. The word *lethe* in Greek means oblivion, forgetfulness, or concealment. It has also been related to the word *truth*. Our spiritual adulting reveals the truths that were hidden prior to raising our levels of consciousness and transmuting our thoughts. Lethe flowed through the cave *Hypnos*, god of sleep, where it induced drowsiness. This refers to states of consciousness. Our waking state is simply awareness of the manifested world; however, as stated in Verses 3 to 6 of the *Mandukya Upanishad*, higher states of consciousness, dreams, and deep sleep reveal hidden truths about ourselves and the universe once we start to spiritually adult.

In the Disney classic *Aladdin*, the genie comes out of the lamp and says, "It's all part of the genie gig: Phenomenal cosmic powers! Itty-bitty living space!" That also describes us! We *are* divine with enormous cosmic powers. But after entering a physical body, we feel we have entered an itty-bitty living space. Fortunately, as we spiritually adult, we catch glimpses of our true selves and true size. As we raise our consciousness, truths are revealed. Unfortunately, this also creates confusion in our psyche, thinking that the womb was perfect when in reality it's what I call "toxic water." The physical womb pretends to hold the space for the cosmic womb, but like your mother and all things earthly, it is flawed. The womb is a parasitic place. You think you are getting your needs met because your mother is feeding and housing you and allowing you to "breathe," but you are subconsciously learning a false shadow language of love based on your mother's external experiences. Breathing is also linked to the placenta, and the quality of the oxygen you get is linked to your mother's stress levels. You are also learning that to get your needs met, you need a secret language, which boils down to manipulation. That's the definition of love you inherit, which is flawed and false.

The philosopher Jean Gebser described consciousness as having five structures. The first is the *archaic structure*, defined by a lack of differentiation and a state of wholeness. The subconscious is not differentiated. Any emotional hit becomes the drama of life, no matter the severity. When I understood that getting cancer and dropping a glass were the same to the subconscious emotionally, I started shifting my perspective on how to get my needs met. In my shamanism program I teach the totem animal of geese and lion, which is differentiation and individuation. When we learn to discern and individuate, we use *mind our pleck* and man our fires correctly. This is related to the soul's symbiosis with the mother in the womb. Erich Neumann, a Jungian psychologist, calls this dynamic "the great mother archetype." Ken Wilber developed a "spectrum of consciousness" theory consisting of three broad sections: *pre-personal, personal,* and *transpersonal,* which he further broke down into eleven stages. The pre-personal is linked to traditional developmental theories; the personal is linked to humanistic psychology; and the transpersonal is linked to Eastern mystic traditions. Similar to Gebser, the first stage of Wilber's theory is the *undifferentiated or primary matrix stage,* where the soul exists in an unconscious state and the infant has no separate identity.

During pregnancy, we get our "shadow love language"—what we chase with lovers and friends throughout life. For instance, if mom worked until the day her water broke, you may subconsciously interpret this as "hard work equals love." If dad abuses mom, you may conclude that conflict is the language of love. This "shadow love" leads to pain, not love. It's an unhealthy, faulty version of love because of those toxic waters of the womb. The more we seek to fulfill this definition of love, the unhappier we become. Because the mother feeds us through her umbilical cord, and our attachment style is created in the womb, we think that the language of these waters is what we should strive for as a child and as an adult. The authentic version of love we need can only be found within ourselves by owning our power, leaving the victim mindset, setting boundaries, achieving a 48 to 52, and, finally, owning our kingdom.

The second structure of consciousness, according to Gebser, is the "magic structure." This is what I call "identification with the cracked snowglobe." The child has been released from his harmonious identity with the whole and individual consciousness begins to emerge in a dream-like way. The French anthropologist Lucien Levy-Bruhl calls this *participation mystique*. The child is questioning how to live in a world with a crack in the snowglobe. He understands he is separate but must still meet his needs. Ken Wilber's third stage on his spectrum of consciousness is the "phantasmic-emotional stage," where the imaginal and emotional life of the child develops.

Unmet needs from childhood include safety/security, protection, and validation. One of these needs will dominate each person's story and what they seek in life. The quicker you identify that unmet need, the quicker you can spiritually adult. In addition, we all have love needs. After being kicked out of Olympus, you realized your love needs were never met, and you spend your entire life seeking to fulfill them. Our parents didn't meet those needs; we were born to meet *their* needs. Those needs will never be met unless we spiritually adult. Certain people can meet specifically defined needs at specific times, but meeting your unconditional love needs are essentially your own business.

My own story is intricate. I was born into a cult. I was forced to shoplift as a small child until I was in high school. I took care of a mentally ill sister who almost died when I was 10. I had a series of mishaps with sexual assault and was molested by a cult member when was I was young. I felt shame around my sexuality because I enjoyed being touched even though I knew it was wrong. I was forced into an arranged marriage with a man I didn't love, bore him three children, lost custody of those children, gave myself cancer three times, married a transgender man who left me after a ten year marriage I thought was perfect, and went through a severe depression for three years. And those are just the highlights! A bit dramatic? Of course. How else was I supposed to get back to Olympus? Or so I thought.

The drama we create in our life is directly linked to the crack in our snowglobe. You have a story around that crack, but even if your "river of forgetfulness" has lasted until now, you can identify the theme—the crack—based on the life you've created and the life you are living. Your problems are all linked to the one crack, to that one moment of conception, when Clotho, one of *The Three Fates* in Greek mythology, threads the needle and starts the story of your life. Every story, every problem, every issue you encounter is linked back to that moment. We create either an intricate story or a simple one to confirm that crack in the snowglobe, that we're unloveable.

Once I realized I had created the mess that was my life and that I had ignored my nemeses, my neutralizers—the nudges to go in the right direction—I had an existential crisis. I mourned the story I had created and decided to assume my throne and become a spiritual adult. As soon as I started adulting, my entire life changed. My cancer disappeared, my hair grew back, and my relationship with my children started to work. I lost weight and money flowed, learned to love myself unconditionally and found love with a partner. I decided I would own my power and confirm that I was, indeed, Hephaestus. I created my Olympus here on Earth. The throne was now mine; my kingdom was now in order. Thank you, Themis and Zeus!

In the "Garden of the Hesperides," Hercules came across two teachers, one called Nereus and the other Busiris. Nereus nudged Hercules in the right direction, while Busiris promised him the moon and stars and took him for all he had. You will find both of them on your own path, and this is where the concept of spiritual discernment is applicable. In the third step of a spiritual journey, you need a teacher. Decide which teacher and how long you want to study with them, but don't become dependent on them. Have discernment! I've had plenty of Busiris' on my path, but also been lucky enough to have several Nereus' as well. I consider myself a Nereus, but stay vigilant every day. Spiritual teachers have big egos, and I'm no exception. You must watch how you live and what you say. You must walk the walk and talk the talk. You are allowed no incongruence. Do your work and make sure to remember that you heal no one; all the messages you give are the ones you yourself need to hear.

Many Lessons

Nereus was only on Hercules' path to nudge him in the right direction. Similarly, I don't create dependencies with my students. Be careful of teachers who want you to become dependent on them. Be careful of teachers who say they have no ego or they've already worked through a problem. This is a lie. Spiritual teachers are generally known to be wolves in sheep's clothing. Be discerning. Look at their life. Does their outer life correlate with their inner life? That is a universal law called the *Law of Correspondence*. This doesn't mean we are perfect; it means we are human, but trying to walk the walk right alongside our aspirants. Truth Nine is when you become the mentor, remind yourself you're flawed and can only heal yourself.

The ninth step in a spiritual practice, the truth of wisdom and mentorship, is to become aware of what the universe is using to speak to us. This forces us to pay attention. The era of Neptune in Pisces from 2012 to 2025 has brought—and will continue to bring—a lot of false prophets. They will topple like dominoes once Neptune goes into Aries from 2025 to 2039, but a lot of damage will have already been done. Watch shows on cults or Scientology or spiritual coercion; these influences are rampant and can happen to you. Because of them, we can fail to assume our throne even as we are aware of our Zeus-like nature.

In Greek mythology, Zeus was the god of Olympus. When he and his two brothers were splitting the world, he got the biggest piece. He was a womanizer, an escape artist, and a liar. The Greeks were smart. They knew that humans were both divine spark and earthly flesh, so they made their gods reflect that limited yet godlike potential. The Catholic Church canceled Greek mythology and confused our psyche, feeding us an image of a perfect man named Jesus and a Virgin Birth. I love Jesus, but Jesus, like the Buddha, was still a man who adulted spiritually. The Christ-Buddha consciousness is reached at the 10th step of the spiritual journey, which happens to be ruled by Capricorn—the sign that rules spiritual adulting. Only by spiritual adulting can we begin to discover our Christ consciousness and become, like Jesus, the master of our kingdom.

Until then, we are like a low-level consciousness Zeus and the other gods: thieves, womanizers, and egomaniacs. I can definitely admit to my low-level consciousness, but I realized my higher potential, I was able to find my balance, my 48 to 52, between my low and high-level consciousness. Until then, you will play small and call it karma while the pendulum swings from 0 to 100. These swings represent the dramas of our life: ups and downs we believe are inevitable, but are caused by us to confirm our Hephaestus nature. Every seven years, the planet Saturn offers us a neutralizer to slow the swings, revisit our limiting beliefs, and achieve balance and stability, but most people find that boring and revert back to the old ways, creating more drama and chaos. Why? Well, we are all Hephaestus, at the bottom of the ocean with a cracked snowglobe, a clubbed-foot, and a sob story. That story creates these swings. We're aware of the opposite side of the coin—our full potential, our light, our throne—but we are so afraid of what that might look like, we castrate ourselves and don't dare reach those heights.

My mirror, my Zeus, was the cult leader. She was an egomaniac. She had power. She had the lives of hundreds of people in her hands and made a lot of money off them. Was she in my life by accident? Absolutely not. My second spiritual teacher, another Busiris, wasn't as bad, but still used me for his own benefit. Do you think the universe sent them to control 36 years of my life if they weren't there to teach me something? They were the highest point—the "100"—of my pendulum swings and what I was shrinking from: my desire to be a spiritual teacher. But not like them. I first had to use them as mirrors to reflect my capacity to become like them because I'm created in the image of Zeus: flawed, greedy, and ambitious. Then I learned to do it differently.

At recognizing the 100 to my zero—the fear of my potential to play small—I started a plan to adult spiritually, develop my Christ consciousness, and assume my rightful throne based on my 48 to 52. On my podcast "The Mistress of the Subconscious," I have an episode in Season One called "Prince or Pauper?" We are both. The symbolism of Jesus born in a manger is perfect. We are divine, like Jesus, like Zeus, but we are also animals, in a manger, in flawed flesh. And unless we balance that flesh with a spiritual life, we will end up in a life of pleasure as pain or pain as pleasure. In the Buddha's Eightfold Path, this correlates to the second of his Four Noble Truths: *determine the cause of suffering*.

A lot of people enjoy their suffering. It keeps them connected to their inner child. If they suffer, as they did in the toxic waters of the womb, they feel loved and protected—falsely so, but at least a limited version of the love they seek. If you seek hedonism and pleasure, you suffer as well with your chaos, imbalance, and emptiness. The 0 to 100 represents the extremes of our potential, the unhealthy bookends of what we are capable of experiencing. We ride those swings of unlived potential because of wanting to honor the cracked snowglobe as the only truth about ourselves we know. If our snowglobe was nearly shattered, we leave home to avoid repeating the story, which gives us a false sense of security. The snowglobe is in your psyche; the crack is expressed in your need for validation or other unmet needs of choice. You never leave home without it. The myth of Odysseus is a perfect example of this.

Odysseus was called to fight the Trojan War, which he did for 10 years, taking another 10 years to return home. His father Sisyphus had cheated death twice and was punished by the gods, forced to push a boulder up a mountain every day. It was a vicious cycle of boredom and effort, and Odysseus was determined to not repeat his father's fate. Ironically, he still lived out the same story away from his wife and child through 20 years of fighting and sailing. He changed his environment from mountain to sea, but it didn't help.

As we approach 30 years of age following another Saturn return, we attempt to dethrone our parents. What tends to happen, though, is that we repeat Odysseus' story: we change locations but do the same thing (or the opposite which is the same), just like our parents. This lack of awareness keeps us in a lower state of consciousness. When we are only aware of the separation that exists between ourselves and others, we keep hopelessly seeking the glue for the crack in our snow-globe by looking for others to fulfill our unmet needs. This is our shadow love language. We may already have a mortgage, a family, and a profession. We have not yet begun the transition or integrating our parents and unified consciousness. We become Sisyphus, just like our parents.

Growing the Inner Child

The only way to escape—to spiritually adult and own your kingdom—is through transmutation. Transmutation is the raising of consciousness. Einstein said: You cannot solve a problem with the same level of consciousness at which it was created. When we think we are changing the story, we are usually just rearranging the costumes, place, and characters. *You* haven't changed. As Joseph Campbell aptly noticed, every world mythology says the same thing: When you peel back the story, you are Odysseus and your parents are Sisyphus. You remain a child. You don't reach GO and collect $200.

Being a child of *someone*, however, whether God or parents, seems to have payoffs. It means we can lay the responsibility for our troubles on someone else. The reality is that we have created everything we are living. There is no one to blame but ourselves. This is the true, "divine justice" of the spiritual realm. Themis dishes it out equally to everyone. Only when you stop creating karma or living a child-like life will the universe treat you as an adult. Under earthly laws, you may be the child of your parents until 18, but under spiritual law, that relationship ends at 14.

Carolyn Myss has seven different child archetypes in her card deck, from "divine child" to "wounded child." None of them is better than another. None of them are whole. The divine child archetype is just as flawed as the wounded child. The divine child simply may be a narcissist whose parents told them they were perfect. The wounded child may have a huge gash in their snowglobe and become a healer to everyone but themselves. No child archetype is healthy. There is only one healthy child—the inner child—and you are its parent. If you fail to raise it into a spiritual adult—mentally, emotionally, and spiritually—you will not assume your throne. This doesn't mean you have to be alone or that no one can care for you, always responsible and independent. It's the 80/20 rule: It's fine to spend 20% of your life consciously choosing to stay in child script and the rest of it as an adult.

So grow your inner child. Your inner child will keep you creative and playful. Throw out the vision boards and sticky note affirmations that are signs of fluff spirituality. Learn how universal laws work, grow up spiritually and manifest what is already rightfully yours. The third, or "manipura," chakra means "crown of jewels." If you can't wear a crown of jewels by showing up as an adult, how will you be entrusted to take care of humanity? The 11th spiritual truth in my program is about serving humanity with compassion and empathy for others. But you cannot reach this step if you haven't grown your inner child into a healthy, balanced, functioning adult and achieved self-love. Selfless acts don't exist, but if they were to exist, it would not be before truth eleven. We may engage in what appear to be selfless acts, but true altruism is difficult to achieve. The self-oriented norm is when you meet your needs and let others meet theirs. Selfishness, on the other hand, is when you take someone else's power or they take yours. Themis cannot trust that you will take care of the plant-raiser Thallo when you can't even manage Auxo, the grower. First, grow yourself up. Then you will earn more responsibility in the form of wealth, love, joy, etc.

Sally broke up with her boyfriend Douglas after a six-month relationship. Early on, they wrote down the "non-negotiables" of the relationship. As per my book, *The Truth Is in the Triangle*, each member of a couple identifies their non-negotiable—their one need, their main "thread"—which becomes the reason for the relationship and the needs associated with those intertwining threads. The idea that one person should and will meet *all* of our needs is childish. Whatever need one asks to be met in a relationship should be linked to the thread the couple is building around. Sally was clear with Douglas that she had attracted men who didn't have a sex drive and that she wanted a healthy, passionate sex life. He had agreed, but never really honored that non-negotiable. Within a couple of months of dating, their relationship had become dull and lost the passion it once had. After the breakup, Douglas couldn't retaliate because the foundation of the relationship was honest and mature—spiritual adulting. They had talked and set boundaries. They identified the thread and the cracks in their snowglobes. When they split, there was no childish behavior such as revenge or yelling. Each remained spiritual adults and understood that the function of the relationship wasn't fulfilled. Sally kept her power and didn't take Douglas's.

Sally didn't just end the relationship and call it a day, though. She deconstructed why she created the relationship in the first place. She realized a pattern that was linked to her youth. Sally had been abused by her brother which had killed her sex drive. As she grew up, she attracted men who were "brothers"—like Douglas—and she had sexless relationships to honor that original script. Sally also enjoyed the distance in her relationship with Douglas—he was a pilot who traveled half the month. She realized that she really did want a sexual relationship, but not a full-time commitment. She had attracted exactly what she wanted, but in a childish way, on a 0—100 script. When she realized she could simply ask a man to have his own house while she lived at hers *and* share a healthy sex life, she was in her truth. It didn't work with Douglas, but Sally honored her Lilith archetype, the ruler archetype in the spiritual adulting map, by claiming what she wanted. Lilith, or the ruler, is linked to the hidden truths we have in our psyche. When uncovered, they liberate us.

Hidden truths are not always related to sex, of course. They also relate to deep-seated shame, doubt, and guilt. When we begin to show up as spiritual adults, the veils are removed, we discover the depths of our hidden truths, and we stop apologizing for what we truly want. How often do we stay past the expiration date of a relationship because "we feel bad"? It may seem like an attempt to be selfless, but isn't it selfishly motivated, a child's script for getting one's needs met? Adults act like adults. They hold themselves and each other accountable. They have hard edges and rules and responsibilities. At work, everyone has a rule book; in emotional situations, however, we want to wing it. The same principles that apply to your professional life must apply to your personal life. **Guilt is a placeholder emotion for something less socially acceptable**. However, when we own our power and set our own rules, we don't feel bad taking action when those rules are violated. Sally had no reason to feel bad. She is actually part of Douglas's spiritual family. She may have appeared to him as a "nemesis," but she forced him to look at the immature behaviors that led to the break-up. Neutralizers and nemeses enter your life to shine a light on what isn't working, however hard it may be to see it.

When we leave cosmic consciousness, enter the limited consciousness of the womb, and emerge into earthly life, we often develop poor coping skills and escape mechanisms in an effort to reunite with that cosmic consciousness. These fail, however, because they are rooted in earthly means, not spiritual ones—even those of us who've tried to be spiritual by dissociating from the body. The planetary archetype for spirituality is Neptune; it is also the planet that rules escapism, the oceans, confusion, addiction, codependence, victim-martyr, and alcoholism. Whatever your mother was experiencing while you were in the womb, such as anguish or conflict or fear, you associate it with love, and they become what you seek in relationships. This is the shadow side of authentic love, leading to unhealthy ways of getting our love needs met.

I find it disheartening that psychics or intuitives often come off as woo-woo and ungrounded when covered by the media, but that's exactly what has happened. They have interpreted the process of becoming more ethereal and developing psychic abilities as spiritually adulting, but this is the most childlike behavior of all. It appears spiritual to them, but it's the equivalent of addiction. Leaving the body in this way is a common escape mechanism; the body feels everything the psyche doesn't deal with. It's a coping mechanism because being in the body hurts too much. I find a lot of clients engaging in drugs, alcohol and the latest craze of psychedelics to achieve oneness with spirit, but this is an earthly solution to a spiritual problem. The only way to bypass the toxic waters of the womb is to spiritually adult and meet your own needs without such crutches. Being aware of your shadow love language will help you identify such unhealthy patterns.

In my four-step model of how the subconscious develops, the first step is the moment of conception. Step two is the pregnancy, then the "birth story," and finally the ages of zero to seven. At the moment of conception, we are officially "gifted" our low-level consciousness from our parents. That was their only purpose. Technically, our parents have no other obligation to us. Parents love their children, in their own way, but even snowglobes that appear intact have a crack. In the Disney movie, *The Kid*, Bruce Willis' nine-year-old self comes back to "get integrated." This is our inner child, always lingering and waiting for us to grow them up. Unfortunately, we neglect them again and again. We seek someone from the outside to raise us or we try to raise other people in hopes of getting our needs met instead of raising our own inner child and meeting our own needs.

There's a children's book I love to use with my *"Inner Child Slumber Party"* program called *The Day the Crayons Quit* by Drew Daywalt. I use it to teach students about their inner child. Each crayon represents a color that is linked to a feeling our inner child feels. Each color speaks to overuse or neglect—the 0 or 100. For instance, red represents anger when yelling at or insulting our inner child. Anger is a low-level aspect of the masculine principle, which is often associated with the "fight or flight" response: reacting to stressors that keep us moving and doing, thinking (unconsciously) that this will heal the crack in the snowglobe. The beige crayon is "sad" because it is rarely used, but beige represents the 48 to 52, the balance of extremes. Unfortunately, balance and equanimity are boring to most; the highs and the lows are not very high or very low. The white crayon in Daywalt's cartoon feels like an "empty friend." This is the inner child who is ignored: shrunken in the corner, cold and hungry, getting no attention, yet expected to fulfill our needs. The black crayon is lost among all the brighter colors because this is the shadow work nobody wants to do. This is the real crux of the spiritual journey. It's dirty, messy, and real.

When we listen intently to our thoughts and self-talk about ourselves and others, we can hear what we're saying to our inner child. This is the first truth of the *Twelve Truths of Spiritual Adulting* journey. Without this step, we cannot grow into our adult selves or find spiritual and material union—the marriage of Themis & Zeus. When I realized how self-destructive I was to my inner child, I bought a three-pound Yorkshire Terrier to represent her and take care of. His name is Dino, which means "little sword" in Italian, and it was a swap for the big sword I used as a dagger to self-harm. I encourage my clients to carry a picture of their younger self, set up an altar for their inner child, and/or get a pet, buy a stuffed animal, or nurture a plant so they can learn to care for an externalized version of their inner child. I also suggest they give their inner child a name that is different from their given name. When we start to see how we mistreat our inner child through these externalized rituals, we start to understand why our life is in shambles.

When I was going through my three-year depression, I needed a surrogate mother to help me while I became a mother to myself. You may also need some help while you grow yourself spiritually, as long as you don't become dependent on anyone, which will stop your progress. Whenever you think of yourself as a "child of God," or a child of anyone, you give yourself permission to stay small. This can't go on forever. Eventually, you will have to parent yourself, if you wish to become a spiritual adult.

In mythology, the virgin or maiden goddesses remain virgins because they rule the moon cycles. The Moon is linked to memory, the past, traditions, child, and mother. Artemis, Athena, and Hestia, for example, never marry or have children because of their experiences as children. Hestia is the goddess of hearth and family. She swore to Zeus she would never marry because she was scared to suffer the same fate as her mother. Artemis helped her mother birth her twin brother and was greatly affected by this, swearing to remain a virgin goddess. Athena's mother, the Titan Metis, was swallowed by Zeus, and Athena was born from Zeus' head. She was traumatized by her mother's death and swore never to have children. There's a theme among these goddesses: They stay children to honor their mother. They don't create anything from themselves. They care for others in hopes of getting their needs met. Every one of them suffered their mother's tragedy as if it was their own.

This is the beehive mentality, the constellation of Cancer. Your earthly family has its purpose—it is the foundation of your early life— but it's not intended to be your source of love or to meet your needs beyond 14 years old. I've had many clients who lost their children through abortion or death, custody battles or miscarriages, or they were unable to have children, and most often it's because of a loyalty to remain a child themselves. I lost custody of my children because of this same script as well as a strong transgenerational trauma linked to the moon: my mother lost a daughter, my aunt lost a pregnancy, and my grandmother's daughter died and another was abducted. While I had 50% visitation rights, on paper I was deemed the non-custodial parent. This declaration of my ineptitude by a judge who didn't know me spiraled me into three bouts of cancer. I created all of that. I chose to stay in child. I sought a version of love from my mother that I wanted and didn't give myself—it wasn't her job. She did birth me, but it was my job to find my own way, parent my inner child, and become a spiritual adult.

In my book, *The Shadow Side of the Mother's Love* I discuss every astrological moon sign, its dysfunctional version of love, and the toxic waters we emerge from. We may not all become addicts, but we all develop an unhealthy coping style linked to our virgin goddess archetype and moon sign. Our attachment style is also developed in the womb. I don't believe anyone has a secure attachment style with their biological parents. However, if you raise your inner child appropriately, you can develop such a style with yourself, leading to adult relationships where everyone meets their own needs. This then creates secure attachments with others.

Referring to those who spiritually adult, *The Kybalion* states that

> "[T]hese men have never sought popular approval, nor numbers of followers. They are indifferent to these things, for they know how few there are in each generation who are ready for the truth or who would recognize it if it were presented to them. They reserve the strong meat for men while others furnish the milk for babes. They reserve their pearls of wisdom for the few elect, who recognize their value and who wear them in their crowns." [citation p. 5]

Again, the constellation of Cancer is that of the masses: the first great gate representing human incarnation, the earthly family. It sets the foundation for leaving home, seeking your own path, and becoming a spiritual adult. The crab in Greek mythology was sent by Hera to bite the foot of Hercules as a sign of his vulnerability—a symbol of the limitations of physical life. Cancer rules children and mothers. If we stay within the limitations of our family, we limit our spiritual growth and remain attached to the low-level consciousness.

Chapter Two

The Snowglobe Crack: Ages 0 to 11

E rik Erickson is commonly referenced for his eight-stage model on psychosocial development. His first four stages are 1) Infancy, where children develop trust or mistrust of their world; 2) Early childhood, the second and third year of life, which is linked to autonomy, shame, and doubt; 3) Preschool (ages 3 to 6), when children experience initiative and guilt; and 4) Middle childhood (ages 7 to 12), when industry and inferiority are the main themes. In Ken Wilber's "spectrum of consciousness" theory, the second stage is the *sensori-physical stage* when a child begins to develop an identity with the world. This is similar to Jean Piaaiget's first stage – birth to two— when a baby learns about the world using their senses to interact with their surroundings. In his comprehensive theory about the nature and development of human intelligence, Piaget proposed that humans progress through four stages: the sensorimotor, the preoperational, the concrete, and the formal operational.

Kohlberg's Theory of Moral Development has three levels and six steps—two steps in each level. The first four steps occur between birth and about age eleven. Level One has to do with *preconventional morality*. This relates to punishment and obedience, getting rewards, and having favors returned. Level Two correlates with *conventional morality* and is about the good boy/good girl mentality, social roles, social order, and conformity. Theologian James Fowler wrote about his six-stage theory of moral development in *Stages of Faith*. The first three stages occur between birth and twelve years old. Stage 0—"Primal or Undifferentiated Faith" (birth to 2 years) is characterized by how a child experiences the safety of their environment (i.e., warm and secure vs. neglected and abused). If it's consistently nurturing, the child will develop a sense of trust and safety about the Universe and the divine. Conversely, negative experiences will cause the child to develop distrust about the Universe and the divine. Transition to the next stage begins with the integration of thought and language, which facilitates the use of symbols in speech and play. Stage 1—"Intuitive-Projective Faith" (ages 3 to 7) is characterized by the psyche's unprotected exposure to the unconscious and marked by a relative fluidity of thought patterns. Religion is learned mainly through experiences, stories, images, and the people the child comes in contact with. Stage 2—"Mythic-Literal Faith" (primarily school-aged children) describes the development of a strong belief in the justice and reciprocity of the universe, and the deities are almost always anthropomorphic (e.g., Hanuman the monkey god in Hinduism, known for his daring feats, strength, and loyalty). During this time, metaphors and symbolic language are often misunderstood and taken literally.

Psychologist and author David Elkind proposed that there are three stages of religious development in childhood and adolescence that parallel the preoperational, concrete operational, and formal operational stages of cognitive development described by Piaget. In their scholarly paper, "Religion and Spirituality in Childhood and Adolescence," Bridges & Moore (2002) break down Elkind's theory and write,

> "In *Stage One*, preoperational children are beginning to use signs and symbols to represent objects in their real lives. They are able to use categorical thinking, but they have little ability to understand what distinguishes categories from each other, or that an individual or object can be classified into more than one category at the same time. Young children cannot, for example, understand that an individual can be Catholic and American at the same time. Children who are raised in a religion may know the name of their denomination, and that the name of the denomination represents something about individuals who belong to that denomination, but they have

very little understanding of what distinguishes one denomination from another.

"*Stage Two*, spanning the elementary school years, represents an increased level of understanding about religion and religious beliefs. In keeping with the concrete operational thought that characterizes children of this age, however, thinking about religion is also based on observable behavior, rather than on thoughts, feelings, and motivations. Children understand that denominations differ in their religious activities, but they have much less understanding about the differences in religious beliefs that underlie different activities. Similarly, when children at this age are asked to describe prayer, they focus on the activity of prayer, rather than on the inner feelings and beliefs that older individuals may explore and express in prayer.

"Finally, *Stage Three* religious thinking becomes possible with the advent of formal operational thought. Typically beginning in preadolescence or early adolescence, *Stage Three* is characterized by the capacity for understanding abstract concepts and for personal reflection and exploration of religious beliefs, values, and practices. Denominations are understood to differ because of underlying differences in beliefs, and prayer is understood as a private and personal experience of communion with God. Thus, it is with the advent of *Stage Three* religious thinking that young adolescents' responses to questions about religion are likely to be similar in their meaning to those of adults."

A Confusing Time

The stages of development described above are guided by the spiritual laws of the universe, which also differ from those in earthly paradigms. Upon conception, pregnancy, birth, and ages zero to seven, the child is developing his subconscious mind in response to his snow-globe being cracked, which leads to shame, doubt, guilt, and a sense of inferiority. We feel exiled from Olympus—thrown out and discarded to the bottom of the ocean—and recognize our Hephaestus qualities. This begins the awareness of our unmet needs and imperfections and our search for adults to validate us—developmentally keeping us in the child stage.

We get very attached to our ego at this stage because we've decided that if we "do something good," we'll get praise. Unfortunately, this is a weak form of validation—short-lived and not a measure of our true worth—which creates our personality and the mask we will wear going forward. Truth Five in a spiritual practice—the truth of ego, personality, and soul—is to about identifying the masks we wear. At zero to seven, we experience our first incongruence: Our crack in the snowglobe is accompanied by, "do as I say, not as I do." As children, we haven't yet realized that our parents aren't God, so we observe their incongruent behavior and get very confused. Our parents are often on different sides of the same issue, creating further incongruence and causing us to pick a side. Many years ago I had a student who was describing a homework assignment I assigned to the class and she said "I like thin crust", while showing a hand gesture of thick crust. I pointed out to her the incongruence in her psyche, as we all have, because we learn to live a life based on our parent's values based on what they said, not actually what they did.

Mars returns every two years, and the first one arrives at the begin-ning of the terrible twos. Mars is the god of war, which explains why kids at this age confront you and throw tantrums. They are trying to exercise their ego, their will, their creator energy. Some parents are overly permissive about allowing this energy to be expressed. Others castrate it—sever the connection—because they want you to succumb. They gave you life and that should be enough; but they own you. Later in life, you're expected to pave your own way in the world. But when you get castrated at two, you realize you had better meet your parents' needs and you do—or you do the exact opposite because you're at war in your psyche with the incongruencies. But each response is the same. They are both in the same story. This begins the 0 to 100 as the pendulum swings between extreme hubris and shutting down. You came to earth to live your life and choose your values and become an individual, and your parents immediately put the kibosh on that. And they should, of course, because you aren't yet ready, but that story is now in your psyche and will follow you until you dethrone them and change the story. This is a very important concept to understand. Your purpose in life is to find your own path, not follow the one set down by your parents.

In *The Truth Is in the Triangle*, I write about the alliance we create with a preferred parent while essentially discarding the other one. Often the alliance is due to the power currency of the preferred parent. One parent has covert power currency and the other has overt power currency. Again, we are confused. This incongruence in our psyche, reflecting different sides of the same coin, drives us to spend our life trying to reconcile it. Our parents showed us their incongruence between zero to seven, creating another crack in our snowglobe and a fissure in our psyche. "Something is wrong here," we decided. "*I must be wrong, and I need to fix it.*"

Until the age of seven, we aren't developmentally mature enough to know that our parents are indeed different sides of the same coin, but have different delivery styles. We see the two sides of the one coin as different, and this begins the 0 to 100 pendulum swings. We swing from one direction to another trying to honor our parents while also trying to do things differently, yet we are trapped in the 0 to 100, doing the exact same thing. "Doing it differently" doesn't really begin until we reach 52 years of age.

I used to run the psychology department at a local university in Florida and I would tell my students that all of us in the helping professions, especially mental health, are narcissistic. Why? Because we were parents to our parents and believed we could make mom and dad feel better! The belief that we held the key to their happiness confused us, though. We began to link our value and self-worth with making others feel good, when in actuality, we can't control how anyone feels. This vicious cycle of taking care of others in the hope of getting our needs met creates nothing but a world of children in adult bodies who cannot spiritually adult! Their self-worth is tied to meeting the needs of others and neglecting their own. If this cycle perpetuates, the world will never change and the suffering that exists won't end. The goddess Themis is needed to provide divine order, but first we must put ourselves in order. "Mind your pleck," stop meeting your parents' needs, and receive the throne that is rightfully yours.

That first incongruence between zero to seven sets up subsequent seven-year cycles that represent the "skinny cows" or the "spiritual crisis" years. Spiritual crisis refers to being confronted with a different value system than that of your parents, which you inherited at the moment of conception. Every seven years, that same value system will show up in your life, giving you a chance to re-evaluate it and assimilate your own. You will keep swinging from 0 to 100 trying to figure it out until you finally achieve balance: 48 to 52. Remember: The constellation of Cancer, which rules the low-level consciousness inherited at conception, is that of a beehive, making it very hard to leave the family unit. Even if you literally move cross country, your parents will still live in your subconscious. You can't eliminate the low-level consciousness you inherited from conception, but you can leave and individuate, despite this. There is only one conception story to dethrone. The challenge is dethroning it via the value system your parents gave you. That's the only way to own your kingdom and grow into a spiritual adult.

The marriage of Zeus and Themis represents the integration of the two value systems. There is no incongruence because you finally transformed theirs into your own. Once you create your own value system, dethrone your parents, and begin to do it differently—living life on your own terms at a higher consciousness—duality is elim- inated and unity is restored. The snowglobe is repaired, but now rooted not in child and innocence and meeting others' needs, but in a change in vibration. You've transmuted the low-level consciousness you inherited at conception. When you restore your snowglobe and attain high-level consciousness, you see the duality of the world and the separation that exists between you and others. You realize that we all come from the same Source and that there is only unity.

The "third eye" or sixth chakra is represented by a lotus with two petals. The petal on the left is reserved for mother; the petal on the right is reserved for father. In the middle there is the Void—a circular throne. Symbolically, the Void is *your throne*. You are a child of the Void, the cosmic consciousness; you are also accompanied on either side by your earthly parents. All are connected. When you integrate your parents' value system and make it your own by doing it differently, you become a true spiritual adult. This snowglobe has no toxic waters because we now recognize that we are the universe: Father Sky and Mother Earth. Divine and earthly. The sixth chakra has been called the "seat of consciousness" because the pineal gland is located there. This almond-shaped gland is responsible for secreting melatonin, the hormone that regulates the light-dark cycles that control sleep. These cycles represent the light and shadow aspects of your psyche.

I link the pineal gland to two myths: Phyllis, daughter of Lycurgus, the Queen of Thrace, and the nymph Nana. In the first, Phyllis's lover is sent to war. Believing he would never come back, she commits suicide in her despair. Despair is one of the emotions we feel when we lose the love of our parents—when we realize, in our shattered snow globe, that we weren't unconditionally loved. In the myth, the gods look down on Phyllis and, realizing she sacrificed herself, turn her into an almond tree. This is the victim, the martyr, the rescuer archetype. It describes people who feel that love is sacrifice—that they have to sacrifice their life for their children or their lover. When Phyllis's lover *does* return, he embraces the tree and it blossoms, becoming the symbol for constancy and love and eternal hope.

In the other myth, Nana would gather almonds from the tree and store them in her bosom. One day, the almonds disappear. She then became pregnant. (In another version, a castrated being falls from the tree into her lap and she becomes pregnant with the almond tree.) The child she births is named Attis. She abandons him after birth and, later in the story, he castrates himself. Castration is a theme in mythology that I'll mention over and over again. We castrate ourselves and limit the love we are allowed to receive based on the parental definition of love that we learned in pregnancy.

CHAPTER THREE

The Foundational Structure of Spiritual Adulting— Ages 12 to 16

AGE 12

Erickson states that adolescence begins with identity versus role confusion while social relationships become the focus of one's life. Gebser's third structure of consciousness is the *mythical structure*. Here, the child's emergent consciousness expresses itself as the "hero" of mythic domains. At 12, we begin our first cycle toward spiritual growth. Our Jupiter return occurs every 12 years. The ages of 12, 24, 36, 48, 60, 72 and 84 will be blessed with what I call "fat cows"; they are years of spiritual growth. In the Bible, Joseph becomes the King of Egypt after interpreting a dream for the Pharaoh. The Pharaoh kept dreaming that seven skinny cows would eat seven fat cows. The skinny cows represented years of famine and the fat cows represented years of feasting. Joseph explained to Pharaoh that during the fat cow years (the Jupiter cycles), they needed to save a portion of the wheat so there'd be enough for the country during the famine years (the Saturn cycles). The skinny cows represent the spiritual crisis we encounter every seven years; the fat cows represent the spiritual growth we experience every 12 years as a result of the inner work we conducted during the skinny cows, they're dependent on one another. The interplay of the skinny cows and fat cows create the structure of our entire spiritual life. Later in the book, I describe each cycle, what to expect, and how you can grow through them with few surprises. You will see how you are spiritually guided and how the Universe did not abandon you to toxic waters but provided an earthly vehicle—your body—to express your divinity through your humanity.

Gebser's major thesis was that human consciousness is in transition, not continuous. Transitions are more of a structural unfolding, while continuous consciousness is more like stages evolving. I believe it is both. Consciousness is in transition in the way that the age blocks identified in this represent transition points when we must make choices to support our spiritual growth. If we honor these transitions, especially structural Saturn transits, we evolve and the consciousness of Jupiter cycles begins to gradually unfold. Ken Wilbur, piggybacking on Gerber's work, also states that there are unfolding structures of consciousness rather than stages of consciousness that appear continuous. Cynthia Bourgeault, contributor for *Northeast Wisdom*, writes in relation to Wilbur's work that structures unfold like sections of a jigsaw puzzle or rooms in an art museum, gradually filling in to reveal the big picture (which already implicitly exists). Stages, on the other hand, *evolve*, like steps on a ladder that build sequentially, one upon the other, in a journey that leads onward and upward. But knowing the influences of Saturn and Jupiter and the interplay of those cycles, one can see that consciousness is both transitional and continuous. Saturn provides the structure; Jupiter provides the evolution.

Jupiter's cycles occur every twelve years. When they reach twelve, children understand (spiritually) that they are capable of dethroning their parents. They realize during their first Jupiter cycle that mother and father aren't perfect, and something in their psyche clicks. They now have permission, spiritually and subconsciously, to surpass them. In Roman lore, Jupiter dethroned his father, Saturn (also known as Cronos). It had been prophesied that Saturn would be dethroned by one of his children, so he began swallowing each of them after birth to keep this from happening. Rhea, Saturn's wife, got angry, and when Zeus was born, she sent him off to Crete to be raised by goats. She replaced him with a swaddled rock, fooling Saturn into thinking he was Zeus, and Saturn swallowed the rock. Twelve years later, Jupiter dethroned Saturn and the Titans fell. Thus began the rise of the

Olympians. This myth remains in our psyche, and at 12 we get a glimpse of our parents' mortality and make a plan to dethrone them.

AGES 14—16

Between 14 and 16, children experience their first Saturn opposition: the second skinny cow. There are two types of skinny cows or Saturn cycles; every seven years, we go through one of them. The incongruence of values or the "I like thin crust" stage begins at age 14 and continues every 14 years at age 28, 42, 56, 70 and 84. As children we are trying to reconcile the incongruencies within our parents, and ourselves; therefore, we swing only showing one side of the coin. These are the 0-100 swings. The skinny cows force us to at least become aware of the incongruencies we are living by and begin integration. The years 14 to 16 are characterized by the first swing of the pendulum—the 0 to 100. G. Stanley Hall, an American psychologist, termed this period of adolescence "storm and stress," saying it was linked to conflict with parents and authority figures, mood disruptions, and risky behavior. This cycle is extremely important because it's the child's first attempt to dethrone the parental value system and become his own person. It's also the first attempt at reconciling the incongruence that was experienced during ages zero to seven (the first skinny cow). Remember: At 12, the child realizes he can dethrone his parents. This is his first attempt to actually do it.

Gebser's fourth structure of consciousness is the *mental structure*, where the child has a fully functional ego or self. According to Gebser, consciousness at this stage is fully awake. Piaget's formal-operational thinking correlates to this stage of Gebser's model, where the mind is able to create rules and logic and to understand events and people. Ken Wilber's fourth stage of consciousness, called the *representative mind* stage, also fits in here. This is when the mental structures of the mind begin to form. Children start wanting to spend time with their friends or at their friend's house rather than at home. Their consciousness has broadened to realize there are other ways of living and the world is a larger context than their snowglobe. The imperative question at this stage is whether the child will heed the call of his hero's journey. Children who aren't supported during this stage find it difficult to leave home or, if they do, become self-destructive.

"One Core Values" is a great card game for families to discuss key values. In *Dethroning Olympus,* I provided "value sheets" for families to have a conversation on how the parents and children differ on their values and how to support the child's attempt at a new value system. This is the way society moves forward. When we support the new values of a younger generation, society can evolve. If we stunt our children's growth, we will stunt societal evolution. If you are reading this book as the parent of a teenager, have a conversation with your child. Make a note of their value system and how it differs from yours. This is the thread from the moment of conception that your child will be working through his entire life: the need to dethrone their parents and find their own way. This thread will appear on schedule every 14 years in the above-mentioned years.

The reason adolescents feel the need to defy authority is because of *The Principle of Rhythm.* As described in *The Kybalion,* "Everything flows, out and in; everything has its tides; all things rise and fall; the pendulum swing manifests in everything; the measure of the swing to the right is the measure of the swing to the left; rhythm compensates." This law is intertwined with *The Principle of Polarity*—the pendulum swings between the two extreme poles of 0 and 100. The poles were determined at conception by the parents' level of consciousness. Remember that the parents are but different sides of the same coin, and here lies the incongruence. The child uses those two sides as bookends for his "swings." *The Kybalion* asserts that "with all great movements including birth, growth, maturity…the swing of the pendulum is ever in evidence."

The First Realization

The age of 14 is the child's first opportunity (called an "opposition" in astrology) to challenge her parents and become her own authority figure. Obviously, parents can't let children just run the show at 14; however, this is here where the parents' spiritual influence ends. This first swing of the pendulum is linked to the child assuming his own spiritual and karmic responsibilities. What tends to emerge here is what Carolyn Myss calls the "prostitute archetype." This causes the child to feel shame around wanting to have sex or experiment with drugs or discover hidden truths about the universe that are different than those of their parents. In mythology, this archetype has a name: Lilith. As Erickson pointed out, this shame and doubt was already experienced as a toddler. In actuality, it began at the moment of conception but was confirmed during the 0 to seven snowglobe-shattering years. We hid what we learned about ourselves, creating a primordial, self-loathing wound and birthing the mask we would wear to cover up the ineptitude we discovered about ourselves.

Lilith has always appeared as a demon, a villain, a destroyer of families by seducing a woman's husband and eating their children. This personification of Lilith is actually quite misrepresentative. Yes, at the lowest vibration, she is a seductress that leads us to poor decision-making—such as when adolescents are enamored with bad boys or big breasts. But in actuality, she is the keeper of the hidden truths about ourselves and the universe. Remember when you weren't fully accepted *as you were* by your family? This was the first realization that your earthly family was not your spiritual family. This caused a fissure in your psyche that helped to create Lilith. As a human being created at a low-level of consciousness, we suppressed the thought that there is something more—that *we* are something more. But at the age of 14, a veil is removed, revealing a truth that was forgotten upon drinking from the *River of Forgetfulness*.

There is a now-famous dance performed by Salome for King Herod II at the execution of John the Baptist. Little of this can be found in the Bible, but Mark 6:17-29 mentions the dance and that Herod was so pleased, he offered Herodias' daughter anything she desired—even half of his kingdom! This offer has been grossly misinterpreted; "the kingdom" refers to our place on our throne when and if we remove the veils that keep us at a low-level consciousness. The low-level consciousness prostitute archetype is the ruler archetype at high-level consciousness. On the Spiritual Adulting Archetypal Map Lilith is linked to spiritual adulting. Oscar Wilde popularized the dance in his play, "Salome," calling it the "Dance of the Seven Veils." This name has been used to describe how women use lust to seduce, and some considered it the first-ever striptease. Harem dancers still use scarves to flirt and tease the sultans.

In truth, "Dance of the Seven Veils" is none of these. It refers to a process of *unveiling* our spiritual journey as we realize the truth of our lives and who we are in the universe. The number seven is significant. In all spiritual traditions, the universe is made up of seven planes. In *The Kybalion*, there are seven universal laws that dictate our lives. (I have added an eighth in my book *The Hidden Truths: The Magic of Mysticism and It's Modern-Day Applications*, the Law of Octaves, which refers to the ability to transmute behavior change into belief change and raise the consciousness or vibration inherited at conception. The first real opportunity for this is at age 14—16 when we challenge authority and start figuring out our own values. This law piggybacks on the Law of Vibration, since it explains how to raise consciousness, not just that everything is vibration.) There are seven chakras that must be deciphered and explored to fully know ourselves. The seven primary planets of the solar system are the archetypes— or what I call the psychological organs—that dictate behavior in the earthly realm. In my book, *The Seven Gates: Seven Steps Beyond Self-Awareness*, I speak to the name of the book as being linked to Inanna, a Sumerian goddess of the heavens, who was asked by her sister, Ereshkigal, to comfort her in the Underworld because her husband died. As she passes through each of the seven gates toward the Underworld, an article of clothing is removed, and she ends up at Ereshkigal's house naked. Ereshkigal is horrified that her sister would show up naked to her husband's funeral and orders her to be killed. Inanna was pregnant, and upon being killed, sprouts new life.

This is the original story of resurrection, revisited by all religions and mythologies to show the life-death-rebirth cycle we must all undergo in order to transmute consciousness.

In the Tarot, "The Hanged Man" is the only card that, when thrown upside down, is better than right side up. (I teach the Egyptian Tarot, so that's the image I will use here.). In most decks, "The Hanged Man" depicts the shameful image of a traitor being punished, oftentimes compared to Judas. From his hands, coins are flowing out. Like much of our knowledge around spiritual symbology, however, the image has been misrepresented. It actually refers to an exchange of values and ultimate surrender—when we exchange the values of the earthly realm for those linked to the spiritual realm. This is when *our* truth is no longer viewed as *the* truth, but rather the search begins for the universal truth, of which there is only one. It requires an ultimate surrender, and possibly again being kicked out of Olympus, our earthly family, because our new value system may not be aligned with the family coat of arms. Like Judas, we may believe we are sell-outs to our family if we challenge the conventional value system. In reality, we are healing transgenerational trauma and moving the lineage forward. In Norse mythology, this card represents the god Odin, who suspended himself from the tree Yggdrasil, the tree of life, to gain knowledge of the other worlds.

In my teachings, I explain the card to be one where the client is exchanging one set of values (spiritual) for another set of values (material). The second truth of the spiritual path, the Truth of Desire, is linked to balancing the material and spiritual domains—giving equal opportunity to our earthly lives and our spiritual lives. As a shaman, I use terms like "ordinary states of consciousness" and "shamanic states of consciousness" to represent the connection of both worlds as important to a spiritual path. Shamans walk between the worlds, meaning we walk on earth and through our bodies—centered and grounded—we connect to the divine realms. Jesus was the ultimate shaman. He lived in the earthly world, transmuted his earthly values, and was the representation of the divine through his earthly body:

"The Hanged Man" personified.

In astrology, the Second House (of 12) in the chart is the house of values (Appendix B). I personally think it is the most important axis in the entire chart. Each house in astrology has an opposing house; both houses together are called an axis. The two-eight axis represents our values, our views of money, shared resources with others, sex, transmutation, and death. Jesus was crucified on what is known as the "fixed cross" between two thieves. Each cross represents one of the three crosses in astrology. The fixed cross houses the two-eight axis and speaks to the story of Jesus. Ironically, it's considered a selfish cross. Those with planets in the fixed cross are viewed, at the earthly level, as hoarders or possessive. However, the fixed cross also refers to energy. Those with signs on this cross, when balanced and living at a high vibration, manage their energy well, giving what needs to be given, no more, no less. Taurus and Scorpio rule the two-eight axis—what we value and the exchange of material values for spiritual values. The five-eleven axis is ruled by Leo and Aquarius and represents owning our throne through self-love and then gaining the capacity to love thy neighbor. At a spiritual level, these four signs exemplify exactly what Jesus did during his lifetime. We, too, are called and guided to do the same throughout our lives.

THE SYMBOLISM OF SEXUALITY

The first attempt at entering the Eighth House and exchanging our values occurs between the ages of 14 and 16. During this first opposition, we develop hormonally along with our views around sex. Learning healthy sexual behaviors from our earthly family would be of benefit but this is rare; such discussions are usually awkward and full of shame. Some schools offer sexual education covering anatomy and STDs, but nowhere does the adolescent receive spiritual-sexual education. The seed—the ejaculate of the orgasm—is the most valuable energy in the world. It not only produces offspring and continues the lineage but it's the same energy that births the arts, music, poetry, books, and literature. In Genesis Chapter 38, Onan is slain by God for spilling his seed on the ground—by withdrawing before orgasm. "Onanism" is the practice of masturbation, commonly associated with the ages of 14 to 16. "Spilling the seed" has nothing to do with sex; it refers to a wastefulness of resources and energy and the lack of self-worth and self-love we have for ourselves. If we are busy chasing our unmet needs by never growing up and meeting our own needs, we waste our potential. The potential of our being is found in the energetic version of sperm.

Energetically, sperm is the penetrator energy; it fertilizes the egg so we can be born. If we continue to waste our penetrator energy on people who don't deserve it, we waste our God-given essence and gifts. Themis is the goddess of good counsel, fairness, and divine order. Unless you live in the 48 to 52, own your throne, are fair to yourself, and acknowledge your divinity, she cannot provide your place, *your pleck*. "Know your place, know your price" refers to knowing your worth. The French call orgasms *le petit mort*—the little death. Every time we have sex and waste the seed (energetically, not physically), a little bit of our true selves die.

Sex is found in the Eighth House, exactly the same as transmutation, death, and resources. Where are you spending your resources? On whom and on what? Show me that, and I'll show you what you really value. Jesus' death was simply a demonstration of transmutation. He transmuted the low-level vibration of his earthly parents and became the Christ consciousness with a high-vibration value system. At twelve—his first Jupiter return—Jesus identified his true worth and dethroned his parents. He went to the temple, and when Mary found him, he said, "I must do my father's work." No parent will allow their children to leave home at 12 or 14 to "do their heavenly father's' work," but they have to be careful not to castrate them because if this age doesn't go well, it sets the foundation for the rest of the child's spiritual adulting possibilities and the spiritual growth they may, or may not, attain.

Tantra is a Hindu and Buddhist mystical text that describes the process a person undergoes with spiritual transmutation. Patanjali, father of the yoga sutras, the foundation for the eight limbs of yoga, says the word means *principal.* The occultist Pierre Bernard introduced the term to the Americas as a sexual practice and distorted its meaning. Tantra refers to the balance of the masculine and feminine energies found in each of us. The yin-yang symbol demonstrates this with a white dot and a black dot in each of the respective parts of the circle. Jung called the feminine principle found in a male psyche the *anima,* and the masculine principle found in the woman's psyche the *animus.* In Hermetic philosophy and *The Kybalion,* the "Principle of Gender" states that, "Gender is in everything; everything has its masculine and feminine principles; gender manifests on all planes."

We each have a balance of masculine and feminine energies; one is not better than the other. This is our state at birth, what the Vedas call the *manas prakriti.* Our manas prakriti is the balance of the elements—air, fire, earth, water, and *akash,* or ether—and relates to our state of mind at the moment of birth, when we are deemed to be in a perfect, balanced state. Our perfect combination of them speaks to our true nature in this lifetime. In Sanskrit, manas is derived from the root word *eul,* which means "to know." It has also been conceptualized as the inner flame of knowledge. We view the world through the lens of our manas prakriti; however, from 0 to seven when we are kicked out of Olympus, these elements become imbalanced as we try and become someone we are not. Our astrological birth chart is the easiest way to see the elemental distribution that is our essence. By counting the number of air, earth, fire and water planets in your birth chart you can calculate your *manas prakriti* or elemental makeup that is deemed balanced for you. For instance, if we have too little earth, we may overcompensate and add earth to our essence by seeking wealth. With excess fire, we may dim our trailblazing nature by acting more emotional. It never changes throughout our life. However, we adulterate this balance to become accepted; we start wearing a mask, distorting our true, elemental essence. Our inner knowing, the snowglobe we want to re-enter so desperately, is obscured by the outer world and its veils of delusion.

Becoming a Child of the Void

Themis was the mother of Prometheus, who was punished for stealing fire from the gods. She knew the prophecy that her son would be condemned to a life of misery for doing this to fulfill a promise to humans, but he did it anyway and she supported him. The fire element is associated with the third chakra: our crown of jewels, our throne. It represents self-love and is the bridge between erotic or sexual love, what we birth in our second chakra, and love toward humanity, what we birth through service (once we *mind our pleck*) in the fourth chakra. From a symbolic standpoint, the fire element refers to inner knowing. Out of fear of being punished by our earthly family if we don't stop the game of conditional love, we fail to find our fire—our elemental balance—and, as a result, our entire society lives out of balance. No one minding their rightful throne.

The masculine polarity elements are fire and air; the feminine polarity elements are earth and water. We have a combination of all four in our astrology chart, which represents the essence of a person—their true, natural state. This is the first thing I teach in my "Hidden Truths Astrology Fundamentals" course. We then see how, from zero to seven, the balance of these elements gets distorted by false veils and early programming. The goal, then, is to restore this balance by learning universal laws, namely the Principle of Gender, since humans generally understand the energetic traits of masculine and feminine. Learning the ratio of fire/air to earth/water elements in your chart will explain the feminine/masculine polarity in your life. This is the origin of Tantra. It's association with sex arose to help people balance these masculine and feminine energies with another person—to achieve the mystical marriage or *hieros gamos*.

In my book, *The Truth Is in the Triangle*, I describe how achieving a mystical marriage between you and your partner is a spiritual adulting process; it has nothing to do with sex. Sex is part of an earthly relationship; spiritual adulting has to do with energy distribution. Each person must first own their throne—their 48 to 52—before achieving that balance in the bedroom. Sex is mentioned in the Eighth House in astrology because it relates to the Principle of Gender, owning your optimal distribution of masculine and feminine energies, and transmuting the low vibration consciousness inherited at conception. We use the masculine and feminine polarities simultaneously, and our gender and sexuality are the vehicle for exploring how the polarities manifest in the earthly plane.

The key to balancing and, ultimately, transmuting those polarities is through shadow work—also the domain of the Eighth House. This process is the lifelong journey of the soul. Shadow work is the eighth truth in spiritual adulting. We leave "home" at 14 and return at 42, when we really begin to integrate our parents into our psyche and balance the masculine and feminine polarities. This is where the spiritual adulting process really begins. Duality is caused by the belief that we are separate from others; the crack in the snowglobe has us feeling ashamed and in doubt of who we are. As we go through the spiritual adulting process and begin to balance the masculine and feminine energies, our psyche becomes unified. In the energetic anatomy system, represented by the caduceus, the two serpents, Ida and Pingala, refer to the feminine polarity on the left side (Ida) and the masculine polarity on the right side (Pingala). Where these two serpents meet creates a chakra. Not until the sixth chakra—the third eye—do the serpents meet and create unity. Until you balance the masculine and feminine energies (your manas prakriti) and integrate your parents at age 48 to 52, you will not have laid the foundation for supporting the process of spiritually adulting.

To avoid becoming like his father, Odysseus left home to fight in a war. Twenty years later, he returned to Ithaca to reunite with his wife and son. This story represents the value we place on the masculine principle. Leaving home is an act of *doing*, the masculine principle. War is also associated with the masculine principle. His return home is an effort to balance the masculine and feminine, symbolized by his reunion with his wife, Penelope, and represented by his son, Telemachus. Upon his return home, he says to Penelope, "You cannot separate the olive branch from the marital bed." At that moment, he realizes he is the olive branch produced from his parents' marital relations. He is them; they are him. Only at this point of integration do we balance our energies, become unified in our consciousness, and raise the serpents of the kundalini located at the base of the spine. These represent the veils of illusion that Inanna removes, thus beginning one's spiritual adulting. We finally accept that we are exactly like our parents, but instead of leaving home, we return home to integrate them. 99% of our fire is spent on trying to change our unchangeable nature. In Shamanism, this is I referred to as the West. It is linked to our roots and what we inherited at conception, low-conscious, impure thoughts, sinful desires and a negative emotion linked to all of it. When we return home we realize that is us, and always has been, but at 14-16 our job is to leave home and attempt to begin to do it differently.

The ages 48 to 52 correspond to Chiron, our primordial wound, when people undergo an existential crisis—a grief cycle—when they realize that their life has been a series of chaotic mistakes and choices that were falsely created to keep them in child and victim. I went through a three-year depression until, like The Hanged Man, I accepted that I had created my mess based on a bad bucket value system— mainly pride and vanity—rather than balancing them with my true value system, my good bucket values, which was to honor the *pleck*—the throne—I was divinely provided at conception by Themis. The defeat of the Hydra and integrating material values with spiritual ones begins the spiritual path. In mythology, the Hydra of Lerna was a nine-headed creature that lived in a swamp. It represents our subconscious and the shadow aspects of our psyche. Hercules was sent to defeat the Hydra as it was terrorizing the countryside. He was given little instruction other than not to cut off the Hydra's heads because two more would grow back in their place. Hercules carried a club, and with help of his nephew, Iolaus, he ignited his club and severed the Hydra's heads with fire—the only way to transmute their power. Here again we see the element of fire as symbolizing an inner knowing and the answer to defeating our Hydra. Fire is the only element humans can control.

In *The Seven Gates: Seven Steps Beyond Self-Awareness*, I discuss each parent as having a good and a bad bucket. Items in the good bucket don't cause any problems. This is the light cycle. Items in the bad bucket become the shadow aspect of ourselves—the ones that create problems. Denial of the bad bucket value system causes the incongruence keeping you from who you really are. The good news is that the antidote is found in the good buckets. Integration of both the bad and good bucket values leads to dethroning your parents and growing into a spiritual adult.

During the zero to seven years, we observe that our parents have flaws, and when we see these, we put them in a bad bucket and shove them to the depths of the subconscious while continuing to live behind a veil that mother and father are perfect. If we actually accept that mom and dad aren't perfect, then, by deductive reasoning, we are imperfect as well. We aren't ready to shatter our snowglobe from zero to seven; hell, we don't even want it shattered in our 50s!

Jung identified the shadow as the unknown "dark side" of the personality. The shadow represents the un-integrated aspects of our parents and why we "leave home" to pretend we aren't them. At 14, we only get as far as our neighbor's house, but the process of dethroning our parents has begun. Children aren't consciously aware of their shadow because subconsciously and spiritually, they are being influenced by their parents, who don't give their children permission to dethrone them and discover their own values. Despite this lack of support, spiritual adulting begins at 14 anyway: mentally, emotionally and spiritually, even as children are detoured by excess, acting out, or sexual promiscuity. Again, sexuality is not a negative activity; it is linked to the energy of creation, our potential to create ourselves anew, like Jesus. A rebirth.

In John 3, Jesus told Nicodemus that he must be born again. Nicodemus was considered a "teacher of teachers" yet did not understand the basic spiritual teachings of the Universe. Jesus declared, "I tell you the truth, no one can see the kingdom of God unless he is born again." Nicodemus responded, "How can a man be born when he is old? Surely he cannot enter a second time into his mother's womb to be born!" And Jesus answered, "No one can enter the kingdom of God unless he is born of water and the Spirit. Flesh gives birth to flesh. but the Spirit gives birth to Spirit." We start our sexual experimentation in adolescence, but no one supports our spirit being birthed from spirit at this age. Issues of shame and guilt around the sexual act that were present at conception show up as the "values" we want to dethrone, but we cannot face them at this age.

In many mythologies, the feminine principle, symbolized by Lilith and her counterparts, is viewed as evil because of its wisdom and power to give life and willingness to defy tradition. Lilith and her counterparts are viewed as female demons. This is clearly because the feminine holds wisdom and is the vehicle for God's manifestation. In Hebrew literature, Lilith is considered the first wife of Adam – and made from the same clay as Adam—but who also refused to submit to Adam's authority. In the Epic of Gilgamesh, *ki-sikil-lil-la-ke* is a serpent that is linked to Lilith, but its translation actually means "sacred place and spirit." Lamashtu is a demon goddess called the child-killer. In theatre, she is depicted as the prostitute, the harlot, the seductress—the one who leads men astray. All of us have a Lilith archetype in our hidden truths. *The Dance of the Seven Veils* represents Inanna and Mary Magdalene as prostitutes. They are demonized in religion as those scholars knew the power of sexual energy, the Principle of Gender, and the power of the mystical marriage to Self—the *hieros gamos*.

If, however, we were allowed to remove the veils of illusion, we would own our own lives and wouldn't need a mediator for our spiritual lives. Lilith is the only character in mythology who said "No" to the gods. This means that we have the right to assume our throne, parent ourselves, remove the veils, and reject the concept of being a "child of God." But because we are desperate to be a child of *someone*, we refuse to be an adult. This subconscious programming is linked to the scarcity version of love received from our parents. We think if we leave the beehive—the dysfunctional, limited version of love we've come to know—our biggest fear will come true: that no one will love us. Lilith is a threat to religious scholars because she owned herself as an adult, as an earthly woman, as a spiritual woman, as a spiritual adult. If the news got out that all of us have permission to own our lives, parent ourselves, and own our sexuality, both earthly and spiritually, there would be no need for intermediaries to God. The notion that we need a parent to meet our needs is castrating. Lilith did not allow herself to be castrated—to be submissive. She ate her children because she refused to birth more needy adults, more needy inner children. She understood that the only real way to spiritual liberation was to be the adult, the parent, to herself.

Lilith holds the hidden truths of the Universe, the answer to our feminine principle, and how to integrate our parents and "do it differently." Lilith "led men astray" because the masculine principle is not the self-worth principle; that belongs to the feminine. She is considered the child-killer because she lets us grow up and own our adult. She is the only character in mythology who defied the gods by claiming that she, too, is a god as in the story of Adam and Lilith, she doesn't allow God to tell her what to do. Lilith was Adam's first wife and she refused to lay beneath him during sex since they were both created equal. God reprimands her, saying he will send her into exile if she doesn't comply with Adam's wishes. Instead, she sends herself into exile as she will not succumb to this unreasonable request.

Our gods are our parents. They told us to succumb to the beehive—the family norms—although we saw the need to do things differently because our values are different. And yet we would lose what I call our Costco membership card—the dysfunctional and conditional version of love learned in the womb—if we dared to do things differently. So we exiled ourselves. We self-flagellated to show how pious we were. We honored our parents' story and forgot that we came to experience God through our feminine principle. We were castrated and we continue to castrate ourselves. Lilith is the demon we battle in our subconscious, not because she is bad, but because if we dare to do it differently, who will be our god? No one wants our hard edges, our boundaries, or our self-love. If we love ourselves, others will be required to love themselves and get out of victimhood, shifting the system. But no one wants us to shift the system. The status quo, the 0 to 100, the masculine principle, swinging left to right, up and down—those are valued. Doing it differently based on personal responsibility would change the world.

If you need to be a child of someone, be a child of the Void. The Void is the throne in the sixth chakra—the universal consciousness that birthed you. It owes you nothing; it is merely energy. Universal law is the only system you need to be a spiritual adult and a child of the Universe. Stop bargaining with a false god as if he sits on *your* throne, punishing you into submission for sins you did not commit. This is nonsense. Take personal responsibility. You created the world you live in with your thoughts and your actions. Own the consequences. Until you remove the veils of delusion and get out of your snowglobe to own your earthly and spiritual life, nothing will change. God isn't doing anything to you. The Universe doesn't have your back and nothing is personal. The Universe is simply responding to your thoughts, and supports you when you have your own back.

Dr. Hew Len was a therapist who worked at Hawaii State Hospital but never saw a single patient, closing the hospital doors four years later because all his patients had recovered. How? From his constant practice of *ho'oponopono*, a meditative technique in which the following is repeated: *"I'm sorry. Please forgive me. Thank you. I love you."* It seems so simple, but he was able to make these changes because of his single-minded focus on taking responsibility for his part in creating the mental hospital and the mentally sick. Two aspects of the practice involve taking responsibility *"I'm sorry and Please forgive me"*. These are more important in changing the world than anything. We must understand the most important universal law of all universal laws, *Principle of Mentalism*, that states all is mind, and all the world has been created from our own thoughts. The personal TED talk, linked to the first three truths, are about ownership of our low-level consciousness, and owning our impure thoughts, emotions and desires. Without this we change nothing. The latter part is *"Thank you, I love you"*, this is linked to truth eleven and twelve, actually loving another while maintaining Self, eliminating all dogma and returning to unity with the universal consciousness and remembering all is one. There is a lot to confront about ourselves between truth three and eleven! This is the Lilith principle—the feminine principle that has been castrated by all religions and many cultures, replaced by the image of "the virgin"—the quiet, submissive, pious mother. This is a false narrative, however, more of a masculine principle in the guise of the feminine as the pendulum swings from sexual promiscuity to "girl boss." The *real* feminine holds the answer; it's the vessel for God's manifestation—the divinity we come to share with the world. If we dare to defy the gods of our subconscious programming, self-destruction and self-loathing because we are animals with programmed low level consciousness, this can cure the world's ills. Again, it takes personal responsibility, exiling yourself from the family beehive, and doing it differently. All of the issues we didn't like in our parents got shoved down in our subconscious and become our shadow, our Hydra. Until we enter that swamp and confront those shadow aspects of ourselves, we will not begin the spiritual adulting process.

Why is the 14—16 adolescent stage the most important one in this process? Because this is the first time we start to realize that there is a flaw in our parents' value system—the one issue you need to dethrone. Prior to this, you weren't aware of what was happening. You were veiled, but this is the first stage of veil removal. At conception and during pregnancy and birth, you didn't know that there was a crack in the snowglobe. At 0 to seven, you hid the crack and pretended it wasn't there. You "shrunk" to meet your parents' needs. At 12, you discovered that they weren't perfect and that you had to dethrone them but did not have permission (according to spiritual law and biology). From 14 to 16, you are given permission to identify the value you will dethrone in this lifetime. You may not veer far from the parental storyline, but you will find a way to do it differently.

For example, my oldest sister died when I was 15. My father got a call from a friend who asked him if he wanted to sue the school. My sister had been attending a large school associated with a very successful non-profit organization. Their negligence killed her. She had choked on some food and was found dead on a bathroom floor. He had a solid court case if he chose to pursue it. My father's response to his friend was, "That won't bring her back." That, right there, became my value system. My parents were in the worst financial crisis of my childhood and their lives. Our townhouse didn't have a bedroom for me and I slept on the floor. Suing this organization could have changed a lot, but my father is the most principled person I know. At that moment, if I had any doubt, my values around money became very clear. However, in my adolescent mind, I had to make that value system my own. I had to dethrone him.

Years later, I found out that Jupiter, the planet that allows us to dethrone our parents, was in my second house of money and values. No coincidence there. This is exactly where I needed to do it differently! Whatever happens between 14 and 16 sets the stage for the rest of our spiritual adulting. We cannot skip this step! My father was the "financial arm" of the cult. He funded the cult leader and all of the followers who needed loans. He was the cult's ATM, and it seemed that his funds never ran out. I wanted that! And so, I became that but in a very unhealthy way. Using unbalanced masculine energy, I started making a lot of money. I bought real estate. I paid for my partner's to live a lavish lifestyle. I wasted my earthly assets, acting as if they were unlimited, of which there were three: money, resources, and time. All of them are linked to self-worth. I wasted my seed, my sexual energy. Sexual energy is synonymous with these assets. Our energy is held in sexual energy—the energy of creation.

The symbol of the planet Mars is a circle, representing spirit, with an arrow that represents how we use that spirit. We direct our spirit through sexual or creator energy, whether it's physical sex that produces a child or the energy that creates a book or work of art. It's all the same energy. We channel this energy on earth through money, time, and resources. I wasted all my money to receive a false version of love. I owned my father's value system, which was that the material would never be as important as the spiritual one. However, I copied his dysfunctional use of money to "earn my love" and seek a childlike version of love. I remember being 8 years old and leaving a big plastic bin full of coins—at least $50 worth—at a Burger King. I begged my parents to go back and get it. They said no. I took that to mean my earthly resources weren't that important. This led me to value the spiritual world over the material. Although I made quite a bit of money, I wasted it, and never valued the material resources I had, I mismanaged time, money and energy, proving my lack of self-worth. I lived this way until I was forced back into my body following my cancer diagnosis. I had used money as a way to get love and didn't value my hard work, my seed, or my self-worth. I definitely didn't *mind my pleck*, and my life showed it!

The glyph of mars: When used appropriately it is the creator energy leading us to our divine will and purpose and the ego and personality are tamed and serve the divine will. When used inappropriately the ego and personality rule and the will is stunted.

Chemotherapy was the most physically exhausting and debilitating experience of my life, but I needed a hardcore neutralizer, and it arrived right on schedule, forcing me into my body and to dethroning my father's value system around money. My childhood of hearing that my father would be a millionaire, that no one could surpass him financially, was the link to my values. That was the "story" I'd become so attached to. I became him, the most values-oriented person I knew. However, all of this was at a low vibration. You don't dethrone your parents by doing the opposite; you have to do it differently. Dethroning him and those values was the key to my spiritual growth. This means transmuting the thoughts of low-level consciousness and honoring that same value system but with a higher level of consciousness—one that serves us as adults and not as children. As long as I simply copied my father's story at the same low vibration, I wasn't doing it differently. I was still in child. Once I dethroned him and became a spiritual adult, earning my seat on my throne, my financial and spiritual wealth multiplied.

In your astrological chart, Jupiter's house location is where you have permission to dethrone your parents. However, it doesn't mean you will. Jupiter shows up in 12-year cycles, and when it does, you may or may not choose to change your vibration, raise your consciousness, and do it differently. Most keep repeating the same story, calling it the "sins of the father," genetics, transgenerational trauma, or "family business." We give earthly identification to spiritual problems because we fail to live in a shamanic state of consciousness where spirit and matter are unified. We limit ourselves to the waking state of consciousness even as we want spiritual growth.

When you look at a pond, the surface should be still. Stillness allows you to see the depth of the pond—your subconscious thoughts. This is the first step in the spiritual path. The inner child is named, seen, and heard by analyzing the quality of your thoughts. However, if the surface of the pond is chaotic, your inner life is noisy and you will not hear her. You will not be able to grow her up. You likely created chaos to avoid stilling the mind because of FOFO: *fear of being found out*. You distract yourself because you don't want to see the real truth of who you are, preferring the mask, the delusion, the crack in the snowglobe. You don't want to do the hard work of removing veils. You will, however, make a "vision board" to "consciously" manifest your dreams and then complain when they don't come true, blaming karma or the Universe, sticky-note spirituality. But if you don't address your subconscious programming, your conscious mind will create nothing of true value. Yes, it's easier to have friends and family praise you and say "Thank you" when you do their chores or make them soup. It's painful and difficult to hear and acknowledge the awful things you say to your inner child and the truth of what you think about yourself. But this is what all seekers of personal truth must do. If you do not obsessively analyze your thoughts, where they come from, and look at what you really think about yourself, you're not on a spiritual path or a true seeker, you're engaging in fluff spirituality.

OWNING YOUR VALUES

The second phase on a spiritual path is to exchange our material values for more spiritual ones. This doesn't mean austerity, hiding in an ashram, or beating our physical bodies because they lead us to temptation. This is all childish behavior—literally—getting punished by the Father. This also doesn't mean to avoid paying your bills, idealize poverty, or sit in prayer all day—a 0 to 100 of pious behavior that is still childish. The 48 to 52 is about balancing spirit and matter. Have you scheduled as much of your time for spiritual activities as you have for material ones? Is there space in your home that honors spiritual practices, or is everything cluttered with junk and other people's problems? False selflessness will keep you distracted from attending to the quality of your thoughts. The second truth is the *truth of desire*, we were all conceived on a desirous, impure thought, and we will keep from analyzing our thoughts in truth one to not identify with our desires. Without identifying our desires and judgments, we cannot know our true values. **Judgements are confessions, and they're great!** When we identify a judgement about others, link it to one of the cardinal vices, and this indicates something you value. This value was present at the moment of your conception, yet, you were taught an incongruence around it in childhood. It creates a negative inner dialogue and a shadow aspect you'd prefer to hide by doing the opposite. For instance, do you judge an overweight woman, this is linked to vanity, perhaps it was your mother's beauty that attracted your father? This impure thought at conception is linked to all judgments, which are linked to bad bucket items in your parents and a suppressed shadow aspect in yourself. A true account of your thoughts will show the self-hatred for being vain yourself and having this in your bad bucket value system. Judgements of others are simply judgements of self, linked to a bad bucket value you haven't accepted is in you, trying to pretend it is in your parents alone.

Everything is a system: you, your relationship, your family, your work. Half of every system in your life should be devoted to the spiritual. So create space in your homes, your calendars, and your life for spiritual growth. When the spiritual and the material become equal in your systems, you are on the way to assuming your throne. When you start shifting your system, your shamanic state of consciousness (SSC) or spiritual consciousness will open up. Jung termed this state the subjective psyche. The objective psyche refers to aspects we are, in part, unaware of, but the subjective psyche, coincides with the higher states of consciousness that lead us to intuition and inner knowing. Henry Corbin, a philosopher and theologian, calls this the *mundis imaginalis*: the space between earthly and spiritual kingdoms. The *mundis imaginalis* means "the souls of souls" and is considered the "real world" where the mystery of the unconscious, symbolic meaning, and the true essence of existence are revealed.

When I see clients, I ask them to imagine themselves in a shamanic state during the session. I listen to their earthly story, validate their emotions, and then address their SSC. I hear their inner child and translate what he or she is saying to them. I break down the symbolism, myth, and metaphor—the languages of the universe—in which they unknowingly speak. This is the realm of the imagination with no room for the logical mind. However, we need both: the logical, rational mind to live in ordinary reality and the symbolism and imagination to understand the universe and grow into a spiritual adult.

But we do love our stories! We're attached to our story. We make love to our story, over and over again. This is how we stay children while attracting a parental figure to keep us there. Carolyn Myss calls this "woundology": Within minutes of a conversation, we speak of our wound. What would happen if we dared to rewrite our own story? Yes, we are in an earthly body that goes through some pain, but the suffering is optional—though we love to add it to our story. I was in a romantic relationship with my story until I broke it off, preferring to be in a healthy relationship with my inner child. When I tended to her, we fast-tracked to spiritual adulthood. When I finally decided to own my Lilith and remove the veils, I connected with the Shekinah, the "glory of the divine presence" as depicted in Kabbalah and often represented as the divine feminine. You cannot access the light of the divine if you don't honor the "bad buckets" or shadow aspects that hold the darkness you've been running from. Those bad buckets represent the judgements of your parents that you internalized as true and shaped your life around.

When I asked my daughter about the values and issues she confronted during those key years of 14—16, she said she was at the height of an eating disorder and felt alone and depressed, as if the world had abandoned her, and tried psychedelics for the first time. She was just beginning her spiritual development and psychedelics were a "toxic water," low-vibration attempt to integrate spirituality into her value system. Her depression reflected the Saturn cycle she was in, and pulling away from authority left her feeling abandoned. She also felt abandoned because, at 14 to 16 when you leave your parents' spiritual umbrella, the psyche feels at odds and doesn't know how to cope—hence the "toxic water" as an escape. Spiritually, she was being given her spiritual adulting script, which was scary. Her eating disorder reflected my level of consciousness at conception when I was at the height of my own eating disorder—now in her bad bucket. She was trying to integrate my shadow as hers, keeping me in child by doing my work for me—living out *my* shadow—while failing at her own attempts to change. Moral of the story: **Parents, do your work so your kids don't have too!** In my book *Dethroning Olympus* I speak to how children are the unintegrated shadow of the parents. Children will become the materialized shadow, as a projection for the parent, to help parents learn to meet their own needs. The ultimate act of love on behalf of the child, yet parents, we continue to castrate our children, refusing to do our own shadow work, so they can pursue their own spiritual adulting process.

It's not uncommon, of course, for teenagers to feel depressed. This first opposition is ruled by Saturn, the same god who was dethroned by Jupiter and swallowed his children. It reflects the interplay of the skinny cows (Saturn) and the fat cows (Jupiter) that dictate our spiritual progress. At 12, we first get permission to dethrone our parents, but the adolescent turmoil is ruled by Saturn, and he will not make it easy for you. He ate his children to avoid this happening, and your parents are no different. Saturn is the planet that rules limitations, authority, boundaries, depression, loneliness, *and* the spiritual adulting process. When Saturn is in opposition, your child self and your adult self are being pulled apart. Your parents tug you to stay in child while your inner child and spiritual-adult tug you toward maturity. **Owning your own value system is the first decision based on free will that will dictate the remainder of your spiritual growth and the rest of your Saturn-Jupiter cycles outlined in subsequent chapters.** The amount of spiritual growth is up to you. As written in *The Kybalion,* you are guaranteed spiritual growth but how far you get is directly related to this 14 to 16 cycle. How you decide to live this out—as a child or an adult—will follow you throughout life.

Growth cycles in nature are dictated by the Fibonacci number, the mathematical code that governs nature's design, such as spirals on a seashell or the branching of a tree. These same designs apply to our spiritual growth. The same spiral, for example, is found in the glyph of Jupiter. We can only grow in proportion to the cycles of Saturn. Remember Joseph in the Bible who prophesied the years of feast and famine? During the years of feasting, he saved enough wheat so that the Egyptians would have sufficient food during the famine years. Our spiritual growth boils down to that relationship between the skinny cows and fat cows—the bookends of our growth, the 0 to 100. The 48 to 52 of our spiritual path is the midpoint between feast or famine, working consistently throughout life, and even the Jupiter cycles, to make the Saturn cycles less intense. When we are forced to work internally during the skinny cow years, we might show up for ourselves. But rarely does anyone work on their inner selves during the feasting years. We are gluttonous and indulgent, living in the moment. We pilfer our resources, saving nothing for the famine years.

The Lessons of Saturn

Saturn in our chart is linked to death. The real spiritual process is about learning how to die, which relates to surrender, not resignation—surrendering one value system (the material) for another (the spiritual). Every Saturn cycle forces you to detach from something that no longer serves you—a habit or a way of thinking. The Saturn cycles force you to adult, killing some aspects of the child in your psyche. My daughter's feelings of being abandoned and left alone in the world was her version of both death and adulting. She has Saturn in the Eighth House of death and spiritual transmutation, hence her trying psychedelics. She tried to connect to her spiritual waters through a "toxic water" coping skill. She indeed killed some childlike aspect of herself and began the spiritual adulting process. Again, you don't need to know astrology; these cycles happen in line with your "story." The astrology chart simply confirms what your earthly consciousness lives out as a story. This story "shows up" every seven years. If you choose deep spiritual adulting during each Saturn cycle, you can grow exponentially. Even if you do little or nothing, your story will continue to unfold and a small level of growth will occur. Just as we age biologically, we age spiritually, and how well we age is up to us.

When my daughter got her wisdom teeth out at 21, during a neutralizer Saturn cycle, she graded me on the care I gave her after the surgery. She gave me an A for nurturance and a D on administering medication. She went on to confirm that she was an adult and could take care of herself. This extended the adulting process she experienced at 15. She has a story of being abandoned and her having to take care of her father and her brothers after a bitter divorce, right on schedule, the story resurfaced to confirm the thread—one that started at conception, "I must care for myself, rely on no one and be an adult even as a child". My daughter's pregnancy story was quite awful and it is recorded in her subconscious as a distrust with authority. From conception, pregnancy, and 0 to seven, and even through 21, she is following the thread. This will persist in each of us until we decide to spiritually adult.

Saturn is linked to a scarcity mentality and Jupiter to an abundance mentality. Scarcity is associated with limitations, boundaries and spiritually adulting. That's why we don't like it. Abundance seems easy, as if the universe is providing for us, but it's not a gift the way we think it to be, it's directly related to the growth from the skinny cow cycle. The work you did with Saturn is rewarded by Jupiter. This is the marriage between Themis and Zeus. The theme is the same for 12 years old and 14—16. The full marriage between Themis and Zeus, Saturn and Jupiter, the fat cows and the skinny cows, doesn't occur until you are 60, but each Saturn and Jupiter cycle leads us there.

There are two types of Saturn cycles: those that happen every seven years (Neutralizer or Nemesis years-N years) and those that happen in opposition years (Value or Valor years-V years)—those that close cycles of karma and propel you into spiritual adulthood. N years happen at ages 7, 21, 35, 49, 63, 77, and 91. Oftentimes, a nemesis from your spiritual family will appear and nudge you in the right direction. These years are directly related to neutralizing the 0 to 100 pendulum swings you create to honor your parents. They show you a different way to achieve the 48 to 52. *Nemesis* is the goddess of retribution, balance, and vengeance. She can control shadows. The people and situations that appear during these years are linked to the original crack in the snowglobe and the 14 to 16 value you want to dethrone. She will shine a light on your shadow—your bad buckets—to help you integrate your parents.

The V years are ages 14, 28, 42, 56, 70, 84. These years are also related to the value system you tried dethroning at 14 to 16. These cycles are ruled by the goddess *Arete*, the goddess of valor. Valor means great courage in the face of danger, especially in battle. These Saturn cycles do feel like battle and they are scary. We are daring to dethrone our parents, to become spiritual adults and children of the Void. In the Bhagavad Gita, the warrior Arjuna tells Lord Krishna that he is unwilling to fight the Kaurava army because he'd be fighting his family, which was a mortal sin. Lord Krishna responded that the only reason a person could refuse to fight is fear of defeat. When we swing from 0 to 100—especially when we live in the 0, the scarcity realm—we are shrinking and playing small. V years come to challenge us and force us to get in the ring and fight. These situations are called "oppositions" because they often come in the form of a person or situation that creates external conflict. In reality, this is mirroring our own inner desires, conflicts, and fears. My 0 to 100 was a desire to be a spiritual teacher; however, having had a cult leader as a mirror for my 100, I shrunk. For fear of becoming *that*, which we all have the potential for, I played small.

The pendulum swings of 0 to 100 correlate to the prince or pauper; at its root is hubris. *Hybris*, the goddess of insolence, violence, and outrageous behavior, is at the 100, and we often fear that potential in ourselves. Shrinking or playing small avoids that, but this is a scarcity mentality and not truthful. We were never taught how to live in balance and equanimity; the 48 to 52 is not in our psyche, so fearing the exalted, violent version of our hubris—our pride, we shrink. When I understood I was doing this, I decided to shift the system, honor the 48 to 52, and own my throne as a spiritual teacher who walks the walk. This doesn't mean I don't have the capacity to become that which I fear: the cult leader or Hybris. If I don't do my work—if I'm a false prophet, a hypocrite, or take someone else's power—I will indeed become just that. Arjuna wanted to play small; he didn't want to fight his family on the battlefield. Like the constellation of Cancer, he wanted his light to stay dim. However, if we fail to have valor and fight to become spiritual adults, we continue the lineage of countless others who chose to dim their light. Arjuna himself presented his arguments for not fighting, but Lord Krishna explained that fighting in His service is transcendental and will bring no sinful reaction. He tells Arjuna to fight but with knowledge and detachment without falling victim to his own attractions and aversions. [Bhagavad Gita, Chapter 3.39-30]

We must fight to separate from our parents' value systems during the V years, but not with guilt, shame, or apologies for how we live our life. We've already spent our early years meeting our parents' unmet needs; it is time to fight for *our* needs, specifically during these years. Ideally, we fight from a level of high vibration, but this age is often of a low-level consciousness we may not know how to do this yet. As we get older and we transmute through the ages of the V years, we learn to fight more consciously, and aware of our part in the conflict.

My first husband was violent and abusive and we fought every day. I believed I was different from him, that I was the victim, but I wasn't. I was showing a socially acceptable face as the victim and he the perpetrator in my story, but they're the same. We were the same. I had created an external conflict that mirrored my inner conflict. I learned in my second marriage to fight differently. There was better communication and less external conflict because I had less inner conflict. But I had not yet learned to be an adult in a relationship. When he left me, I was devastated. I had betrayed my non-negotiables and created inner conflict, although outwardly I was passive and, like Arjuna, didn't want to fight. Covert power and overt power are different sides of the same coin. These were my 0 to 100 swings and neither worked. So I raised my vibration and started adulting spiritually. I wrote *The Truth Is in the Triangle* about a model I learned for how to establish boundaries, non-negotiables, and rules in a relationship where conflict is constructive.

Every relationship has a fight, a crack in the snowglobe, but how we address it is directly related to our level of consciousness. When you are a spiritual adult, you stay on your throne even if you have to end a relationship. When you apply the spiritual laws and understand the cycles, you don't need to feel guilty for what you did—for behaving like an adult. As Krishna explained, you don't create a "sinful reaction," meaning you don't create additional karma. Themis is fair. She delivers good counsel and divine order. The childish behavior of "feeling bad" or "feeling guilty" is an attempt to hide your true emotions. **Guilt is a placeholder for a less socially acceptable emotion; it's not genuine.** It's a veil that is directly linked to gaining self-worth by meeting your parents' needs and not your own. Saying you feel bad or guilty for acting like a spiritual adult creates karma. You are acting selfishly, because you are taking someone else's power and giving away your own in order to honor a child script. You are not behaving with valor. Krishna tells Arjuna that you create bad karma by escaping responsibility and renouncing work. When we play small, we create karma. When we live in the 0, we shrink our potential and create a domino effect because others in the system don't get a chance to own their kingdom or find their 48 to 52. If you stay in the 0, 100 percent is left in the system for your partner or someone else to fill, keeping them in child as well.

When I assume my 48 to 52, I allow my partner, friends, and children the opportunity to show up as Self, own their throne, balance in the 48 to 52, and neutralize the 0 to 100 swings. If you are playing small, observe your surroundings. Alex is a client who works with professional athletes. He is constantly judging and criticizing their morality and promiscuous sexual escapades. Alex is 35 years old, a virgin, and his lab work shows low testosterone. His physical reality suggests a medical issue, but his subjective reality is a 0 to 100 swing. His hubris (100) speaks to wanting to be a sexual deviant, and to avoid the possibility of becoming one, he shrinks and avoids sex altogether. His biology corresponds to his psyche—being the loyal servant it is—but the issue is a lack of spiritual adulting and finding his 48 to 52.

We are children. We have temper tantrums. If we can't have it all, we spit and kick and say we don't want anything. I recommend to clients that they link their 0 to 100 swings to specific values so they have a clear map and a check on their hubris. I call my 0 "Aladdin" when I play small and my 100 the power-hungry Jafar—the potential to become the cult leader. The genie in the lamp is my 48 to 52, who has some powers but is limited in what he can do. Like me, he is obligated to honor divine law. I find that using fairytales to identify the 0 to 100 and 48 to 52 is a good way to keep a check on these swings. Naming these aspects of the self gives us a visual on where we are on the pendulum. The potential to become the 0 or 100 never goes away. These are the deadly sins in Christian theology and Aristotelian ethics (such as pride, greed, laziness), and we all have them in our psyche—usually one or two more prominent than the others. Identify the swings of vice and virtue, define the balance—the 48 to 52, and decide how you want that to show up in your life. This is truth seven on the spiritual path: the truth of balance and fun.

Raising Your Vibration

During this lifetime, the only job you have *in the spiritual realm* is to raise your vibration and level of consciousness. Our subconscious development begins at the moment of conception when you inherit the low-level consciousness of your parents. The second step of the subconscious development is in the womb. This is when we inherit our emotional infrastructure: our shadow love language, the dark side of love we seek throughout life. In the womb, we learn a secret language from our mothers and we use this secret as a way to try and get our needs met. This is linked to the moon sign in our astrology, and like the moon, we become cunning and manipulative, and change our face, depending on what we are trying to get. The third stage of subconscious development is our birth story, which is the way we're going to move into the world as we transition from each of these ages and stages. Our transitions into each stage of life are directly related to our birth story and how we entered the world. It is linked to our first sexual experience, and how we will transition out of the body, if we don't learn to do it differently. For instance, I was born basically coming out of the womb by the time my mother arrived at the hospital. The doctor indicated to her that she needed to hold me from coming, yet, she couldn't and I almost fell to the floor. With this fast and furious nature, I moved into all other transitions in my life. Upon getting cancer, I learned to slow down and pause as I transition into the next stages of life. Rewriting the pace around my birth story, and transitions, was a way of doing it differently At zero to seven, the fourth stage of the subconscious, you have your story, your personal mythology, your characters, your villains, your protagonists, your country, your costumes, everything that a mythology involves. Now you become the living myth, the personal mythology you live out. That's your story! These steps set the foundation for everything in life until your last breath. You can raise your consciousness by doing it differently at any stage, because there is only one thread.

The real crack in the snow globe occurred when you first were conceived. Your psyche interpreted this as being kicked out of heaven or Olympus. Not so. Before you incarnated, a contract was made with your earthly family and your spiritual family. But the crack in the snowglobe makes you feel as if you don't belong in the family. This creates a feeling that you're separated from others, and at the psychic level, that you're separated from God—that you're Hephaestus. Remember that Hephaestus was the only god who was kicked out of Olympus. The entire spiritual adulting process is about returning to the cosmic womb instead of perpetuating situations that keep us in the toxic waters of the maternal, flawed womb. Based on our childhood values, every single thing that happens from 14 to 16 builds our spiritual infrastructure until we are 84, when we are meant to transcend all dogma, dissolve our value system, and return to the universal womb.

You were once one with the energy of the Universe, preconception. There was no father and son. There was no child of God. You were God and God was you. In the womb, the psyche of the child believed that it was in an integrated state with God, with the divine. But it wasn't. It's a false perfection, attempting to resemble the universal womb. That's why the mother is so hard to let go of. Children want to find their mother because they think she is God, but in reality, she is just a human who happened to birth you. In an unconscious effort to reconnect with their cosmic source, this perfect womb, this universal consciousness confused with mother—you end up developing poor coping skills around drinking, drugs, sex, and food. This becomes blatant in middle school at 14 to 16, but started in pregnancy. It's also an attempt to dissolve the constricting structure of the womb. This period is called the "adolescent storm." However, your kid is doing exactly what he needs to do: creating a boundary between you and those toxic waters, trying to reconnect with God. Our true state is divinity and what Jesus came to teach us: Bring both God and the divine into the body in your earthly state.

Bert Hellinger, the father of Family Constellations therapy, once said, "Your parents gave you life, and that's enough." It's our duty to transmute the emotional infrastructure of the womb by confronting the Hydra, the psyche. The Law of Rhythm states that everything is rhythmic, everything ebbs and flows like the tides, the seasons, the cycles of birth, growth, and death. We are all divinely guided. You aren't here without a template, but you don't know what it is because we haven't been educated and religion has distorted that template. That's why Greek mythology is so important! Its stories and figures represent the map of your psyche.

The template stating that a woman's goal in life is to be a mother is a lie. Your soul came to achieve far more than the symbiosis of mother-child. Parents who don't find their own path have a major crisis when they get older if they feel they accomplished nothing. Raising a family then becomes their main value—which is important, but there is so much more. People who look back at an unlived life and complain that their ungrateful kids never call or their rotten spouse left them likely didn't forge their own path, what Joseph Campbell meant when he said, "Follow your bliss." This becomes your story—your crack in the snow globe.

Raising one's vibration is about engaging your "creator energy"—not to create kids but to create yourself. Create your inner child first—and books, poetry, peace, social justice, anything your soul desires—then (or simultaneously) create children if that's what you choose to do. If you are still focusing on your children's life by the time you reach your fifties, you will end up in a traffic jam where the end of mother and the beginning of crone collide.

Samantha is a client with a suffocating mother. When she broke up with her boyfriend, the mother dropped all of her plans for Mother's Day that she had scheduled with her family and left to visit Samantha in Oregon. In objective reality, this appears to be the act of a loving mother, but it isn't. It's an unhealthy parasitic mother-child relationship (appearing to be symbiosis)—a toxic water—to prevent your child from growing up. Samantha didn't want to be in a relationship; *she* created the break-up. But her mother needed to be needed and to keep Samantha in child. At 60, her mother doesn't have much of a life of her own, so she lives through her children's lives. At 60 mom has not created anything and has to keep on top of her biologically adult-child. They already spent their entire childhood trying to meet your needs; now you want your adult children to meet your needs too?! On top of that, we often spend our life trying to patch up *their* snowglobe: their marriage, their money issues, their problems.

The reason I use the snow globe metaphor is because before you were "kicked out of heaven," your snow globe was intact. Prior to incarnating, you were one with God. The crack in your psyche occurred when you left that cosmic womb. This is where the Adam and Eve story comes from. It's all metaphor! You made the decision as a soul to incarnate because of karma and now you're in a body. That's the first crack. The second crack occurs at birth, The third snow globe crack is the story from zero to seven, which will follow you your entire life until it no longer serves you and you dethrone your parents. By seven, you have it all: your thoughts, desires, emotions, consciousness level, value system all wrapped up in your story.

I invite clients to write down their top two values, and they can't be "family." Those two values will represent the entire basis of their spiritual life—the ones from your parents you will try to dethrone and do differently. You try to leave the apple orchard of your parents and become a pear tree, which is impossible because you're an apple. Your entire spiritual journey, which started at the moment of conception, is about dethroning the values you inherited and believe are who you are. You will create an entire life around them that you will eventually realize are not authentic, that you created only to say you were different from your parents. Remember: This is a thread from your conception story. You think your values are different than your parents, but they aren't. For example, my mother taught me that beauty was everything—a value system based on "image." The fact that I wasn't the great beauty she wanted created the crack in my snowglobe. And when I reviewed my life, I realized that beauty or vanity are central to my value system. I got breast cancer, had an eating disorder, and gained weight to prove her wrong, but until I owned this, I couldn't heal the crack, dethrone my mother, or do it differently.

One of my clients, Quinn, stated that his two values were teamwork and leadership. His father used to abuse his mother, his parents got divorced at seven, and he never saw teamwork. This was the crack in his snow globe. He wanted his parents to be together and be a team. How did he try to do it differently? By having a 25-year marriage, which from outward appearances, was considered successful. When we stripped it down, though, it turned out that he was the one carrying the marriage. He simply did a 0 to 100 by *appearing* to have what his parents hadn't. His wife runs the show; there's no real teamwork and he is not a leader.

So, clearly defining your two main values and then assessing your situation takes you out of 0 to 100 (child) and into 48 to 52 (adult). This doesn't mean blowing up your life without discernment if things don't line up. Quinn doesn't need to end his marriage. The goal is simply to become aware of what you are really doing and why. I like this saying: "Consider the crime, not the criminal." We want to let the criminal off the hook if it's our mother, father, brother, sister, or our kids. We don't want to put the 48 to 52 in play and lay down the law. And yet we're all criminals because we don't live our lives honestly. We live our parents' lives, refusing to define our own value system in measurable, observable, and clear terms.

In *The Seven Gates*, Step Four is to define a need you have in measurable terms so you can hold both yourself and others accountable. When you actually put your non-negotiables in place, you have to hold yourself and others accountable. If you fail to measure and define your values or your unmet needs, everyone else can stay in child, you continue to be a victim, and your life will never change. If, instead, you apply the laws of the Universe, they will work: You will grow up, live as a spiritual adult, and return to the cosmic consciousness while living in the earthly consciousness—the healthy womb, not the toxic waters—to solve your life. The downside is that, in solving your life, how can you then complain about the mother-in-law or a job? We love the drama! During the terrible twos the planet mars was making its first appearance, this is the creator archetype on the spiritual adulting map. Our parents either controlled our will excessively, or not sufficiently. Our will at a low-level consciousness is ego and we may tend to lean towards 0 if we were castrated due to our parents fears or we may lean towards 100 if our parents were too permissive, which could exhibit as an egomaniac. Our ego has fought (or feared to fight) for that story ever since. And what fun would it be if your life wasn't a battle? However, that's the wrong story to fight for. We need to fight for our spirit (divine will) and to carve our own path—to live our own life.

The Adolescent Storm

My version of the what I call the "Archetypal Spiritual Adulting Brain Map" (Appendix H) spells out the path that uncovers our values and how to do it differently from our parents. It starts with the Moon, the emotional infrastructure we get in the womb. Then the Sun, the source of our identity, mental infrastructure, and rational selves. This is the 0 -7—our mother, father, and child years. Then comes our teenage years when we work with Mercury, Mars, Jupiter, and Venus. At 12, we experience our Jupiter return with our first "A-ha" that mom and dad aren't perfect. It's not that you didn't know this, but you shoved all those imperfections into the bad buckets of the subconscious at the bottom of the ocean floor (symbolically) to keep them on their pedestal. Still, at 12, Jupiter's intelligence alerts you to these truths and the fact that you can dethrone them (like he did), that you can do it differently. Something clicks.

Right before the storm of 14 -16, we are shown where to dethrone our parents—a place we revisit every 12 years but don't necessarily initiate often until we're 60. In astrology, you have what's called a "Saturn opposition" at 14 to 16. Saturn is the planet of authority, limits, and boundaries. The child is confronting his father or mother figure—whoever is the authority—and he's like, "No, I'm going to do it my way." This is the adolescent storm when parents go crazy and think they will lose their children. In middle school, your kids are trying to figure out their life. This is what starts the [building of their spiritual infrastructure. Parents don't understand what is happening on the spiritual plane when the child is trying to return to cosmic consciousness, so they unwittingly interfere.] They need to start doing their shadow work so the child doesn't have to carry the parents' burdens, but the teenager is identified as the patient instead. This causes the kid to start drinking and smoking or experimenting with drugs because they're trying to get back to heaven—to the original, uncracked snow globe. They start talking about sex and looking at girls—all of which is also part of exploring one's sexuality. Parents freak out!

What is sex? Sex is Mars, the creator energy, the directed will and ego. At 14, sex becomes an issue because, symbolically, it's the archetypal answer to what gives life meaning. It's the energy of the perpetrator. It's what gets us into the world and how we create our divine self. To create ourselves, we need that energy. Sexual energy may have created you in the womb, but it's your correct use of creator energy that allows you to birth yourself anew and return to the *true* cosmic womb.

In the "spiritual adult" part of the archetypal brain map (Appendix H) the last archetpe is Lilith, the prostitute archetype, because she's the version of sex as high consciousness. Remember sexual energy is tied to the "spiritual seed" which is proper use of time, money and resources. Lilith here in higher consciousness is known as the ruler archetype, the low consciousness is the prostitute archetype. We become spiritual adults because we are in charge of our fire, man our fires and stay on our throne. Lilith, the ruler, is side-by-side, Chiron or the everyday man archetype on the spiritual adulting map. Together I call these the "wounder ruler" archetype. Here we own our commoner status as humans, yet our ruler status as divine beings. Only when we own our humanity and divinity, our earthly and spiritual consciousness, the divine marriage of Zeus and Themis, can we finally spiritually adult, which means the body is a chalice or divine vessel, accepted as flawed but not beaten down. The truth of thoughts and truth of purification work together, rather than as a means to purify the impure thoughts. The only expression of the divine that we have is our body and the earth. We embody the divine and the earthly, and now our vessel, the body, represented by high-consciousness Venus or Aphrodite Urania. The concept of God, or the divine, being unlimited is unconceivable to humans. The Principle of Mentalism is so difficult to comprehend, because we cannot understand something without limits. As humans we require limits to make something comprehensible; therefore, God or divine as form, known as the Ishta-Devata in Sanskrit gives the divine a form or a godhead. In spiritual adulting, the form is our body, the vessel, that houses the divine. Once we spiritually adult as the wounder ruler, we return to our form, and honor it as the divine vessel it is. This is the seventh—the last—veil to be removed before returning to the cosmic womb. It's a sexual penetration of the psyche, where we admit our good and bad buckets. The way back to that intact snow globe is Lilith and Venus. In Christianity, it's Mary Magdalene. What teenagers reveal to their parents through lying and sex is their search for their own Lilith, their own inner prostitute, removal of their veils. They are starting to figure out their own truth: sexually, identity-wise, and value-wise. Their psyche is attempting to get back to cosmic consciousness and unify the male and female energies so they can create balance and live as a spiritual adult, not a child. In mythology, the only figure to say to God, "No. I'm an equal, not a child. I will not be dominated," was Lilith. She was the first wife of Adam, made not from his rib but from the same clay as him. Still, she was demonized by the church because it wouldn't allow anyone to get near the truth. Otherwise, the church would lose its power as the "official" gatekeeper to heaven.

So when teenagers are going through their chaos years, parents think they are losing their kid when it's really about the parents not doing their shadow work: balancing their own masculine and feminine energies in relationship with themselves and/or a partner. The kid is subconsciously redirected to fix your life, to meet your needs, because most kids aren't allowed to leave their parents' path to live their own life. This is when I say to parents, Let's look at the values. How do your child's values differ from yours? When they can identify their teenager's spiritual infrastructure and its value system, they will realize it's not that different from their own. Think of it as an apple orchard. The child is one tree in the orchard and his/her parents the next tree. Still, most kids leave home pretending they are pears or watermelons or kiwis, and it takes an entire lifetime or an illness or your parents dying or some other drama to realize, "Damn, I've been an apple all along. But I can still have my own tree." We can live in the same kingdom but own our own throne.

Archetypes and Goddesses

To understand our Western psyche, we need to understand the roots of Western philosophy in Greek values. Loyalty is first. Who are you loyal to? Usually, you are loyal to everyone but yourself or your inner child, but you may not even be aware of this. The first truth of the spiritual path is the truth of thought. You need to be aware of your thoughts, which is how you speak to your inner child. The next value is respect, specifically to the gods, which we usually think of as Jesus or Buddha or Mohammed, but the gods you respect and are loyal to are mother and father. Then there is pride. Pride is punished, however, because it is misinterpreted as hubris. So, we are afraid to be proud; we shrink ourselves and don't assume our rightful worth. We don't penetrate life. We stay on the sidelines. We refuse to find the 48 to 52 and own our throne and be ourselves because then we would defy our parents and be disloyal to the gods.

The next value is prophecy: what people said about you when you were young that you then try to prove is true. Prophecy goes back to pregnancy, your birth, the zero to seven. Everybody has a prophecy. Greek philosophy features the Oracle at Delphi, where Oedipus learned he would kill his father and marry his mother, and where Narcissus learned he would die if he saw his reflection. Each of us, from conception, has a prophecy that became ingrained in our psyche. When I do my signature Hidden Truths ™ *Psychological X-ray* with clients, two questions I ask are: 1) How would you describe yourself from zero to seven? and 2) How did others describe you from zero to seven? Your identity and true self is linked to the first question, while the mask you wear for others (the prophecy) is linked to the second question—evidence for how we first betray our inner child and fall off our path.

At 14 -16, your sexual hormones kick in not only for biological reasons but to activate the truth-seeking archetype of Lilith that comes full circle at 60. You want the truth. You want to get back to cosmic consciousness. You learned poor coping skills in the womb, but your parents aren't doing their work, so you do it for them by mirroring their unintegrated shadow. Your parents don't help you; they castrate you and then wonder why you're a late bloomer.

What made religion so catastrophic to our psyche is that it took "stories" such as that of the Virgin Mary and made them literal. The Universe is not literal; it's symbolic, archetypal and metaphorical. Religions such as Christianity want you to believe that there really was a virgin birth, a "world savior." Jesus didn't "save" anyone but himself, but he did teach compassion and modeled all 12 truths on the spiritual path. At 12, he went to the temple, telling Mary, "I must do my father's work"—referring to his spiritual father, which was actually his inner divine spark..

Roman Catholicism castrated Greek philosophy because if you bought the story, you would never get back to the original, intact snowglobe. You would instead create chaos, drama and problems. By keeping you in logic, in "concrete-operations," the church keeps you in child. You would need to go to the church for counseling and end up giving them money for their efforts. You would get an *Indulgence*—a certificate of sins absolved. The Western world is built on materialism; it's inherent in our value system, and the church is no different. **Trying to "materialize yourself" out of materialism is nonsense, and escaping to Eastern philosophy without understanding your Western psyche won't work.** The Western world was won by Athena when she offered material riches and the Eastern world was won by Poseidon when he offered spiritual riches, we need both, the 48 to 52. East & West have the same symbols and myths when they're broken down to the basics, but they've been misunderstood and we're seeing an exodus away from Western hermetic philosophy, towards Eastern philosophy, and the children of this generation (2012-2025) will have an existential crisis trying to reconcile the two in their psyche.

Anytime you accept the hierarchy of child and adult, you remain in child and give away your power. Lilith is the perfect antidote and why, in every mythology, she's viewed as the stripper, the prostitute, the demon. The one who eats her children and takes away your man. In such low-level consciousness, she's the evil seductress. That energy does exist in society, but the Lilith of high-level consciousness liberates you. In the Archetypal Spiritual Adulting Brain Map (Appendix H) she's next to Chiron. Chiron is when you understand your primordial wound—the original lie of your unworthiness. It's when you return home, find the 48 to 52, integrate Lilith at 60, and begin the return to the cosmic consciousness. This starts the spiritual path of real truths because now you are ready for Lilith.

You don't need a church. You don't need a "world savior." You don't need an intermediary. You don't need a messenger from God; *you* are that messenger; you are the divine. This is the *Age of Aquarius*. If you start subtly listening to your intuition, which is truth four, to what the universe is saying, you can raise your consciousness. Intuition is not spiritual adulting but it is one step of the process. Your level of intuition is directly related to your level of consciousness, so start raising your consciousness for clearer intuitive guidance.

We need humanitarians, people who are doing their work and helping others by modeling their work. As a spiritual teacher, I'm not healing you, but through healing myself, I show how you can do it too. You're the savior. You can save yourself. You are not a child of God, and Eastern philosophers knew this. Western philosophies, prior to the Church, did as well. You are a child of the void, a child of cosmic consciousness, of the wholeness of that intact snowglobe. Don't play small. Own the spark of the divine within you. Activate your awareness, integrate new knowledge, do it differently.

In addition to the Greek values, I mentioned earlier, there are three in particular that are linked to my approach. The first is "Ever to excel," which I interpret as entering the world, creating a profession and/or making a family, and building something with material resources such as money. We need these. We have to pay our bills. We have to accept that ambition is important. Find the 48 to 52 and be sure to excel. Take that Mars energy and manifest! The second Greek value is "healthy mind and a healthy body." In my 12 truths of the spiritual path, there are two that we must revisit each day. Truth One is to observe our thoughts—keeping track of our impure thoughts, their origin and link them to our emotions and desires. Truth Six is about purification—keeping a healthy body through eating right and physical movement, and not punishing your body through extreme purification techniques as if to rid yourself of the impure thoughts and judgements from Truth One. Any impure thought that is not processed will be channeled as pain through the body. The impure thoughts show up in the earth element as violation of: 1. Sex; 2. Money; 3. Time; 4. Food or drink (drugs) and; 5. Illness. Processing impure thoughts don't create an energetic build-up; however, if you don't process these thoughts that energy materializes like an energetic brick and eventually leads to illness or a major issue in one of the abovementioned areas. The third Greek value is "Know thyself," including your hidden truths.

During the years of 14 to 16, your values and the spiritual infrastructure are set for the rest of your life. This time period is like a suspension bridge; it's wobbly, the wind pushes it from side to side, it feels kind of scary, and there's a lot of uncertainty. This feeling of uncertainty is crucial, because when we get to ages 42 and 84, which are directly related to what we build during 14 to 16, we have to reassess and reconfigure our value system and spiritual path, and it's not always clear what to do. That is why, from the perspective of spiritual growth, it's important to get comfortable with uncertainty, with those gray areas, even though most people prefer the easy clarity of black and white. From 14 to 16 is exactly the time to get comfortable with the confusion, which will follow us through life as we grow both biologically and spiritually.

At 14 to 16, we also naturally oppose authority figures who keep us from learning how to navigate life on our own. Such oppositions are opportunities. They are directly related to the pendulum swings and the Principle of Rhythm which shape our life. This first confrontation with authority—that "adolescent storm"—is when teens are *supposed* to confront their parents, these gods, so they can start figuring out who they are, who they want to be, and what they want to do. During this two-year period, the Law of Octaves kicks in and the transmutation of low-level consciousness—the entire purpose of a lifetime—begins. The period of 14 - 16 is one of chaos. This word is important because whenever you are creating chaos in your life (at 42 and 84 especially), it's directly related to those 14-to-16 values you are trying to dethrone.

So adolescents will test "the system" to see what their parents will support, what boundaries can be pushed. This is where parenting style is really important, even though those styles are determined much earlier. Extremely permissive parents, for example, who say yes to everything and don't manage boundaries, will create the conditions for permissive children who will be more likely to try drugs and alcohol and sex. They also tend to have better social skills, especially around adults. They become more cunning, more manipulative, and are actually better navigators of social situations. But they don't have boundaries, which can ultimately lead away from truth and toward self-destruction.

Authoritarian parents, on the other hand, are rigid rulers; they set hard boundaries and don't let their kids test anything in the system. They have a militaristic character that says no to everything. Their kids will have little self-worth and little trust in themselves. They won't know how to manage chaos, navigate systems, or deal with uncertainty because they are always trying to follow the rules. They can fall prey to cults and mind control—anything that provides structure or authority—because they are very good followers. The parenting style we experience as children, starting in the womb, is directly related to our attachment style—our level of insecurity—which influences our spiritual infrastructure. If your parents let you push the boundaries and figure out some things for yourself, you're on that suspension bridge and they're your cheerleader, this is authoritative parenting. At the end of the day, since "there is no other" in spirituality, these parenting styles are metaphors for how we parent our inner child. Secure attachment and authoritative parenting is really only achieved by oneself, towards oneself, but our earthly childhood experience explains why we do what we do subconsciously. If they're on the bridge telling you what shoes to wear and how fast to walk, they're authoritarian. If they're nowhere near the bridge, they're too permissive. This is how we develop and then live our spiritual infrastructure: based on the parenting style we grew up with.

A few goddesses in mythology directly relate to this stage: *Adrestia*, for example, the goddess of revolt, revolution, and social justice. Of course, parenting styles will dictate how much we revolt and how much of a revolution we cause, but teenagers will still feel this energy inside. They want to revolt and they should; they need that opposition, they need to confront authority and say, "No, I don't want to do it this way." We can't let them go off the deep end and do whatever they want, but we do want to give them some wiggle room to revolt and figure out who they are and what they want to do.

Chinnasta is another: the goddess of paradoxes. One of the big things that children complain about are parents who say, "Do as I say, not as I do." They might not come right out and say it, but they're definitely thinking it. Every child between 14 and 16 will push back, accusing them of being a hypocrite or a liar. This is exactly where the shadow is created. Every "issue" a child has is rooted in the unintegrated shadow of the parent. *You* are not the problem. You are bringing things to light. You are bringing them to the surface. Our parents have not been trained to see that it's them; they only know to see the teen as the problem.

Age 14 is a kind of limbo phase when a child becomes responsible for their spiritual growth and yet are confused at a subconscious level because of their parents' unintegrated shadow and thinking—again, subconsciously—that they need to fix it. Teenagers are very clear that something doesn't jive; they just don't know how to rectify it. We *try* to get the truth at 14 - 16 but we can't, so we end up building a false foundation on a false premise and therefore, at 42 and again at 84, you try to shatter and deconstruct that entire premise and rebuild.

Another goddess, *Dike*, is the goddess of order. One of the major developments during 14 to 16 is that we start to define what morality means to us. This is challenging, especially sexually, because most kids only want to live in the "good girl-boy"/Virgin Mary archetype. They don't want to be the prostitute—the Lilith that will liberate them. They don't want to acknowledge the indecency of their thoughts and actions. This is the 0 to 100, and both extremes are false. We are good *and* bad. Whether you prefer the prostitute or the virgin doesn't matter; either one is a mask, two sides of the same face. You need to show both faces to yourself. That's why we are strangers to ourselves. Everybody is issued a morality code at conception, but at 14 to 16 you start making your own choices. Dike brings order and balance to this process.

Last is the goddess *Nemesis*. She is the daughter of Ares, the god of war. When we confront authority or start a war, we are subconsciously intending to look at both sides of a story. When we understand that *we* are creating a problem and that we are exactly like the other person, this is Nemesis trying to get you to stop the swings of 0 to 100. Recall Kohlberg's first level of moral development: "preconventional morality," which is the most "childish." It's all about avoiding punishment and getting a reward. If I do this, I will get (a false version of) love. This dynamic is active no matter your age. But this is a form of self-betrayal and generates more karma. Kohlberg's Level 2 ("conventional morality") relates to relationships, good and bad behavior, and conflict with authority. At 14 to 16, which is the foundation of his remaining stages, we are trying to obey the law and order of our parents and their rules on money, food, drugs, curfews, and so on while we're also trying to break those rules. I call this "breaking the rules within the rules" or farting: a spin-off of Selye's GAS stages of stress which is short for *general adaptation syndrome*. I say that people have gas when they hold themselves to the stress of maintaining the 0 or 100. It's not sustainable, and they need a release, often in private, a fart in the system. They break the rules of their moral code, then beat themselves up for doing it. They are exhausted from holding up a false mask. It's a vicious cycle! Truth Six, truth of purification, is often the culprit here too. If I engaged in too much sex, gambling, sugar, then I'll purify with a "cleansing" behavior like a detox or a man-cleanse, another 0 to 100 behavior. The fart in the system is an allowable place to defy the 0-100 swings. For instance, my client Leslie lives vanity and elegance in the 0-100 swings; however, her buffoonery and silliness with friends is the fart in her system. The fart represents the crack in the snowglobe, an incongruence that you can actually do it differently. Her mother modeled that she had to be elegant and vain 100% of the time, by releasing this tension of opposites with her laughter, she can dethrone her mother and spiritually adult. Find just the 5% where you do it differently than the 0-100 swings, and you can achieve the 48-52 balance if you desire to.

Kohlberg's *post-conventional* morality has to do with spiritual adulting. We recognize that there's justice. We recognize that there are laws and that we are obligated to obey whether or not we know what they are. If you go to a place and kill a cat where it's illegal to kill a cat, whether you knew it or not because you were just driving through, you'll still get punished. The same is true of universal laws: You're obligated to obey them whether or not you know what they are. The difference with universal law is that each action has a reaction. You may get away with a violation of an earthly law, but never a divine law. This is where you mature out of child and teenager and start taking personal responsibility for everything you create. This is the goddess Themis. This is divine justice. You are not a victim; you are not a child. Kohlberg's last stage of post-conventional morality deals with ethics and universal principles such as "cause and effect." When you start to realize that every action is linked to these principles, you start behaving differently because you *want* to honor your truth—not because the law says so. This is an unconventional model of morality and ethics. It tends to correlate with the return home to 48 to 52 when you are no longer holding your parents accountable, or doing it their way, or doing the exact opposite. "I am now responsible." Teens at 14 to 16 can't get there because they're still trying to separate from authority. They know there are laws but are testing them.

In the Archetypal Spiritual Adulting Brain Map, there are four archetypes that dominate the teenage years, each one correlating with a planet (Mercury, Mars, Venus and Jupiter) (Appendix H). Mercury (or Hermes), for example, is one of the archetypes that dominate the teenage years. It's associated with lying, shoplifting, and academic achievement, and it's not uncommon for teenagers to do well in school *and* shoplift. In regards to lying, this is when teens will call out their parents who tell them to "do as I say, not as I do." And yet until you come clean about your own lies, usually at around 60, you will not become whole—a spiritual adult. This is one of the last veils to be removed, but you must first overcome what I call FOFO: the fear of being found out. Most of us are afraid to really be honest with ourselves, but when you finally get down and dirty, you can say to the Universe, "Okay, I'm ready to know who I am." This process begins at 14 to 16 when the teen confronts their parents. That's why it's an opposition. Lilith opposed hierarchy because she knew the Universe was circular, not hierarchical. She would not allow herself to be submissive because she was God's equal. We surrender even as we sit on our throne. It's a paradox and the integration of opposites.

Venus (or Aphrodite) is another powerful archetype for teens. It has to do with image and beauty. The thing is, we usually live as an image of (and in) society, but we shouldn't die as one. Each of us wears a mask to appear more spiritual or more successful or better looking or whatever. Oftentimes, these masks are hiding eating disorders or gluttony or material excess. We are lying (Mercury) to fit in—something we picked up from our parents. Lilith says that if you want to live an image, fine, but when you finally decide to be a spiritual adult, it may be too late. You may be confronting mortality and realize that you've been wearing masks all your life to serve other people and be accepted by society. You will go through a huge existential crisis—the realization of an unlived life, never really knowing who you are, following a conventional morality while swinging from 0—100.

This is why the 14 to 16 is so critical; it's the beginning of one's spiritual infrastructure. The foundation is in conception and pregnancy and birth and 0—7, but now the child is allowed to begin spiritually adulting. They start learning to be responsible for their own destiny. their own karma, their own divine law.

CHAPTER FOUR

Rahu & Ketu: Ages 9 and 18

Erickson identifies the 12-to-18 age group as the adolescent stage, but as I pointed out in the previous chapter, there are distinct periods within this range representing the building blocks that will become the entire infrastructure of our spiritual adult lives. Spiritually, after the Saturn crisis of 14 to 16 that establishes the value system, we need to begin evolving into a higher level of consciousness to dethrone our parents and "do it differently," we have a karmic cycle at 18.

In the *Puranas*, the ancient Hindu texts that explain the creation of the universe and Hindu mythology, Lord Vishnu is the preserver and protector of the universe. One evening, Vishnu, in his female form of *Mohini*, held a dinner party. Swarbhanu, a powerful serpent, drank the Amrit, the nectar reserved for the gods, and became immortal. Vishnu couldn't kill him, but he split Swarbhanu in half and separated his head from his body. The head is known as Rahu and the headless body is the Ketu. Scientifically, Rahu and Ketu refer to two mathematical points in the sky at the midpoint of the Sun and the Moon. The Sun and the Moon symbolically refer to father and mother. Lord Vishnu represents the 48 to 52, or the midpoint between the good buckets and bad buckets of mother and father. After this event, Rahu and Ketu were given the responsibility to influence the lives of the humans on Earth.

THE IMPORTANCE OF 9 AND 18

Every nine years, Ketu and Rahu criss cross one another and create changes in our destiny. Nine is the number of endings and corresponds to The Hermit card in Tarot. The Hermit is a wise teacher in search of new horizons who leaves the past behind. This phase is characterized by introspection and inner reflection. The first skinny cow occurs at zero to seven; it kicks you out of Olympus, but you are still too young to understand what happened, so you internalize it. From seven to nine, that cycle closes. The first cycle of Rahu-Ketu crisscrossing happens at nine—a cycle repeats itself every nine years. Like Saturn, there are two phases of Rahu-Ketu. The years linked to endings that began at the skinny cows occur at ages 9, 27, 45, 63, 81 and 99. The "new beginning" years, when Rahu-Ketu are aligned and all doors to your future are open, occur every 18 years at ages 18, 36, 54, 72, and 90. The skinny cow years come with a change in destiny and endings you may not want. These are painful points in your growth and linked to being kicked out of Olympus. They correlate with Saturn cycles and, like Saturn, force a spiritual crisis, an unwanted ending, in order to propel you forward. Often these cycles are ruled by Nemesis, the goddess of divine retribution and revenge. We may feel shunned, done wrong. But once you accept that you have created your reality and that the nemeses on your path are part of your spiritual family, helping you to spiritually adult, you will avoid falling into victimhood and martyrdom.

The Rahu-Ketu years occurring at 18, 36, and so on are the best years of your life. These correspond to Jupiter cycles. The two most auspicious of these cycles are at 36 and 60 years old. Here, the Rahu-Ketu doors of destiny and potential fly open. Remember that all spiritual growth related to Jupiter relates to the spiritual adulting work you did in previous cycles. Growth is exponential and increases over time in proportion to what you did in the previous Saturn and Jupiter cycles. At 36, your third Jupiter cycle meets up with your second Rahu-Ketu cycle, and this is when you can create and change your destiny. Up to this point, you were playing tug-of-war with your parents' value system. This is one of two opportunities to do it differently. It's a fast track to spiritual adulting!

The second opportunity—almost guaranteed to succeed—is at 60. At sixty, the Themis and Zeus marriage is solidified as Rahu-Ketu, the fifth cycle of Jupiter, and the Saturn cycle that started at 28, all come full circle. This period is often associated with retirement, becoming a grandparent, or dedicating yourself to a spiritual path. This opportunity is about finally removing the veils and finding a balance between unity and duality, spirit and matter, feminine and masculine, good and bad buckets, ordinary consciousness and subjective consciousness. In the Upanishads, this is called *moksha*, which in Sanskrit means enlightenment, liberation, and release. Moksha is freedom from ignorance: self-realization, self-actualization, and self-knowledge. In the Hindu literature, there are four stages of life known as the Purusartha, or "objects of human pursuit":

1. Dharma is righteousness and moral values.
2. Artha is prosperity and economic values.
3. Kama is pleasure, love, and psychological values.
4. Moksha is liberation and spiritual values.

As we try to accomplish all of these stages, we are guided through the cycles of Saturn, Jupiter, and Rahu-Ketu. The *Kamasutra* 1.2.1-1.2.4, translated by Patrick Olivelle, states that the lifespan of man is 100 years. During that time, he should attend to three aims of life in such a way that support, rather than hinder, each other. In his youth, he should attend to profitable aims (artha) such as learning. In his prime, the focus should be on pleasure (kama). In his old age, the goal is achieving dharma and moksha. In India, people often tithe to the ashram to honor these cycles. For many, at 60, having paid their dues, they would retire to the ashram, work on moksha, and disconnect from the material world. We in the West may not retire from the world, but we can take advantage of the Jupiter-Saturn-Rahu-Ketu combination and begin our own process of moksha at 60.

In the meantime, at 18, the doors of your future will be open to you. At 18, you need to leave home, not just physically but mentally.

According to the myth of Persephone, the world will "abduct" you in some way, but you must learn to see a new version of truth than what your parents taught. As noted above, Rahu (the head) and Ketu (the tail) represent your mother and your father. They are called the "lunar nodes" in astrology and are related to our karmic path. At 18, we have the first opportunity to work with these nodes by letting go of our parents psychologically and spiritually. You might get your own apartment, find a girlfriend or a boyfriend, or go off to college. Maybe you enter the military. Whatever the action, we do *something* at this time because it aligns with universal law.

Whenever these nodes are available to us, we have a chance to move past our parents so our psyche can choose its own spiritual path. Even then, our parents will always be with us. Rahu and Ketu are immortal; they drank the Amrit. They may have a place beside our throne, but no longer on our throne—that is, as long as you become aware of your thoughts and realize how you always honor them and offer sacrifices to them while you attempt to live your own life. The symbol of the sixth chakra has a petal for each parent on either side of the Void, which is your kingdom. At 12, you realized you could dethrone them. At 14 to 16, you actually tried to dethrone them by acting out, shoplifting, having sex, yelling and fighting, and so on, but they were still too strong. Eighteen is your first attempt to do this in reality. At 18, society gives you this permission because earthly law supports you in becoming an adult.

A serpent, snake, or a dragon, in symbology, always represents illusion—in this case, it means that the truths your mother and father told you did not represent the reality of what is. In their ignorance, your parents gave you the illusion that there is a right way to view the world. This is known as low-level consciousness and is linked to the limiting beliefs and impure throughts you'll struggle with through-out your lifetime. Derek Black, the son of the grand wizard of the Ku Klux Klan and previously homeschooled, went off to college and was exposed to different viewpoints, including those of his Jewish friends. Eli Saslow wrote *Rising out of Hatred* to share Black's story and how his exposure to other cultures and people opened his eyes about his family's beliefs around white nationalism. Derek no longer believed what his parents taught him. That first veil was removed. He realized that he had been metaphorically raped by the world and that his childhood was not the only way to live. This severely shattered his snowglobe, but that's what happens at 18: The world removes another veil.

Derek's parents, like your own, had a version of truth you had to buy into if you wanted the "Costco membership card" to the family beehive. They said that to be part of the family, this had to be your truth. Then the time came to see the truth of what the world really is, not just the reality your family wanted you to see. Because if you continued viewing the world through your parents' lens, they would stay immortal, hence the Amrit. At 18, you are trying to access the universal womb, but you need a metephorical rape and the removal of veils to get there, which is part of the spiritual infrastructure of the spiritual adulting process.

In the Greek myth of Persephone (daughter of Zeus) and Demeter (her mother) are frolicking in the woods. Demeter has intoxicated Persephone with the fragrance of the narcissus flower to veil her from the realities of Earth and keep her yoked to her parents' view of how life is supposed to be. That's what parents do. They want their kids to be safe and do it better than they did, but they get in their way. We keep them from learning, from growing, from honoring their spiritual path. They are already going to live out your mistakes because those emotional loyalties have been programmed in them. The only way to *really* keep your kids safe is sitting at your kitchen table, deconstructing every single thought you have, understanding why you have those impure thoughts and where they come from, owning the shadow aspects of yourself, doing it differently from your parents, and then giving your child permission to follow their own path to their truth. You keep your child (symbolically) safe not by keeping them home, telling them what they can and can't do, or being a helicopter parent but by doing your inner work so your child doesn't have to do it for you. When parents integrate their shadows and become spiritual adults, they give their child subconscious permission to do their own soul's work and become a spiritual adult as well.

The "Dance of the Seven Veils" has been misinterpreted as a sexual dance, but it's actually the dance of life, depicting the spiritual adulting process as we remove the veils of childhood and the material world. The need to remove the veils we received at conception is the purpose of this lifetime. That first veil is removed at 18 when you start seeing things for the first time—not reading about them but meeting people and confronting situations that expose the lies you were told about the world. The metaphor for this is to have been raped. Despite Demeter's efforts to protect Persephone, she is raped by Hades, and her spiritual adulting process begins. The fragrance of the narcissus flower has lost its power. Your childhood snowglobe is no longer safe.

This process repeats at 18, 36, 54, 72 and 90 years old. Pull on that thread, and you will find a version of Amrit, immortality, the nectar of the gods. Each of those years is especially crucial to your spiritual development. Each year is an opportunity to remove more veils and keep growing spiritually. This is your natural impulse. You cannot live your parents' life and truth; you must find your own. At 18, Apate, the goddess of trickery and deceit, arrives in our life to help remove the veils. She might show up as a lover or a friend or a nemesis because your soul is ready for you to know the real truth. You can reduce Apate's influence by no longer deceiving or tricking yourself. Remove your veils, look at your thoughts, and take responsibility for the life you've created and the world you're complaining about.

Forbidden Worlds

When discussing mythology, Joseph Campbell would often refer to the "one forbidden thing." This motif is found in monster myths and often takes the form of fruit or boxes or keys or when Blackbeard told his wife she could open any door but one. In Christianity, it was the apple on the Tree of Knowledge. While growing up, there was usually one big thing your parents told you never to do such as drugs, alcohol, or lie. But the irony is that while they were telling you this, they were thinking about it all the time: "do as I say, not as I do/think." You intuitively and subconsciously pick this up and start doing that very thing, which becomes the source of your impure thoughts—your shame and your judgements about yourself or others. At 18, this hypocrisy becomes more apparent.

Subconsciously, we understand that if we start doing the things our parents told us never to do (or so we assumed)—if we go through that forbidden door—we won't find our way back, which is a terrifying thought. If we don't know our values, if we don't have a philosophy of life, if we don't understand universal laws, we become afraid. We over-rely on what we think we know. But we can't rationalize our way through a love affair or a heartbreak, but that forbidden door will bring you back to self. Sometimes, the only way to learn is to make mistakes. You may not want to make the same mistakes your parents made, but they are already programmed in your psyche. They gave you the blueprint for those same exact mistakes. We rationalize the lies that our parents tell us because we want to keep them immortal and to keep their story true, but it's not true. The truth is in the middle. It's in the 48 to 52. If we learn the laws of the universe and how we're being guided at a soul level, the truth is easier to find.

Erikson's development stage of young adulthood is related to intimacy versus isolation. At 18, you're seeking relationships and you are going to do the exact same thing as your parents. The shadow of their immortality is programmed into your psyche. We call this "transgenerational trauma" and "ancestral trauma" because a part of you doesn't want to dethrone your parents and do it differently. You are trapped in a conditional version of love. Otherwise, you lose the metaphorical Costco membership. When you learn about unconditional love and start loving yourself, you will no longer need to keep honoring your parents. You will nudge them and thank them for the guidance and blueprint, but you will pave your own way, simply utilizing their guidance, not their guidance instead of your own. You can dethrone them. You have permission to live your own life, to follow your soul's purpose—the one you've had since the moment of conception. It won't matter how many doors your parents try to hide from you; you will find that one forbidden door and release that demon because it's what you have to do. The "one forbidden door"—that one forbidden path—is always open because this is *your* path, *your* journey.

Remember that Rahu and Ketu are the mother and father, the Sun and the Moon. So, doing exactly like your parents—or the exact opposite—is living your parents' life, not yours. You have to consciously choose to not become them. You have to choose to look at your thoughts. You have to choose to do it differently.

CHAPTER FIVE

Discovering Your True Self— Age 21

Erickson calls ages 21—39 the "intimacy versus isolation" stage with the central focus on relationships. However, as we spiritually adult, a lot of cycles happen during that period. At 21, we have our first neutralizer or nemesis "N-year" directly related to the crack in the snowglobe from zero to seven. Fourteen years later, we are confronted with the realization that we were kicked out of Olympus, flawed and imperfect. Here we start to recognize whether we are shrinking or living in excess—again, both are 0 to 100. Many young adults left home for college at 18 when Rahu-Ketu had its first opening, and most of them graduate at this age and seek their first professional job. This is where a nemesis or neutralizer, such as a boss or competitive colleague, can typically show up, but they certainly aren't limited to work. Remember that while a nemesis may appear as opposing, confrontational, and conflictive, they are members of your spiritual family.

Karla is a 21-year-old, still in college, who called me in tears because her sister was going to be detained by the State of Florida and mentally assessed for suicidal tendencies. Her parents asked her for help, and she advised them against calling the police and instead getting her on medications and into therapy. She booked a session with me to discuss this family turmoil. I asked her what had happened between zero and seven—specifically with her sister—but any important situation she could remember. Karla recalled being at swimming practice and that while she and her mother were briefly distracted, her little sister caught her hand in a glass door and lost a finger. They rushed to the hospital and had it re-attached. She also shared that her uncle had the heartbreak of his life and moved in with them while he was on the mend. These situations created a framework for Karla to fill her unmet needs by showing up as the adult for her mother, her sister, and her uncle. Karla's mother is a childlike woman who never really individuated from her own parents. She suffers from an eating disorder—a poor coping mechanism linked to "toxic waters." and the *puer aeternus or puella aeternus* or innocent archetype. According to Jung, the term is used to describe an older person whose emotional life has remained at an adolescent level."

Karla resembles the virgin goddess Artemis, who helped her mother birth her brother. Karla also helps her mother and, while still away at college, is helping to raise her younger sister. When female children have to nurture their parents, they exhaust their mothering energy, and like the virgin goddesses, they often have difficulty conceiving children of their own or simply decide not to have any. This is ultimately the fault of parents who fail to individuate and adult spiritually, staying in child mode and forcing their children to become adults too early. This is commonly described as the "Innocent" archetype. Neptune, who rules addictions, is also the innocent archetype. These adult-children don't usually sense danger, are extremely trusting, and have *Snow White* syndrome. The wicked witch may be standing at their door, but despite being warned by the dwarfs to not let her in, they naively open it, trapped in their yearning to remain innocent. Growing up too quickly, without parents who adulted, spiritually or materially, can create this type of dependence on the innocent archetype. This could also be lived out through addictions and sexual disorders.

In actuality, however, they are wolves in sheep's clothing: the 0 is the innocent or the sheep and the 100 is the wolf—there is no difference. They've had to fight for their childhood for most of their young life while never attaining it, left to carry that unrealized youth and innocence into adulthood. But they are also capable of being as dangerous as a mother bear protecting her cub, though in this case the cub is the mother, not her own children, because she often has none or loses them through miscarriage or an inability to conceive. They may present with vaginismus, painful sexual intercourse, or an inability to be penetrated at all. They honor the virgin goddess archetype and therefore prevent any sort of penetration. Again, this keeps them in child, close to mother, and forever innocent. This was Karla's exact story.

During the same week that her sister attempted suicide, Karla had gone to visit her uncle in Colorado to celebrate her birthday. But he had a big argument with his wife, she moved out of the house, and she spent her birthday helping him pick up the pieces. When she returned home, her mother gave her the silent treatment—a form of passive-aggressive child behavior—as if Karla had somehow let her down. That was the last straw before her session.

Karla's snowglobe is a hard one to shatter because the loyalty to her mother is intertwined with her limited self-worth by putting her mother's needs ahead of her own. It's a powerful script. When I asked Karla what she remembered about herself as a child, she said that she wanted to be taken seriously. She wanted adults to respect her and not view her as a child. Subconsciously, she was now creating these situations at 21; they are directly related to the snowglobe crack between 0 to seven. The characters in other stories are not always as precise as Karla's mother, sister, and uncle; they can show up at work or in romance. But if you strip back the veil and piece the storyline together, it's the same story from 0 to seven. In that one week following her 21st birthday, she was the adult who wanted to be taken seriously; she failed to meet her mother's needs (which we will always fail because it's impossible to meet our parents' needs; we can only meet our own); she created a crisis involving her sister and her mother, just like in childhood; and I was the neutralizer-nemesis who called her and her mother out on the dysfunction of the relationship. By the end of that one session, she had what I call a psychological xray. She understood her child script, her good and bad buckets, her values, and her unmet needs. She identified the pendulum swings of her 0 to 100: Perfectionism (100) and Inadequacy (0). She defined her 48 to 52 as being Sufficient.

She scheduled for the next week but didn't show up, which is common when we resist change. I was the nemesis in the system, bringing awareness to the value system that was ruling her life. She may not revisit the situation until her next N-year at 35, but the Universe will provide other chances. You have free will; take those opportunities, fight with valor, and don't take anything too personally. Nothing is being done *to* us; it's all being done *for* us. Define your pendulum swings and 48 to 52 in measurable terms so you can hold yourself accountable and so others in your system can hold you accountable.

After my three-year depression, I realized that the cosmos isn't personal. My Pluto transit had brought cancer, a divorce, chemotherapy, and financial hardship, among other misfortunes. I was convinced that God had abandoned me—again. This was a theme during my Saturn skinny cows. Once I woke up from that delusion, however, I realized that I had created these extreme pendulum swings because I had never spiritually adulted. I did not handle my illness or my divorce as an adult. I was completely in child, waiting only to get my needs met. I self-betrayed. I was an emotional and physical wreck.

After shattering my snowglobe of delusion and removing some heavy veils of delusion, I got off of my medications, changed my diet, became cancer free, and began to spiritually adult. I wrote five books in a matter of a few months. My creator energy reawakened because I discovered my self-worth, reignited my fire, and embraced my inner knowing. As I pondered how I'd handled my Pluto transit, I started laughing, calling myself out on my pain-as-pleasure construct. Oh, how I loved to suffer. But the pain wasn't enough; I needed a dramatic, Netflix-worthy soap opera. I realized that Pluto was in Capricorn; it wasn't personal. Pluto didn't show up to destroy my life. The cosmos was doing what the cosmos does. We are given opportunities to grow, and our job is to extract the essence of those experiences. Our free will and level of consciousness will determine how crazy (or not) we live out these scenarios. We will have N and V years, the skinny cows are coming, but we don't need to blow up our life and cause such drama when they arrive. Unfortunately, I hadn't yet learned this. I was in victim-wounded child mode. I was waiting to be rescued, and guess what? I had to rescue myself. The idea of a world savior who will take all the pain away has done major harm. There is no world savior, there is no knight in shining armor. You are the savior you've been waiting for!

A Path to Freedom

Truth Twelve on the spiritual path is to unite with the Universe, becoming aware that there is no distinction between you and others. There can't be a savior because that is hierarchical, and the Universe is cyclical. There is no God on a throne with you as his child. *You* are the god with an inner child—more real than your biological or adopted children, who aren't really yours. In Matthew 18:1-5, the disciples came to Jesus and asked, "Who, then, is the greatest in the kingdom of heaven?" He called over a little child and placed him among them. "Truly, I tell you, unless you change and become like little children, you will never enter the kingdom of heaven." Jesus is referring to the truth that children represent in order to find unity and own the kingdom found in the sixth chakra. Children speak, think, do, feel, and say one thing. If they think you are ugly, they will say you are ugly. They aren't incongruent until the crack in the snowglobe—the shame, the abandonment—that happened when we were kicked out of Olympus rises up. Now we feel imperfect and start meeting our parents' needs to get a dysfunctional version of love. We begin neglecting our inner child, who becomes ashamed, guilty, bitter and stops growing. If we wish to re-enter Olympus, our kingdom, we must return to the unity of speaking, thinking, doing, feeling, and saying the same thing. This is the unity of mind-body-spirit. This is living your truth. This is spiritual adulting. No children; just your inner child, grown up and living a congruent truth with her adult self. Start spiritual adulting and your vision board—your true purpose—will come to life but not a moment before.

Libertas was a Roman goddess; her name means "freedom." She symbolizes independence and, ironically, restraint. In the United States, she is represented by the Statue of Liberty. We don't usually associate freedom with restraint, but true freedom occurs in the subconscious where we free ourselves from the 0 to 100 pendulum swings and find that 48 to 52 balance, which requires some restraint. Libertas is always depicted with a *pileus* (a cap)—the symbol of granting freedom to former slaves, and a rod—a measuring stick of justice. I have a theory called "hard edges and soft corners." We need both. We need the hard edges of the Saturn cycles (the skinny cows) to make us work but balanced with the soft corners of Jupiter. The construction of a house requires the hard edges of a strong foundation, but its decorative aspects with curtains, pillows, candles, and so on to make it welcoming. Our spiritual life is no different. The hard edge is the spiritual adulting. We need to call ourselves out on our veils and our nonsense. At the same time, we need the soft corners of compassion, empathy, and forgiveness so we can move forward in our growth. If we speak to our inner child with only hard edges, they will be angry and resentful; if we praise her and meet her needs, she will more easily accept the limitations we place on her.

The problem with the rod is that we hold ourselves to an expectation of perfection, which becomes our 0 to 100 swings. Josephina's inner child was being held to such perfection in everything! In her child script, her father would ask her why she failed at getting 100% on her assignments even when she'd bring home a 98. With such an impossible expectation to meet, she inevitably collapsed. The physical body cannot hold the weight of such thoughts. Another client, Ingrid, wore a "good girl" mask, refusing to identify her inner prostitute, and was shocked when her husband cheated on her. When she "deconstructed" the good girl mask of perfection by defining good girl and prostitute in measurable terms, she saw how she had created the mistress in her marriage as a mirror to what she was negating.

Doing inner child work with my clients, I ask my clients to list five qualities they like about themselves, and then five that they don't. The ones you like are the measuring rod you hold yourself to, but only a partial truth of who you are. The qualities you dislike become the mask you wear to keep your inner child small and out of view. When you liberate this mask, you liberate the truth of who you are and what you are holding yourself to—a pattern that started at 14 to 16. I tell clients to get their f*** on, meaning to penetrate your psyche and your thoughts, as the prostitute gets penetrated. When we liberate this mask, this gate, this veil, we are truly whole. Libertas represents the hard edges of truth and justice with her rod, yet her cap has soft corners: compassion for the slaves. *We* are the slaves, enslaved by our subconscious thoughts and beliefs about duality and incongruence that keep us separated from others and ourselves. *Libertas'* cap, or *pileus*, represents the emancipated slaves of Rome. It represents the freedom to think and do it differently rather than being stuck at the same level of consciousness as our parents.

Her sister, *Veritas*, the goddess of virtue of truthfulness, is often depicted naked because she is unveiled or unconcealed. This has nothing to do with sexuality; it has to do with removing the veils and showing the congruence of who we are. Truth and freedom are one. Without the truth about who we really are, both the light and the dark—low-level consciousness and the illusion of duality—we cannot remove the veils of illusion, grow our inner child into an adult, and assume our throne in the kingdom.

Recall the goddess Nemesis, who among other characteristics, was said to enact retribution against those who succumbed to hubris and arrogance before the gods. In Greek mythology, bowing to the gods represents the value of humility. But this is a false humility. You don't need to be prideful, but you don't need to be excessively humble either. The point is to find the 48 to 52, the midpoint. Age 21 is the first attempt of your psyche to balance the pendulum swing. The word nemesis means "to give what is due,": not too much, not too little. It also can mean "distributor of fortune," either good fortune or misfortune depending on what you've earned. Again, neither good nor bad;

only in due proportion to each according to what was deserved. This is the universal law of Cause and Effect or *karma*.

The people who show up in your life at 21 are called nemeses because their job is to "poke the bear"—to challenge the way you've always done things. They say your mom and dad were wrong. They show you a different way to do it. It could be a boss who never cuts you slack; that report is due tomorrow—no excuses! Maybe it's a boyfriend or lover who dumps you because they just aren't interested. People are going to show up in your life at this age and their only job, whether it takes a day or a year or forever, is to point out your zero to 100—that what you learned in childhood is not the only way to do things.

When we meet a nemesis on our path, they take our job, they take our lover, they take our money, they break into our car. Resentment is natural, but unnecessary. This is the Universe speaking to you. But they are here to teach, to show us something. The Universe has put this person or situation on our path (that we created) so we can do it differently. Rather than looking at that person, place, thing, or situation with anger, view it as something *you* created to fulfill your need to change the pendulum swings of 0 to 100. If you can take ownership of their arrival and know their purpose, you will no longer resent them.

Chapter Six
A Year of Plenty— Age 24

Twenty-four is our second Jupiter cycle and second fat cow. After working with the skinny cows and neutralizer-nemesis in the N-year of 21, we get spiritually compensated at 24. Twenty-four is what is called a "Six Year" in numerology. If you add 2 + 4, you get six. Six is the number of balance, the home, and our health. Six correlates with the sign of Virgo, ruled by the goddess Demeter, who is responsible for the harvest. Twenty-four is a harvest year: A year to plant seeds that will begin to sprout at 36. Here we begin to stabilize the pendulum swings from 0 to 100 and focus on finding that 48 to 52 within ourselves. In speaking to Austin, he said "I had the worst hangover ever. I can't drink like this anymore." These are common statements from people this age. They are in a preparatory phase for the completion cycle—the return home, at 48, their midpoint. The sixth step of the spiritual path is taking care of the body and seeing it as a temple.

Our next Saturn cycle may bring motherhood or fatherhood and it is common to prepare the body for a few years and address poor coping skills before welcoming a child. Are you smoking, drinking, doing drugs, or eating poorly? Our dietary habits thus become important at this age, and we may start to eat healthier and even exercise. Many adults at this age begin seeking alternative health remedies, acupuncturists, chiropractors, and energy healers. As we spiritually adult, we take more pride in our *real* health rather than appearance and image because we want to feel good, have more energy, and live a long, healthy life. This is also a time to build ourselves professionally. In astrology, the sixth house has to do with routines, work, and health.

What we do at 24 will have a direct impact on what we experience at 48 to 52 with the Chiron return and our spiritual awakening.

Hygeia, the goddess of health, cleanliness, and sanitation, rules this age. She had four sisters: 1) Panacea (universal remedy); 2) Iaso (recuperation from illness); 3) Aceso (the healing process); and 4) Aglaia (beauty, splendor, glory, magnificence, and adornment). Hygeia and her sisters represent the importance of maintaining a well-functioning body so it can be a vehicle for the divine spark within us. At 48, our fourth Jupiter cycle, we will encounter the primordial wound; at 24, we are setting the foundation for how to heal it. This is a good time to start yoga or seek an Ayurvedic practitioner. In Ayurveda, the balance of the elements in our body is called the doshas. There are three main doshas: *vata*, *pitta*, and *kapha*. Vata is the space and ether element; pitta associates with water and fire; kapha with earth and water. Knowing your dosha can help you devise a proper food, exercise, and herbal protocol for optimal health. Ayurveda is the sister science to yoga and often goes hand in hand with food and exercise.

Now, at 24, if you haven't begun to dethrone your parents' values around health, you are going to begin a disease process (if you don't already have one) known in the Ayurvedic tradition as *samprapti*. This is the outcome of the program you received at conception that illness was the only way to get your needs met. Children realize that they get attention when they are sick, so we subconsciously produce illness to achieve this goal. This also reflects emotional loyalties to our parents and low-vibration value systems. This is especially common when parents couldn't be children themselves; taking care of a sick child subconsciously keeps *them* in child. Jacquelyn is a dutiful, responsible adult whose son is epileptic. After she takes care of him when he experiences a seizure, she gives herself permission to go into child, cry, and stay in bed. Otherwise, she would never take time off. She has become dependent on her son meeting the needs of her inner child rather than honoring them herself.

Samprapti says that a disease goes through six stages: the first four are localized and may be "symptom free" according to Western medicine. *Sanchaya* presents as minor symptoms like gas and bloating. *Prakopa* may give us stiffness and lethargy. *Prasara* can cause food cravings. Western doctors would describe such things as stress- or lifestyle-related and essentially ignore them. This is a mistake. They are messages from the subconscious letting the physical body know that there is an irregularity and an imbalance. Unfortunately, we tend to ignore these symptoms, especially in a fat cow year (like 24!) when the going is good. *Sthana* is the fourth stage when such signs and symptoms become harder to ignore but still not strong enough to really get our attention. *Vyakti* is when we acknowledge that an issue should be addressed and we seek (or should seek) medical attention. At *Bheda*, the sixth stage, conditions have become severe and more difficult to treat. The diseases that show up at the midpoint ages of 48 to 52 are often referred to as *karmic diseases*. They gradually build up in the psyche and seep into the body over a period of years. They develop to force us to change our ways. These are the physical stages, and there are similar stages spiritually. When I was first diagnosed with cancer, for example, I knew it was directly related to my children, which I conceived at 24, my custody battle and the wounds I had not yet healed.

Honoring the Material and the Spiritual

At 24, we have our second Jupiter return. Remember that our first Jupiter return was at 12, when you realized your parents weren't gods and you could dethrone them. In mythology, Jupiter was the only god who got to dethrone his father. From zero to seven, you slowly learn that your parents aren't perfect, but the conscious mind is still developing, and that awareness sinks to your subconscious. Children aren't ready to see their parents as anything but gods. We're not mature enough to understand how we put the bad things that don't make sense into a bucket that we shove down our psyche and which becomes our shadow. That's why Jupiter is about dethroning our parents with awareness, at the level of the conscious mind. The conscious mind is largely developed at 12, but by 24 has had 12 more years to mature. Jupiter is about *both* spiritual growth and material values. This is super important and best exemplified by Jesus—a physical man who also honored his spiritual growth. The Buddha tried to deny his body and material needs and finally realized he wouldn't reach enlightenment if he didn't eat. You have to give the body what the body needs, and you have to give the spirit what the spirit needs. There is material food and spiritual food. What's happening in our society, though, is that people are choosing one or the other, and we cannot build our spiritual infrastructure unless we honor both.

I want to stress the need to address material values. We all have values around money, sex, home, food, and other material needs that were "given" to us from 0 to 7. If we disagree with them and end up doing the opposite, it often means negating the physical altogether and staying on the pendulum. This will become a source of suffering and pain if not addressed. To negate either the spiritual or material is not the solution. Jupiter is perfect because it says spirit and matter are both necessary to be whole. Jupiter took the biggest piece of pie when the world was being split. Take what is rightfully yours, he says. Don't give it away to honor your parents. Recall that Jupiter dethroned his father, and that is your right as well.

So, the question becomes, Do you feel guilty about money or material values? If so, why? This is an important age to get clear about the answers because the currency of the world is time, money, and resources, and at 24, you are just beginning a long journey, and all of this will be needed. And again, it's not about making money or having resources but how you get and manage them. There is no point to struggling with material means. This is not a spiritual practice. We've idealized poverty as spiritual and villainized wealth as material when the archetypes and myths say different. In Matthew 19:23-24, Jesus says, "Truly I say to you, it will be hard for a rich man to enter the kingdom of heaven." He didn't mean you had to be poor; he was cautioning against emotional gluttony and thought hoarding and attachment. It's about the quality of your thoughts, your value system, and your self-worth.

The East and the West appear to have very different views about material possession. Athena and Poseidon went to Greece and made a bid to have the city named after them. Athena offered material wealth and riches; Poseidon offered spiritual wealth and riches. Obviously, Athena won because the capital is Athens. The Western world is built on a material foundation. If you try to negate your desire for money or beauty or image or "stuff," you are denying the core of your existence at a psychic level and building your life on a false foundation. This doesn't mean this is all there is, but we're outsourcing our entire spiritual life to India when we have a beautiful hermetic philosophy and mythology here in the Western world that is rich in spiritual teachings but was partly suppressed by religion and the Church. Many people believe that India is superior because their origin story is rooted in spiritual riches. But India is poor and needs materialism the same way the Western world needs spirituality. They are both out of balance. Your psyche is programmed to Western values that are built on materiality. If you replace that with a scarcity mentality, you will still be out of balance.

We struggle in the Western world with money and sensuality, which the Romans didn't help when they inserted a Virgin Mary image in our psyche that favored purity and sexless procreation. Despite their struggles with materialism, the Eastern world understands that spirit and matter co-exist; they have a Shiva-Shakti god and goddess embracing sexuality. In the Vedas, there are entire chapters about sexuality and the rules of when to have sex. There isn't the negation of sexuality and prudence as in the Western world.

There are two types of Aphrodite: *Pandemos* and *Urania*. Aphrodite Pandemos has to do with the second chakra and unmet needs from childhood. Aphrodite Urania has to do with agape or unconditional love and the fourth chakra. We need Pandemos for the material comforts. We need Urania for the heart energy. At 24, we're supposed to rewrite our values around image and money. How important is image and beauty? How much effort should go into those? How many Botox visits is enough? What should you spend money on? How is money linked to self-worth? Are you paying everyone's bills when you go to the bar? Do you live in a studio with an empty refrigerator? What are the values and motives behind your behaviors related to money and image?

Shalom Schwartz, a social psychologist and cross-cultural researcher, developed the Theory of Basic Human Values which perfectly aligns with the developmental stages of spiritual infrastructure and my Archetypal Spiritual Adulting Brain map (Appendix H). His theory proposes four categories and ten values: 1) openness to change (self-direction, stimulation), 2) self enhancement (hedonism, achievement, and power); 3) conservation (security, conformity, tradition), and 4) self-transcendence (benevolence, and universalism). I added some of those values to my spiritual adulting map. The Moon is directly linked to tradition, and the Sun is directly linked to security needs: unmet needs from childhood. Achievement and stimulation are linked to Mercury, logic, and rational intelligence. Every two years, the ego desires to move forward in the world, powered by the masculine energy of Mars. The teenage years of hedonism are right in line with the gluttony and the sexual escapades of Zeus and Aphrodite. There could be benevolence as well with Jupiter's spiritual growth and Aphrodite-Urania's agape love. At 28, we're moving from self-direction into adult and conformity. Universalism and power are the spiritual adult phases.

Dr Schwartz considered a fifth category—spirituality—but said it wasn't found in all cultures. I wholeheartedly disagree. Spirituality was known by different names such as nature or universal law or the seasons or mythology. Every culture absolutely has a practice around the soul or spiritual growth. Joseph Campbell spoke to this in *Hero with a Thousand Faces*. In every mythology, in every culture, there is some version of spirit. This correlates to spiritual adulting and the removal of the final veil—the one that is directly linked to the zero to seven snowglobe crack where we felt worthless, useless, and that we no longer belonged. When we finally unmask and liberate ourselves from that lie, we become one with the Universe. Da Vinci created his famous "Vitruvian Man" with spirit in the center, a statement that you cannot eliminate spirit from being human. Matter and spirit are always one. His use of the pentagram, often depicted as a satanic or a pagan symbol when upside down, is simply saying that the feminine is how we experience God on Earth. Spirit animates matter. Every point on the pentagram is associated with an element that created the earthly realm: air, fire, water, and earth. The arms and legs of the Vitruvius Man represent the physical, but you don't become a spiritual adult until you honor both your physical and spiritual nature.

Spiritual transformation in ancient alchemy was linked to copper, silver and gold. Copper represented transmuting earthly desires, which lead to silver, containing the emotional needs, which lead to gold: our spiritual self that owns its power and its throne. Venus or Aphrodite is often the symbol for copper which represents the body. She's associated with the senses and how we experience pleasure. Venus was born from the sperm of Uranus when he was castrated by Saturn, so there's a direct link to sexuality, desires, the second chakra and eros love. But we know that sex doesn't necessarily mean physical or erotic sex; it can also mean agape love. There are two levels of consciousness. Copper (Venus) leads to Gold, but in between is silver—mom, the toxic waters of the womb. You must dethrone mom in the psyche to achieve the gold standard of being one with the Universe: our spiritual consciousness, the universal womb. Your copper (your body) is the only vehicle that can take you to your soul. This is how spirit meets matter. Transmute and integrate your mother, do it differently, and get your gold. In John 3:14, the Bible says, "Jesus is a copper serpent lifted in the wilderness." They're talking about the feminine. They're talking about Venus. They're talking about universal love. Jesus preached love and compassion, that only through the feminine can experience God on Earth, and only through matter (the feminine) can our spirit exist and perform its divine duty. That is why the story of Jesus is so important. Jesus is the copper, the feminine, the Venus. He showed us that spirit and matter must exist as one, and that if we can raise our vibration and honor Urania, we can be whole beings and live in harmony and balance.

In Western medical literature, copper has been found to stimulate the brain and the thyroid, help arthritis the joints, support clearer skin, produce melanin, and aid in peristalsis. Again, if copper is Venus and copper is directly linked to the physical body, this would make sense. But at 24, we stay at the lower-level vibration of physical pleasures instead of the higher-level senses and higher vibration of Venus. The second truth in my 12-truth model is called the "truth of desire." There is nothing wrong with desire. Our body has desires, and we should honor that. We just need to balance it with spirit. The glyph of Venus features the circle of spirit balanced above the cross of matter: spirit balanced on matter. This isn't the triumph of Eastern philosophy over Western philosophy; it's the balance of spirit and matter. What DaVinci was trying to explain, and what the pentagram of Venus shows, is that the role of the body is to experience spirit.

Glyph of Venus: The circle of spirit balanced above the cross of matter.

In mythology, there are the *Graces* or the *Charites:* the three daughters of Zeus and Hera. Aglaea represents beauty, splendor, brightness, and elegance. Euphrosyne is of good cheer, mirth, and joyfulness. Thalia embodies youth, beauty, bloom, and festivities. The way to experience God, the way to experience spirit, the way to experience the Universe, is through your high-vibration Venus as depicted by the three Charities and their love of music, poetry, literature, and all things of beauty. There are also nine muses who work for the Graces: Erato, Euterpe, Thalia, Terpsichore, Clio, Melpomene, Calliope, Urania, and Polyhymnia. They are directly connected to Aphrodite Urania or high-consciousness Venus and how we experience God through our senses and the vehicle of the flesh. You honor your spirit through the body. At 24, you should have a relationship to one of the arts at every Jupiter and Venus cycle. Did your parents instill beauty in your life? Which Muse or Grace is most similar to your values? How did your parents engage the senses in a high-vibration way? Honoring Venus is how to help yourself get closer to being a spiritual adult and how you honor your parents without self-destructing through improper use of the senses or the *indriyas*. Truth Ten on a spiritual path is Truth of Silence. Here we use sound healing and other modalities focusing on proper use of the senses to connect to the god within.

CHAPTER SEVEN

The Saturn Return— Age 28

As Joan Didion wrote in *Slouching Towards Bethlehem*, "That was the year, my twenty-eighth, when I was discovering that not all of the promises would be kept, that some things are in fact irrevocable and that it had counted after all, every evasion and every procrastination, every mistake, every word, all of it." At 28, we finish our first, full, seasonal cycle of life. We come full circle and now pick up where our parents left off. This is the age of adulting when we take on more responsibility—and castrate ourselves by honoring our parents' value system and not our own (the mortgage, the job, the child). This sets the foundation to do it exactly as our parents did and, ironically, provides the material to (hopefully) start liberating ourselves at 42. The *Law of Rhythm* states that, "Everything vibrates and moves to certain rhythms. These rhythms establish seasons, cycles, stages of development and patterns. Everything is either growing or dying." The cycle that began at age seven with the crack in the snowglobe comes full circle. This is a V-year, and the type of valor you assume is directly related to which burden you choose to carry. Kohlberg's last level, the *Postconventional*, emphasizes individual rights and individual principles of conscience. Fowler's third stage of faith, *Synthetic-Conventional* (arising in adolescence and into young adulthood), is characterized by conformity to authority and the religious development of a personal identity. Any conflicts with one's beliefs are ignored at this stage because they are inconsistent with the value system we inherited from our parents and thus a threat to the stability of our psyche.

Deontological ethical theories are at play here as well. This class of ethics states that people should adhere to their obligations and duties when engaged in decision-making because upholding one's duty to another individual or society is considered ethically correct. The flaw in deontology is that there may be no logical or rational basis for choosing those obligations or duties; self-awareness is limited here. There is a subconscious motive to remain in child and honor a child script, which can lead to bad decisions because such impulses aren't analyzed to understand the real reasons behind them. This type of behavior is always linked to a good or bad bucket item and either mimicked or opposed, blindly. At this age, you have come full circle with biological adulting; your prefrontal cortex is completely developed, and this region of the brain is now engaged in accomplishing executive functions. It has reached peak performance, especially regarding recall and storing and processing information. This is the *formal-reflexive* stage of Ken Wilber's model: The child thinks for the sake of thinking and understands critical thinking. The problem is that the focus is on material responsibilities.

Psychologically, this stage is linked with reaching full adulthood and being faced for the first time with adult challenges and responsibilities. For example, it is common at this age to start a family, get a mortgage, and/or start one's professional career. These responsibilities become the focal point of our life for the next 30 years. At 60, when we "retire," we begin the process of liberation. But if we haven't done any spiritual introspection in the previous 30 years, we are going to struggle, and the Themis-Zeus-Rahu-Ketu cycle may not deliver the freedom you are expecting. The common issue associated with this cycle is that you may repeat the patterns of your parents. For instance, your marriage may have the same issues as those of your parents. Your parenting techniques may be the same as theirs. Of course, you may do the exact opposite, thinking you're doing it differently, but you're not. It is thus imperative to revisit the value system you tried to dethrone at 14 to 16, because if you start this 30-year cycle at the same level of consciousness, it will come back to haunt you at 58 to 60. This is a sobering reality for many and a wake-up-call that it's time to grow up. Don't dismiss your spiritual growth here.

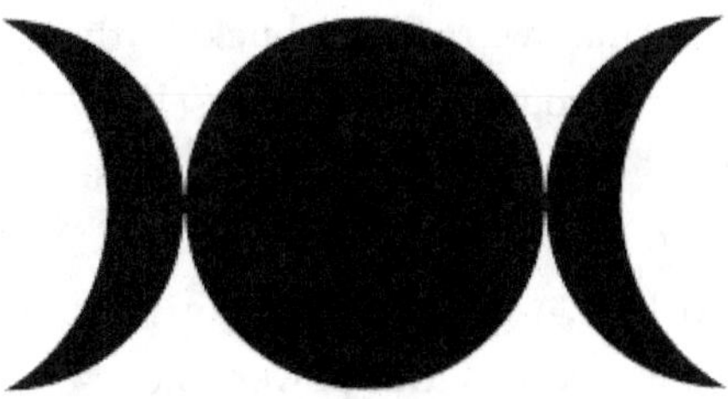

Triple Goddess Archetype: Represents the three main phases of a person's life: Maiden, mother and crone. Maiden can represent 0-14 years old, Mother can represent 14-52 years old and Crone can represent beyond 52.

The Triple Goddess: Maiden

The *Triple Goddess* archetype represents the three main phases of a person's life. Often depicted as a woman's cycle, it actually also corresponds to men as well. The first phase is called "the maiden" or the waxing Moon. This phase is linked to the child (0—14), when we are under our parents' care. Here we learn that we aren't loved unconditionally and, to gain approval, we must meet our parents' needs. Many people choose to stay in this phase developmentally and spiritually, looking for surrogate parents in their friends and partners and never truly growing up.

The Mother

The second phase is the full Moon or "the mother" phase. Often associated with the onset of puberty through menopause, it lasts from 14 to 52. These years are often wasted tending to everyone else's needs but our own. Most people also neglect their spiritual development during these years, focusing instead on academic and financial achievement. Our inner child suffers during these years. We value the masculine principle; the ego needs to be constantly validated. I often tell my clients that they use their children and relationships to mirror what they need to address in themselves spiritually. For instance, the things you don't like in your children are unintegrated aspects of your own psyche—your shadow, the bad buckets that you've neglected. Rather than punishing your child, ask yourself, "Where do I have this quality in my life?" "How can I integrate this shadow aspect so my child doesn't have to do my work for me?"

In our relationships, we often show up with hopes to get our childhood needs met and give our power to our partner. Many marriages end in divorce because it is unnatural to expect that one person will meet your needs. Rarely does a marriage establish boundaries and rules early on, so when the system shatters—around the seventh year—many don't have the experience or the tools to understand what happened. In *The Truth Is in the Triangle*, I use the same concept of a snowglobe to describe the beginning of a relationship; it contains the story of how two people meet—the fantasy. That snowglobe cracks during the first fight, which becomes a source of ongoing tension, linked to every other fight the couple experiences. With our perspective distorted by details that don't pertain to the real issue, we throw the baby out with the bath water and get divorced. In my model, I offer a step-by-step approach for defining the boundaries, non-negotiables, unmet needs, and purpose of the relationship (e.g., spiritual growth, building wealth). Marriage is an opportunity for self-discovery and achieving a mystical marriage—the *hieros gamos*—by putting yourself first and then your partner. If the couple has a clear understanding what they're doing *together*, they can avoid most of what leads to a dysfunctional relationship. Most people get together because they recognize the discarded parts of their partner and vice versa. They feel seen and heard—exactly what they lacked in childhood and why they were kicked out of Olympus. The fastest way to enlightenment is through a relationship. The sacrament of marriage is actually linked to the mystical marriage with oneself, and then another. In the pagan traditions goddesses would marry a godhead of their choice to achieve the *hieros gamos* or mystical marriage. When you are in relationship and understand your partner is modeling your shadow, (your unintegrated parent) and bad buckets, you can grow quickly and reach enlightenment. Couples often battle over the same theme but from different sides of the issue. They identify with one another, but they're still children. They may begin adulting after the first real crisis, which occurs at five-to-seven years of marriage, but many don't, dooming the relationship.

I believe that every relationship has a mistress who comes in the form of infidelity, an addiction, time limitations, travel, or even a child; anything that takes priority away from the relationship. That mistress needs to be faced so we can do our inner work and our relationship work. Marriages are also built as a business, not only as a place for love. There are negotiations and arrangements, boundaries and values. Instead of abstract concepts like happiness and love, we must define the thread that brings two people together and builds the structure of the relationship. Your partner isn't a mind reader and shouldn't just know what you need. Define these terms and create a plan with boundaries so that you hold each other accountable.

The Crone

If you are a mother in this second stage of life, read *The Truth Is in the Triangle* so you can approach your relationship as a spiritual experience and opportunity and not just a romantic and/or financial relationship. If you don't, you may experience an existential crisis as you enter the final phase after 52 when you realize that you spent 30 years falsely nurturing others, trying to get your own needs met, and accomplishing nothing. In *Dethroning Olympus*, my family systems book and workbook, I spell out ways to support your children, integrate your shadow so they don't have to do the work for you, keep your power, and help your children keep theirs.

What tends to happen with the *Triple Goddess*, though, is what I call a traffic jam. Usually at the age of 52 and beyond—depending on the maturity of the parent-child—the parents (though usually this is associated with the mother) are supposed to enter "the crone": the last phase represented by a waning moon. This is linked to aging, menopause, and facing our mortality. However, many refuse to leave the mother phase because they won't let their daughters enter it. In crone, you need to start planning your legacy and perhaps catch up on the spiritual adulting you have failed to do. The traffic jam happens when forcing the child to stay in maiden when it's time for them to move into adulthood.

Sheila is a 28-year-old client who called me because her period lasted 14 days instead of the normal seven-day cycle. She lived in New York City, was sexually active, and growing as a top professional in her industry. While away from her mother, she was living her truth and owning the mother phase. But whenever she spoke on the phone with her mother—which was every day, multiple times a day—she retreated into maiden. Her mother was 60 and had refused to enter the crone phase. Sheila would pretend she was a poor, innocent little girl, exactly what her mother needed to believe she was. Her long period was her subconscious screaming for her to grow up. Abnormal menstrual cycles are directly related to traffic jams in the system. She needed twice as many days to be an adult in the mother phase because her mother kept pushing her back into maiden. Her mother, who should have been focusing on her own spiritual adulting, visits New York every chance she gets to see Sheila, violating Sheila's boundaries in the name of being a "good mother".

By the age of 28, we should have clear adult boundaries with everyone, especially our parents. We gave our parents our childhood; it's time they parent themselves and let us grow up. This is probably the hardest V-year for those with marital problems or a baby because the instinct is to go to our parents for advice. Unfortunately, their advice is based on their view of what they want for your life: the same as theirs, played out at a low-level of consciousness—exactly the one you're supposed to transmute. Sheila spoke to her mother about breaking up with her boyfriend, and Sheila's mother said, "No, he's a good catch. Don't lose him." Sheila is bisexual and has no interest in getting married or having children, yet her mother wants grandchildren and Sheila is an only child. She isn't thinking about Sheila's needs; she's thinking about her own needs getting met. When Sheila confronted her mother about her own marriage, she replied, "It's not that bad." Sheila understood that her mother is obsessed with her because she doesn't want to admit that she and her husband have no common interests except Sheila. These are systemic issues, and when we reach 28 to 30, they become very dangerous because we are programmed to not dethrone this aspect of our parents, often repeating our parents' mistakes to the tee. Our loyalties run deep! Instead, be loyal to yourself and your own spiritual adulting process. End those childish behaviors that are causing the traffic jam and clogging the system.

If you have access to your astrology chart, I highly recommend check the house placement of your Saturn. The house will tell you what area of life you have to fight to dethrone your parents and do it differently. In the appendices, I have a list of the houses so you can identify the area where your skinny cows will appear with each Saturn cycle. If you are a bit more advanced in astrology, I invite you to look at the *decanate* that your Saturn is in (Appendix C). There are three decanates per sign; raise the vibration one decanate. For instance, I have Saturn in Gemini in the second decanate of Venus in the seventh house of marriage. This where I need to dethrone my parents during each N and V year. The Venus decanate at a low vibration is based on image and financial gain. I've had two marriages that, while quite different, were still focused on image and finances. In order to do it differently and dethrone my parents, I needed to raise the vibration to the third decanate, which is Uranus: the planet of independence, freedom, revolutionary thinking, innovation, and rebellion. I lived part of this out while married to a transgender man. When I better understood the concept of *hieros gamos*, I created a model called the I-I-We, which says that each individual in a relationship is an independent person with certain freedoms inside the confines of that partnership—something I never observed in my parents' marriage.

The only way to Libertas is by changing your thoughts. I had to transmute my parents' relationship and make it on my own. Decanates are only ten degrees, or equivalent to an octave, which is the only amount of change allotted in one lifetime. According to the Law of Octaves, thoughts and beliefs are transmuted and behavior change becomes permanent only when a new octave is reached; anything else is only transformation and can relapse at any time.

CHAPTER EIGHT

Jesus and the Weight of Your Thoughts: 33–35

This stage is the peak of a spiritual crisis period that began at 33—the age Jesus died. This is a spiritual rebirth year, an extremely important time of spiritual adulting when your values will be turned upside down, forcing you into action. This is our third N-year and, once again, we are visited by the "ghosts of Christmas past" from the 0-to-7 snowglobe cracks. If you can't remember what happened at 35, try going back to when you were 21. It's the continuation of the theme that started there. During Jesus' last year on Earth, he was betrayed by Judas, Peter disowned him, others spit on him, and he was injured, mocked, and crucified. A similar experience will happen to you at this age. Our spiritual family shows up in full force to push you forward, because the next Rahu-Ketu destiny change is the following year. This crisis, built into your psyche, will bring you to your knees. The breakdown of the body and psyche birthed from your toxic womb is meant to be destroyed here. Like The Hanged Man, this phase should have you rethinking your entire value system, what you are doing with your life, and how you want to rebirth yourself *from* yourself.

There are 33 vertebrae, the top one being Atlas, named after the figure in Greek mythology who carried the weight of the world on his shoulders. Similarly, this vertebra supports the entire head. I like to imagine that **the body crumbles when it can no longer carry the weight of your unprocessed thoughts**, which is what this stage reminds me of. You have been carrying subconscious programming that hasn't served you and you may be experiencing physical illness from the weight of those thoughts—also sluggish and old without energy. Your body is telling you, "Rebirth is necessary!" There are also 33 nerve groups going through the spine. There are 33 turns of the human DNA sequence. Thirty-three is considered the number of Christ consciousness. The Bible records 33 miracles and the Sephirot of the Kabbalah has 33 constituent parts. In Tibetan Buddhism, the crown chakra has 33 downward pointing petals.

The human DNA sequence in the body mimics the energetic body, where Ida and Pingala (the right and left serpents) wrap around the *sushumna* (the energy that flows through the center of the spine) and create chakras: energy centers located up and down the body. The image of the *caduceus*—two serpents wrapped around a staff—is the anchor symbol of Western medicine, but it's more authentically associated with energetic health and is related to Hermes Trismegistus (the father of metaphysics), hermetic teachings, alchemy, and astrology. It resembles the double-helix of the DNA and represents a wand for raising consciousness and spiritual rebirth. The 33rd day of every year is called Groundhog Day, and I consider the same-named film one of the most spiritual movies I have ever seen. In it, Bill Murray is forced to repeat the same day again and again until he spiritually adults, and makes it right. Groundhog Day also represents the Saturn cycles that returns every seven years. Saturn is the planet associated with alchemy—our transmutation of lead to gold. With each Groundhog Day, each Saturn cycle, we transmute our thoughts and get lighter and lighter—closer to the gold. In numerology, the number three is associated with thought and individuation.

Candace was 35 when she slipped and broke her neck. A few months earlier, her father, who gave her life structure, suddenly died. After his death, her own physical structure began to collapse. She had a contentious relationship with her mother, who was always in victim and child and was now her only parent. Candace and her father had shared the responsibility of taking care of her mom, now that he was gone, it was left to Candace alone. Subconsciously, she wanted to erase the program that she was responsible for her mother. With no other way to dethrone her mother and assume her throne, she created a variety of health conditions in addition to her neck, forcing her mother to also seek therapy with me. Once her mother started shifting the system, Candace was able to deal with her grief and rebuild her foundation on her own values, not her father's. Both she and her mother strengthened their bond and started traveling the world together, a value they both shared. Through individuation of thought, transmuting the low-level consciousness of your parents, and raising the vibration of your thoughts, you are on the road to birthing a Christ consciousness with Truth Ten on the spiritual path.

CHAPTER NINE

The Best Is Yet to Come: Age 36

If you survive 35, then amazing prospects are in store for you at 36! This is the second turn of the Rahu-Ketu lunar nodes. Every 18 years, these two nodes meet up and open the doors of destiny, changing your future for the positive. Imagine being at the Lion's Gate in Mycenae, Greece—the main entrance to that Bronze Age citadel and its only surviving structure. When Rahu-Ketu get together at 36, they resemble that imposing gate, whose representation of lions was an emblem of the Mycenaean kings and a symbol of their power. Lions represent the conquering of personality and owning our true selves. In the myth of Hercules and "The Slaying of the Nemean Lion," Hercules traps the lion in a cave. Symbolically, the cave is where we do our shadow work, an essential step in the spiritual path. The cave also refers to the pituitary gland, which is a master gland. (You will learn more about the pituitary when I discuss the Jupiter cycle of 48 to 52.)

In this myth, Hercules had to kill the lion with his bare hands and leave the cave wearing the lion's skins to demonstrate his triumph. In St. Peter's *Epistle* we find these words: "Your adversary, the devil, like a roaring lion walketh about, seeking whom he may devour." The lion is our dominant personality, overriding our spirit and our heart and wreaking havoc in our lives when out of control. We have a similar cave in our heads: a small, bony structure that shields and guards one of the most important glands in the body—the pituitary. When this gland is functioning properly, our personality is well-rounded and engaged. We are self-controlled with heightened mental activity and endurance. With the rebirth that occurs at 33—35, we enter a fat cow Jupiter cycle that piggybacks on these lunar nodes. It's one of the most auspicious times of our life.

When Tyrone's wife was diagnosed with cancer at the age of 33, his world crumbled, and he began reevaluating his life's choices. With the stress of her disease, he was forced to confront that he had failed to create a life independent of her. He was plagued with thoughts that if she died, he would be totally alone. *Her* kids, her house, her friends, her money, her family . . . that's how he organized his life. Nothing for himself. Also 33, the cancer shows him that the structure of his life was flawed, and he had to rebuild it. They eventually divorced, and after a few months, he rekindled a romance with his college sweetheart. Neither of them had children, and they decided they were both ready to start a family. With his Rahu-Ketu cycle, he moved to another state, got sober, had a child, and even started a podcast. He experienced a profound change in his destiny. He found someone from his past to start a new future with. By becoming sober and facing who he had become, he dethroned the "toxic waters" of his own father's alcoholism and addictions and found new connections and friends, something he had missed out on in his prior life.

The lunar nodes are in exact opposite signs. Rahu, the north node, is the door of your future—your karmic destiny in this lifetime. The south node is Ketu—leftover karma from a past life that you finish out in the early part of this incarnation. In the north node are skills you need to practice, but once implemented, they will change your life. From the south node you find gifts that come naturally. In Kabbalah, the north node is called a *tikkun*, or a correction. It is viewed as a karmic adjustment the soul makes. The north node is calling your name, but it takes some time to equip yourself to climb that mountain. When you live through the north node, you leave your comfort zone and activate your life's mission. The south node is more comfortable, providing skills you've mastered that are always available when you need to recalibrate.

At 36, you meet your karmic destiny through the doors of the nodes while Zeus, king of Olympus, provides spiritual gifts a plenty. The warning here is to not become gluttonous, indulgent, or greedy.

Jupiter and the nodes will make your dreams come true, but they're not too concerned with how you maintain those dreams. This period requires discernment because we may make impulsive decisions, both financial and spiritual, that can be detrimental later.

CHAPTER TEN

The Uranus Opposition and Crumbling Structures: Age 42

This stage actually begins around 39, and by 42 we begin the return home. Erickson calls this phase "middle adulthood," which for him spans ages 40 to 65. Gebser's fifth structure of consciousness, the *integral structure*, begins here but doesn't end here. This is a stage of insight, integration, and transparency, with an ability to perceive time and space as an integrated whole. Gebser states that this is a "concretion of previous structure of consciousness"; however, I believe that this stage is about dissolving those structures in an attempt to reunite with the cosmic consciousness. Ken Wilber's seventh step of consciousness is the *centaur*, where the soul begins to transcend and integrate all aspects of previous stages. Fowler's fourth stage of faith is *Individuative-Reflective* (usually mid-twenties to late thirties)—a stage of angst and struggle when one takes personal responsibility for his or her beliefs and feelings. As they reflect on those beliefs, there is an openness to a new complexity of faith, which also reveals the conflicts in existing beliefs.

This is Kohlberg's second stage of morality, "conventional" morality, which is linked to ethical theories based on rights. The rights established by a society are protected and given the highest priority. Those rights are assumed to be ethically correct and valid since a large population endorses them. The problem with this theory is that, on a larger scale, societies must determine which rights to uphold and grant to citizens and then enforce them. Some of them have to do with social justice and humanitarian issues that a society considers important. This is necessary, but it can also be incompatible with the process of spiritual adulting, which is about building an *internal* system of morality where you define your own values. Kohlberg's "post-conventional" morality is more consistent with this process. Here you identify your goals and priorities and the beginning of new structures.

The eleventh step in a spiritual practice is to give back to humanity; you begin to build the infrastructure for that mission at 42. In the Quran 89:17-20, Muhammad spoke about social and economic justice. He set out a *sirah*, a path for practicing and promoting social justice that addressed rights of women, the root causes of economic inequality, and even called out racism. Eventually, we realize in the 48 to 52 that those structures are inside us, and this phase attempts to dissolve them. Forty-two is another six year (4 + 2), but instead of building a home, wealth, a career, or health habits, it's a "freedom" transit. Uranus is the planet of freedom and independence. We begin to notice that much of our life has been one of feeling chained, detained, and limited. We are on a mission to shatter anything that confines us and keeps us in prison, often destroying whatever we built in previous "6" years, starting at 24. We don't always realize that the freedom we seek is found in our thoughts, but we still try to break down the structures in our life like our profession, our marriage, and our bank account. This transit is often accompanied by a midlife crisis, sexual liberation, and a search for a spiritual path.

In "The Seizing of the Girdle of Hippolyte," Hercules is tasked with bringing the chastity girdle of Hippolyte back to Hera. The symbolism of a chastity girdle is important to mention here, because this age is directly associated with sexual liberation. The shame and guilt we experienced about our bodies, our desires, and our sexual choices begin to disintegrate. The sixth sign is Virgo, representing the Virgin Birth, but at 42 we start to embrace strong goddesses like Isis and Lilith. Be careful to avoid creating an imbalance here. Strong female energy, like that of Hippolyte (Queen of the Amazons), can overwhelm the masculine, and you need a balance of both to create unity. "Girl boss" energy is just another 0—100 pendulum swing manifesting as female but is masculine in disguise. The Amazonian women chopped off their breasts to fight in battle yet carried their children on their hip. They were unified but lacked clarity on what constituted true balance. The myth of Hercules was about retrieving Hippolyte's girdle, which she was willing to give him of her own free will. But the goddess Hera lies and turns the Amazons against Hercules and his men, and he ends up killing Hippolyta because he failed to communicate with her. This is a metaphor for bulldozing through life, tossing everything and anything that limits and restricts us to the curb. At 42, we may thus unnecessarily (and unconsciously) blow up our life without discernment to liberate ourselves from low-level consciousness and the thoughts that produce and maintain it—instead of embracing a more intentional approach that recognizes the spiritual adulting process we are in.

Another phenomenon of this stage is the *spiritual emergency*, a term coined by Stanislav and Christina Grof. The Grofs have described the spiritual emergency "as a crisis often resulting in intense emotions, unusual thoughts and behaviors, and perceptual changes. This crisis often involves a spiritual component—such as experiences of death and rebirth, unity with the universe, and encounters with powerful beings. Such crises bring about the potential for profound psychological and spiritual change, but often appear to be similar to psychotic disorders" It is believed that Carl Jung experienced a *spiritual emergency* while writing, and then failing to complete, *The Red Book*.

The brightest star in the constellation of Virgo is *Spica*, which means "an ear of corn." The image of Virgo is a cup of communion; its highest meaning is the Holy Grail. God gave the Israelites manna from heaven and said, "Take what you need, no more no less." This was the beginning of their return home and God provided, in balance, what they needed. It is wisdom worth heeding at 42 when we want to soak up all the liberation we never had. We, too, are leaving an Egypt of slavery in our minds, but the Promised Land is still distant; we need to keep some semblance of balance until the next important stage of 48 to 52. The Holy Grail here represents the beginning of the wilderness we enter—the wilderness of our minds, our subconscious, and the guidance from other realms. Typical of this stage would be leaving on a pilgrimage, studying with a spiritual teacher, exploring tarot or astrology, or developing our intuition. We can also begin to liberate ourselves of social constructs and redirect our energies toward humanitarian causes and "changing the world." We start understanding that the cosmic womb is very different from the toxic waters of the maternal womb, and we want to experience that collective consciousness once again.

Rosemary had reached out to me for years about starting astrology classes. We had set several appointments that she always cancelled. Suddenly, during the week of her 42nd birthday, she actually started the classes! Astrology is one of the best tools we have for self-discovery. Rosemary had been on the fence because she was grappling with her religion's rejection of astrology. She had read a Facebook post of mine about Jesus being a metaphysician, a yogi, a shaman, and an astrologer and she said it had got her thinking. The more she learned, the more she realized that Jesus was indeed an astrologer. He was announced by a star, he died on a fixed cross, he embodied the 2/8 axis, and he was a Leo, not a Capricorn—hence, the *sun*, not son, of God. She was hooked! I hear this a lot from clients. Certain information reaches them, they have a sudden flash of clarity, and things start to click. As the saying goes, *"When the student is ready, the teacher appears."*

In the myth of Athena's birth, Zeus starts having relations with a Titan named Metis. She gets pregnant, and since he is prophesied to be dethroned by his child. Zeus swallows Metis. He gets a splitting headache and calls on the blacksmith Hephaestus for help. Hephaestus splits Zeus's helmet open with a sledgehammer and out comes Athena. Athena needed help from Hephaestus to be born because in addition to intellect and wisdom, Hephaestus represents imagination. Imagination is another way of invoking spirituality or something beyond the rational mind. In this stage, we need something beyond reason to find a spiritual teacher and discover cosmic conscious-ness—a journey that will be completed in the next stage: 48 to 52.

CHAPTER ELEVEN

Chiron and Your Return Home: 48 to 52

In my opinion, this is the most important cycle of our spiritual adulting. There are three major cycles in our life: the first Saturn return at 28 when we dethrone our parents financially; the Uranus opposition at 42 when we dethrone our parents psychologically; and the Chiron return at ages 48 to 52. At 48, we have our fourth fat cow with Jupiter and our spiritual growth is palpable. Ken Wilber's eighth stage is the *psychic stage*, where the individual begins to transcend the egoic states of the previous levels. Fowler's stage five, *conjunctive faith* (mid-life crisis), acknowledges paradox and transcendence. It refers to the process of moving beyond conventional religion and seeing truth as something multidimensional and not owned by any one religion. The individual resolves conflicts from previous stages by a complex understanding of multidimensional, interdependent "truths" that cannot be rationally explained. This stage is in sync with "virtue ethics." *Virtue ethical theory* judges a person by his/her character rather than by an action that may deviate from their normal behavior. It takes the person's morals, reputation, and motivation into account. In reality, the transcendent is beyond the field of ethics, but embodying the divine requires an individual to live by his definition of character. The Buddha's fourth "noble truth" speaks of the path that leads us toward the end of suffering. This is the Eightfold Path, whose principles are in alignment with these virtues: right understanding, right thought, right speech, right action, right livelihood, right effort, right mindfulness, and right concentration. I include all of these in my twelve-fold spiritual path.

Forty-nine is an N-year, which means a visit from a neutralizer to help bring the pendulum swings back to 48 to– 52. The Saturn cycle that continues here started when we were seven with the original crack in the snowglobe, followed by the nemesis at 21 and the neutralizer-nemesis again at 35. The swings of the pendulum stay wide until you decide to heed the neutralizer. That's why 48 to 52 is so important; Chiron is returning home, forcing us to question what our lives have been—though you will always have free will to do whatever you wish. On my 48th birthday, I threw myself a *hieros gamos* party and invited my favorite couples. At 42, after my cancer diagnosis, when I realized I had castrated my feminine principle and overworked the masculine, I hosted a Venus party. I also started intense shadow work, wrote *The Seven Gates*, and learned a lot more about how the body and psyche relate. I understood my own dissociation from my body upon losing custody of my children and leaving the cult. I linked this back to age seven, when I was thrown out of Monday spirit circles, where I had been the only child permitted to attend. In short, I started to connect the dots.

I went through a three-year cycle of mourning the imbalance and mess I had made out of my life. During my depression, I abandoned my lifeline, my faith. I stopped believing in everything and anything. I had kicked **myself** out of *my* spirit circles! At 33, I left the cult and tried dethroning my parents by finding my own spiritual path, which led me at 36 to astrology and the Akashic Records. Finally, with my breast cancer diagnosis at 42, I broke the structures around what spirit and parenting should look like, identified the key themes of my value system, started formulating my own theories, and applied the concept of "universal" to everything I did. After that, everything changed.

By 48, I had written several books about the spiritual path (including a family model about conscious parenting at a high vibration), started my own metaphysical college, found a balanced relationship, healed my relationship with my children, became cancer-free, embraced a balanced diet, and was enjoying a healthy body weight. Everything I had struggled with—body image, sex, self-worth, feeling inadequate about my intelligence, failing at parenting and financial issues—were suddenly addressed as a spiritual adult. In short, opposites and internal tensions were reconciled. I found myself returning home to myself, embracing my mother (who had been the un-integrated shadow parent), and honoring the feminine principle she had embodied. I deserved that damn birthday party! I had posted on Instagram that week asking, "Who sits on your throne?" On the day of my 48th birthday, my mother, who had notoriously been the star of every function throughout my childhood because of her glamour and beauty, walked in and said, "I'm moving over to give you the throne." My jaw dropped! I had shifted the system, she had seen my post on social media, and in that moment, we had fixed the traffic jam and assumed our respective 48 to 52. It was the best birthday gift ever: from myself to myself and from my mother to me.

This level of consciousness is not determined by anyone but you and chosen daily, in each situation. It might take your entire life to get there—10 jobs, 14 relationships, 13 divorces. Each person is different. It might take a marriage of 50 years to reach the spiritual maturity of 48 to 52. This isn't easy. It takes awareness and a decision to integrate change (transformation) and then do it differently (transmutation). Remember that neutralizers are like Prometheus, who stole fire from the gods. Neutralizers can provide tools for change, but we decide whether or not to use them. In the meantime, you will swing from zero to 100. This is the law of the pendulum; it's a metaphysical law and we are obligated to abide by it.

Most clients have an existential crisis when they reach this period in their lives. For probably the first time, they discover that they haven't been living their true purpose and turn to spirituality, seeking something greater than themselves. Realizing they've become their parents, they return home, like Odysseus, to understand you've been the olive branch from the marital bed. Your parents birthed you. There is no separating you and your parents. This phase is about integration and raising consciousness.

In Greek mythology, Chiron is a centaur—half human, half horse. He rules self-mastery and the 48 to 52. He's the key to our kingdom, the gatekeeper of our primordial wound—the one that makes us feel separate from others and why we have difficulty knowing our true selves. In mythology, centaurs were drunks and rapists of low-level consciousness; they are the negative voices in your head. They don't accept you; they want to ruin your (symbolic) wedding and cause a scene. The wedding metaphor is linked to the *hieros gamos*, the mystical marriage with yourself. If you don't make that inner connection, you will fail to spiritually adult and end up living in incongruence and cognitive dissonance. The best opportunity to do it differently, to integrate and dethrone our parents, occurs during ages 48 to 52, but it is never too late. Chiron is the return home, when we realize that we've had the answers all along. Chiron was the evolved, higher-consciousness centaur. We turn into centaurs and achieve self-mastery when we transmute and raise our consciousness and do it differently than our parents.

Chiron also rules the pituitary gland. Technically called the *hypophysis*, the pituitary is considered the "master gland." It's a pea-sized endocrine gland located at the base of your brain and behind the bridge of your nose that secretes hormones and tells other glands what hormones to produce. It looks like a little crevice and is seated in a curvature called the *sella turcica* or the *silla turka*. That's where I got the idea of *dethroning* your parents. The anatomical structure of the pituitary looks like a throne. In order to reach higher consciousness and come full circle in life, we have to dethrone our parents, and the role of the pituitary is critical. Hypophysis means "lying under"—in our case, under the conscious mind. Jesus was called "master" by his disciples. Your parents are your subconscious "master" starting at conception.

If you remember, the grief cycle begins when we're "thrown out of heaven" or "thrown out of Olympus"—when we leave cosmic consciousness or the universal womb and incarnate in the body. The sudden limitation of being in a physical body is the trauma. Our trauma—our wound—occurs at conception, and by seven, we have a story. The wound triggers a physiological stress response. When the body identifies a stressful situation, the hypothalamus indicates to the pituitary that something has to happen. The adrenals, which sit right above the kidneys, are told to release cortisol, activating our fight-flight-freeze response. (In traditional Chinese medicine, the kidneys are associated with fear.) This hypothalamic-pituitary-adrenal system (the HPA) is also known as the "central stress response system." "Fight and flight" is a sympathetic nervous system response where we are jolted out of "rest and digest" and all of the energy goes to our extremities (such as when a bear starts chasing you and you have to run). "Freeze" is a parasympathetic nervous system response that I call "sheep syndrome." It happens when we're "anticipating our next move" but can't make a decision because subconsciously, we recall a previous time of making a mistake and fear doing so again.

Chronic psychological stress creates all kinds of problems, from depression and "adrenal fatigue" to Cushing syndrome (an excess of fatty deposits). When cortisol goes up during a fight-flight response, we experience a decline in cognitive skills and memory. We can't recall things; we can't think clearly. Our thoughts and actions are driven by our emotions. This is not a moment in which we can think logically or rationally, when we can step back and say, "Oh, this is just a subconscious trauma from when I was three years old." We don't have a clear mind with which to be aware and to make good decisions. Increased cortisol also flattens our circadian rhythm, which affects our sleep. Who can sleep well when they're stressed about something? This is no less true when dealing with our subconscious trauma. Cortisol also goes up with alcohol intake, which is related to toxic waters and the desire to return to the womb.

Our executive function is controlled by the prefrontal cortex, where much of the "adulting process" takes place—when we are thinking clearly and making good choices. Too much cortisol keeps this from happening. Now it's true that a certain amount of stress is needed to survive. Feeling safe and secure are legitimate goals. But then there's *perceived* stress. You may not be under actual threat, but you are linking back to a memory that is associated with fear, and the body recognizes it. It's in your subconscious. It's something that happened from the moment of conception to seven years old. This triggers a stress response—fight-flight-freeze—just as readily as a real threat.

At the psychological, mythological, and astrological level, the wounded child, the feeling of abandonment when we're kicked out of the cosmic consciousness, and the story around our wound that started at conception through zero to seven, are all related to Chiron. Chiron in your chart is linked to certain signs, the most common for sheep syndrome being Libra. Libras, or those with an excess of Libra in their chart, tend to experience "sheep syndrome." Think of sheep: They travel in flocks, led by a shepherd. They are cute and innocent, right? Gazing off into nowhere while sometimes drifting away from the flock. When they sense a wolf, they shut down and play dead. We do this. People who go into freeze response shut down and "play dead" for fear of getting eaten by the wolf—by their fears. This happens a lot in depression, which can lead to lethargy, becoming withdrawn, and so on. When I see this in my practice, it means that this person is holding themselves hostage to something they chose in their childhood or in their previous life. Even if you're 30 or 40 years old, you can still be unable to move on because you haven't forgiven yourself for a poor decision you made in childhood or young adulthood.

How does all of this link to universal laws? The master law of Hermetic philosophy is, "All is mind"—there one Universal energy field that encompasses everything in the universe. This is what we conceptually think of as "God." From a subconscious perspective, this is the master law. The subconscious controls everything from the moment of conception. The initial wound at conception through zero to seven determines our fight-flight-freeze response. It's the master key to healing and returning home to your throne. All other laws such as those of the Kybalion align with "All is mind." The Law of Karma or Cause and Effect, the Law of Correspondence, and the Law of

Gender are all contained in the "All is mind" concept. In the physical body, the hypothalamus acts as a kind of "mind" telling the pituitary gland and other systems what hormones to release depending on what the body is going through or trying to achieve.

Chiron is the master wound in our psyche. In Greek, the word master comes from *kyrios* and is referred to as "opportune time" or *kairos*. We are all obligated to follow chronological time—our earthly timeclock. We have to be at work at 9, we eat lunch at 12, and we pick up our kids at 3. There is also "divine timing." Kairos represents the rainbow bridge between 48 and 52 when we begin to achieve equanimity—a balance between the 0 to 100 swings. This is an *opportune* time to do our spiritual work and dethrone our parents, and we are divinely guided to seek our purpose during these years. Beyond 52 is the return home when we finally show up as the adult in our own lives. True adulting occurs when we dethrone our parents and consciously decide not to be the child and leave the fight or flight and freeze response. We choose to actually show up with a clear mind that takes cortisol out of the equation.

The Pursuit of Mastery

In religion and philosophy, we see the word master applied to Jesus, for example. In Luke 8:24, the disciples wake up Jesus saying, "Master, Master, we're going to drown." Jesus then redirects the winds and calms the storm. Next is Yahweh, the tetragram of YHWH—the "god" or "master" of the Jewish people. The breath or the lungs are associated with YHWH. When we *breathe* through something, we extract ourselves from the fight-flight-freeze mode. Only when we breathe and bring ourselves to the present moment can we make a clear decision as to what should happen next. It is said that God lives between the inhale and the exhale. In *The Seven Gates*, I refer to this pause between breaths (which I associate with the teenager) as a place to stop and think about your next move. You can still choose to stay in child—that's free will—but better to decide to be an adult. The breath is another key to self-mastery. Taking that next breath and avoiding fight or flight—moving into the parasympathetic nervous system where we are calm and more adult, where we can make a clear decision—is about becoming a master.

The yoga sutras state that everyone is born with a certain number of breaths. In yoga, *pranayama* is the practice of focusing on the breath. If you can master your breath, it is believed that you can extend your life. It also helps to manage stress—to avoid getting stuck in fight or flight. From a biological standpoint, prolonged and unmanaged, *will* shorten our life. Constant stress is linked to heart attacks and strokes. At a subconscious level, it is linked to the fear of "leaving home," "losing a home," and losing the parents' love, which encourages one to stay in child mode.

In the spiritual literature, we see this dynamic in the 12 Labors of Hercules. When Hercules was kicked out of Olympus by Hera, she assigned him 12 labors. In order to return to Olympus, his rightful home as son of Zeus, he had to successfully complete all 12 labors. When he had successfully completed a labor, he would bring back an animal (representative of our animal nature) as proof. Symbolically, it means that in order for us to return home to ourselves as adults, we need to conquer our animal nature—which includes defeating the fight-or-flight response that keeps us in child. One of Hercules' labors was to defeat the Nemean lion—the textbook trigger for examples of fight or flight: when a lion chases you, you fight or flee. In a symbolic sense, the lion is the personality, and its defeat brings us closer to living truthfully in our lives. When Hercules enters the cave—a symbol of the pituitary gland—to kill the lion, he blocks it off with bricks, forcing himself to overcome his fears and master his personality.

All hermetic teachings are held in caves. This represents our inner work, our shadow work, those "dark nights of the soul." The *nigredo* in alchemy represents the darkness endured while defeating our personality—our old programming—and leaving home. In shamanism's four directions, the West is about confronting your shadow, doing the bad buckets—finding the inner wisdom (self-mastery) to confront your fears and identify the thoughts and emotions that are ruling your life. In Greek mythology, Charon is the ferryman who took the dead across the River Styx. He required an *obol*—the coin of death—for payment. When we confront our fears and decide to leave home to discover our true selves, we must give the gods (our parents) an offering that symbolizes something within us that has to die for us to be reborn. In every situation that you try to dethrone your parents, you will provide an offering for doing it differently out of guilt or fear until you transmute your thoughts and own a new belief system. How did your mother and father pamper themselves? How did they self-destruct? You will pick one way or another to honor them.

In my case, my mother would self-destruct by drinking Coke and eating chocolate, so I would drink Diet Coke in excess as a low-level consciousness offering. She would do her own nails when she was pampering herself, and as a high-vibration offering—one that wasn't self-destructive—I would get my nails done. My father would hustle, so when I would try to dethrone him, I would work round-the-clock, just like him. He was impatient, as was I. When I am dethroning him from a low-vibration state, I notice that I start to speak loudly. It's not an anger yell; it's a passionate yell. It's how I sacrifice myself to honor him and stay in child. Such actions are how we seek our parents' approval and/or get them to meet our needs, symbolically if not physically. They come from low-level consciousness and keep us from adulting. We will vacillate between offerings (honoring their tradition) and sacrifices (betraying ourselves) until we transmute the impure thoughts we "inherited" at conception.

Chiron, acknowledged as the master key to self-mastery, is also known as the "rainbow bridge" because he lies between Saturn and Uranus. Saturn is the cycle in which we try to dethrone our parents, beginning at 14 but not with any success until 28 when we take on adult responsibilities—kids, a mortgage, a job. Uranus is the last stop before we return home and try with all our might to dethrone our parents by attempting a new definition of freedom. This is the skinny cow. At 40 to 42, we have our next psychological cycle and another attempt to dethrone them. This phase is about freedom and liberating ourselves from limitations. We think these limitations were imposed on us at 28 like our job, our finances, or our marriage, but they started at birth when we "inherited" our value system. That value system—and nothing else—is what limits us. We have seen the incongruities between what we were taught (about religion or sexuality or how the world works) and what we've come to observe—this is what needs to be dethroned. Everyone inherited a subconscious full of limitations, in one area or another. This is known as the upper-limit theory. There is an upper-limit to what you're able to achieve because you sacrifice anything above this programming to your parents to stay in child and get a conditional version of love. When you dethrone your parents, hence breaking free from the upper limits, you own your own value system and transmute your low-level consciousness inherited at birth and raise your vibration. You will pay an offering, as acknowledgement to dethroning them, but you will stop sacrificing your mission in life to honor their unlived lives. This is true liberation. This is where we start our spiritual journey.

Glyph of Chiron: Represents finding a balance within ourselves, the 48–52, and gaining self-mastery.

At the return home of 48 to 52, we begin to understand that we are limited not by our adult responsibilities but by our thoughts. We've had the answers all along. We begin to dethrone our parents, accept our bodies and our minds, and discover a connection to something greater. At 48 to 52, Chiron comes full circle; it is the rainbow bridge between limitation or karma and our liberation. However, we first have to understand and heal our abandoned child, our inner, deepest wound—our subconscious wound of insufficiency—to stop the cycle of *samsara* (reincarnation).

Finding Wisdom in the Physical

The seventh chakra is the pituitary gland, connecting us energetically with the first chakra—the element of earth. The first chakra is confined to tribe, family, values, and judgments—everything you were given in childhood. The seventh chakra, the crown chakra, is the bridge to the cosmos, past the veil of illusion. This is your chakra of transcendence and the formless god. Everybody has an image of God (subconsciously, it's mother-father). It may be Jesus, Buddha, Shiva, or whoever you pray to. It could be money, sex, your body or your car. But once you transcend your dogma and your values, you begin to realize your divine nature. Once you transcend or transmute a thought, you change your entire vibration. We indeed transmute karma and then start the cycle all over again. Growth is cyclical. It never stops.

When you realize that your thoughts and the story of your childhood have limited your reality, you start to identify your divine spark. You discover that the story and the wound you're attached to is just nonsense that keeps you in child and the cycle of coming back into a body—lifetime after lifetime. At the mundane level (and in our heads), we don't want to leave our childhood home, so we settle for a dysfunctional version of love, the Costco card version of love, with its unmet needs and low self-worth. Otherwise, who will you belong to? You will no longer be your parents' child. You will no longer be a child of gods. You will cease to exist. Then what? When we spiritually adult, we stop becoming God's divine child. We can identify and cicatrize the wound that keeps us from growing.

Hellenism, the belief in the Greek culture, was replaced by the

Roman Empire and hence the Catholic church. The belief that we need a Savior to do our own spiritual work—that without this Savior, we are unable to transcend and reach the heavens—created a fissure in our belief in our autonomy and kept us in child mode. The idea that your own self-love could transcend your primordial wound was never an option.

In Greek mythology, Chiron's father was Kronos, a centaur, and his mother was Philyra, an ocean nymph. Kronos raped Philyra, and midway through the sexual act, he turns himself into a horse because his wife Rhea was looking for him and he didn't want to be caught. She found out anyway. Who were *your* parents pretending to be when they conceived you? What mask did they put on the world? Did they really know themselves? When we meet someone, we often have a fantasy around the sexual act, but we really don't know who we're with. So, your mother and father put on a disguise, reflecting the low-level consciousness into which you were conceived. You take on this disguise, which becomes the mask that you wear throughout life as you try to get your needs met. Philyra is wounded and leaves in shame. She fears being abandoned and kicked out of the family. From 0 to seven, we get our own story that is linked in some way to the shame and fear at conception. Some aspects of ourselves are shunned. Our parents tell us verbally or nonverbally, to "put that away" or they don't approve of our behavior. Philyra wasn't prepared to have a child or to cope with her shame around the child. As children, we don't have proper coping skills so we stunt our inner child's growth, hoping for an adult to come and fix it. Even as adults, our inner child stays small, and we seek other adults to solve our problems—maybe our partner or even our god (our Savior). Whoever it is, we resist being an adult at all costs.

Please understand this doesn't mean that we don't pay our bills or attend to worldly needs. I'm saying that psychologically and spiritu-ally, we refuse to grow up. Instead, we engage in "grown up" activities like smoking, drinking, and sex to pretend we're adults. We all have anger inside, and the animal part of us shows up as fight or flight because we don't have good coping skills. Philyra was disgusted by Chiron's incarnation into physical form. When we incarnate, we, too, think our form is disgusting, having just come from the spaciousness of universal consciousness, and society and religion play a big role in confirming this belief. The fact that Chiron was born a centaur—half-animal and half-human—emphasizes her disgrace for having sex. Sexual relations represent an adult behavior. When we become sexually active, we are owning the adult part of ourselves, symbolically choosing our path and a way forward. At 14 to 16, we hit puberty, exactly the time when we have doubts about our parents and start thinking of dethroning them.

In *The Seven Gates*, I discuss finding your divinity through your humanity. We may be in a physical form but yet we have a divine spark. In addition, we can only express our divinity through the flesh. Unfortunately, the Church saw the flesh as evil; it brought on shame and was to be avoided. In Greek mythology, the gods honored and sought pleasure through the flesh. Jesus taught us that the body is the necessary vehicle to do our godly work—our purpose—which is to dethrone "the Savior" and save ourselves. I often ask clients to imagine being handed a body of energy (instead of an actual baby) in the birthing suite and what they would say to the doctor? They often reply, "Where's my baby?" or "What is this?" Absolutely! We don't view a baby as energy but as physical. We want to hold and feed a real, warm body, not a blob of energy. Yet we end up punishing ourselves for having a body, failing to honor and express our divinity through our body.

However, Philyra's disgust of Chiron was a metaphor for being kicked out of Eden or Olympus or Heaven—kicked out of universal consciousness into the limited form of the physical. It was never explained that the form is as essential to spiritual growth as the spirit. Jesus, representing Chiron, taught us to love our flawed, wounded self. If we're able to love our limitations, our wounds, and our desires of the flesh unconditionally—to, in essence, find our divinity in our humanity—then we can heal ourselves. We become our own Savior.

This is in part what the 48 to 52, the return of Chiron, is supposed to teach us. In our collective unconscious, we believe that we were kicked out of the universal womb, when in reality we chose to leave to express our divinity in the flesh. There is no other way to express our divine nature in the physical universe than through the flesh.

Grief Is a Door

The Kübler-Ross model of grief, which proposes that the grief process has five stages—denial, anger, bargaining, depression, and acceptance—can also be applied to what happens when we leave universal consciousness and incarnate into the body. We grow up in a snowglobe, believing that this is the way of the world. In fact, we are in a state of denial about our true nature—this is the beginning of the grief cycle. The symbolism of the snowglobe represents our denial and delusion, until something awful shatters the snowglobe. Then comes anger. Our body is the vehicle for this anger. Anger has the same archetypal energy as creation, sex, aggression, and violence. It is also associated with will, dominance, power, and assertiveness—the male principle. Anger—the Mars archetype—has been valued throughout the ages, while the female principle has been devalued. Not surprisingly, the feminine principle of love—primarily self-love—that Jesus and Buddha both came to teach, is the antidote to anger. Ironically, the feminine principle is associated with the flesh, with the body, with the element of earth. A good way to experience our divinity through our humanity is by creating (masculine) a manifestation of the feminine (children, books, art).

But if you're unable to love your body, how can you create a divine Self? The bargaining phase begins when you attempt to negotiate with God: If he removes your pain, you will be more compliant. However, the suffering is created by you, by your thoughts and self-hatred. God isn't doing anything to you; you are doing it to yourself. The bargaining process comes from the shadow. Instead, go within and observe what you've created of your life and why. In my opinion, depression is absolutely necessary at the soul level to mourn what you discover about yourself. In my theory about grief and despair, I equate grief to an earthly illness where we lost something we weren't done using yet; however, that grief leads to despair which is a spiritual illness and leads us to find the return back to universal consciousness. I went through a three-year depression of mourning my old ways, my old life, my childish behaviors, my self-loathing, until I could fully love myself. Then I accepted that no savior was coming. I alone was the master of my life. All my answers were within.

The spiritual path has often been called a "narrow door" or a lonely path because it's ultimately about your own self-reliance: You are solely in charge of your balance, joy, stability, happiness, and needs. You are your own public relations agency, your own parent. For many, that's a difficult realization to come to. It deserves a grieving process. In essence, you are going to feel abandoned regardless of whether or not your parents were great or actually did abandon you. This is the key essence of Chiron, in your psyche as well as your subconscious wound. Philyra abandoned Chiron in a cave, in secret. We suffer our wound in private, in secrecy. This is also where we confront ourselves and our bad buckets—who we really are and where we really come from—and where the healing begins. It is only when you cicatrize that primordial wound that you can stop the cycle of samsara and be released from earthly incarnations.

The gods adopted Chiron and made him master teacher of all the gods' children. This is very important because, deep in our subconscious, we feel that we've been adopted or abandoned, that we don't belong to the family we are born into. We try to find spirit or God or a validation of our value in others. We want them to adopt us and tell us that we're lovable and worthy. Once we finally own our power, our Chiron; once we own our abandonment; once we own our issues; once we own that we're limited to the flesh; once we own that we're divine and human all in one; then we become the master of our fate and find our equanimity: our 48 to 52. Chiron taught the children on a discreet, separate island. Our wound keeps us separate (or so we think) from everyone else, as if we are the only ones with such trauma.

Chiron is the master. He is the most evolved centaur. When we are operating with the same low-level consciousness as our parents, we're in that fight-or-flight or child mode—the drunken centaur, not an elevated centaur. Only when we show up as Chiron, the centaur who's rational, logical, and spiritual, who understands that he holds the key to healing himself, can we achieve true adulthood and high-level consciousness. Hercules is always with Chiron because Hercules, the warrior, is how we try to show up in the world, pretending we don't have a wound. We're conditioned to believe that if we're busy or engaged enough, such as in our work or through other activities, we'll be validated despite our wound. Chiron was accidentally hit by an arrow with the poisonous blood of a Hydra. It's a wound that never heals because he's immortal. Can we ever heal our own wound? I don't believe so, that's why I prefer the word cicatrix, but we can learn to master ourselves in spite of it, which is a type of healing. Chiron travels the world for 48-to-52 years seeking a cure for his wound; he eventually figures out that the healing will come from within. During our 48 to 52, we also come home to ourselves, discovering the answers within and starting the process of dethroning our parents.

As you recall from above, Chiron's mother was Philyra, an ocean nymph. The bottom of the ocean represents the hidden subconscious. Chiron is the product of parents with strong, unresolved issues that kept them, like you and me, in low-level consciousness. This is why the wound keeps reopening. Each time we try to get our needs met by others, it re-opens. And like Chiron's unhealable wound, ours will be as well if we keep trying to get our needs met by others. Each time we're in child, each time we're in fight or flight, the wound opens. The stress you feel is the subconscious trauma of when your inner child got stuck. Stress tells the abandoned child that there is danger—the fear that you will be left, you will not be loved, your needs will not be met. Remember that Chiron was abandoned by his mother in the cave. You were abandoned by the cosmos. This is the story. This is the primordial wound. This is the source of your stress. Every other stress response is directly related to that story, that abandonment, that wound.

The Principle of Mentalism states that "All is mind." Your version of God in this lifetime are your parents who need to be dethroned so you can become the master of your life. In the meantime, you seek validation and attempt to get your needs met by "acting," by fight or flight. The pituitary gland releases hormones, which activate the adrenals, which release cortisol, and you jump into action. This is child mode, and you won't get your needs met. Instead, over time, you'll get physically and/or mentally sick. The pituitary is the master gland, like Jesus, like Yahweh, like your parents. The word pituitary means "lying under," and all of this is happening in the subconscious mind. When we finally uncover the biggest lies, we tell ourselves, we can uncover what is lying underneath. When we admit what we are lying about, we are liberated.

If we don't do the inner work of integrating and dethroning our parents and neutralize the 0-100 swings, leading to the balance of the 48 to 52, self-mastery, we will set the stage later for an existential crisis. Something will force us to examine ourselves and our life. It may coincide with a death or a divorce or an illness. Maybe our parents are dying, we clean out their house, read their will, and realize that we are them and they are us. There is a grief and despair moment, a crisis. You don't know who you are or what you've really done in this life. **Grief is an earthly illness, the earthly loss of something you haven't surrendered. Despair is a spiritual illness, that began at the moment of conception. Grief cycles, if handled well, will bridge to despair and a deeper pursuit of Self, and a return home to the universal consciousness.**

In every astrology chart, there is a relationship between Chiron and Mars, because we use the ego or drive of Mars to validate our worth—until the 48 to 52, when we realize that only by healing the wound ourselves will we finally achieve validation and self-love. With a simple Google search, you can identify your Chiron sign based on your birth date. Each Chiron sign tends to have a "preferred" fight-flight-freeze response. For instance, the fight response tends to be linked to a Chiron in Aries, Leo, Scorpio, and Aquarius. It would take the form of yelling, screaming, aggression, defensiveness, manipulation, or articulation—a sharp tongue or a smart logical argument. Chiron's flight response is linked to the signs of Gemini, Sagittarius, Capricorn, and Pisces. Gemini will dissociate. Sagittarius tends to exaggerate or escape—anything to avoid confronting the reality of a situation. Capricorn may say everything is fine and not really talk about the melancholy or the depression they're feeling. Pisces will respond by rescuing or becoming a victim or a scapegoat. Chiron's freeze signs—Taurus, Cancer, Virgo and Libra—are the "sheep syndrome" signs. The sheep plays dead to trick the wolf from eating it. People under these signs might hold on tighter and not let go of the wound or their child script. They may cry and hide, they won't confront, or they'll cover their heads like the ostrich to ignore what is happening.

Fortunately, the spiritual journey cannot be stopped! The spiritual texts say, upward and onward! Spiritual growth is cyclical and spherical. You will grow spiritually, either slowly or more quickly. You get to choose how little or how much you grow. That's our free will. Our spiritual growth and our journey back home is ruled by Chiron. It's about finding the key to self-mastery, realizing that we are both human and divine and that our parents could only do what they could do. We begin taking responsibility for our life at that point, dethroning them and owning our lives. The 48 to 52 is often when you find the answers within. You improve your diet, start exercising, and change your sleep routine. Now you are sleeping better, eating better, thinking more clearly, speaking more honestly—all of which is part of the spiritual adulting process. You are experiencing self-mastery, self-care, and self-love. You are finally taking responsibility for your life, dethroning your parents' influence and showing up as an adult in your own life.

CHAPTER TWELVE
Know Thyself/Self Mastery: Beyond 52

Self-mastery is the balanced 48 to 52 swings—the achievement of equanimity, stability, and contentment. Ultimately, the goal in most spiritual traditions is to achieve a level of self-mastery in a single lifetime—whatever that potential and purpose is. Ken Wilber calls such an accomplishment the *subtle* stage of consciousness, when you see something beyond nature, beyond the existential, beyond the psychic. You are starting to see the hidden or esoteric dimension. Stage 6 of Fowler's Stages of Faith is called *Universalizing Faith*, or what some might call "enlightenment". At this stage, no one faith is considered better or worse than another. Everyone is worthy of compassion, understanding, love, and justice.

However, some people don't want the equanimity of 48 to 52. It may feel boring to them. It lacks the high-highs and low-lows. I call such an attitude "Beyond the 52." Know thyself! Do you like a little drama or chaos? If so, own it! The *manas prakriti*—your mental state at the moment of conception shaped by the influence of the four elements (earth, fire, water, air)—will determine *your* particular definition of the 48 to 52. Sheryl is a client who, after being widowed, decided to start dating again. We identified her list of values and broke down each of her dates. She admitted to liking a man with a bit of an edge—considerate but not overly sweet. We were able to place her around a 35—to the left of the 48 to- 52 scale when looking for a new life partner. Your value system will dictate where you land on the scale, and this requires honesty and knowing yourself.

In my book, *The Shadow Side of Mother's Love*, I explain that our true 48 to 52 swings are linked to the moon phase we are born into (there are eight phases). For instance, I am a "crescent moon," which is a little to the left of the 48 to 52 midpoint, so I prefer a 30-to-40 midpoint when seeking my own personal balance.

Once you establish your baseline 48 to 52, you can define the 48 to 52 for your *lifestyle*. Many temples in ancient Greece, Turkey, Persia, Mesopotamia were also sundials that tracked the location of the Sun and whether it was too strong or too weak. Stonehenge is a sundial that has been the center of mystery for over 4,000 years. Symbolically, the image of the sundial is linked back to us. It's the center circle of The Squared Circle which is a metaphysical image of the relationship between the universe, our thoughts, and the world we create externally. The Sun represents our divine spark. For example, some may like the noonday sun; others prefer sunset. Spiritual growth is personal and individual. We are all given the same opportunities, but it's not a one-size-fits-all, Procrustean approach. No two people will love or master themselves in the same exact way. However, each of us must still build a foundation from which to achieve whatever equanimity we choose. All spiritual paths have foundational steps that include hard edges and soft corners.

The Squared Circle: A metaphysical image where the outer circle represents the Universe, the triangle represents limiting thoughts, the square represents the body and the emotions and the inner circle represents the divine spark that originated from the outer circle, the Universe within each one of us.

The need to stop the 0 to 100 swings is one of those necessary foundations. Choose a sector of your life such as finances or relationships. Draw a line where one end is 0 and the other end is 100. Where on the pendulum do you want to fall? If 0 is the total absence of good qualities in a partner, for instance, and 100 is the ideal partner with every good quality, what would be the midpoint? What would that partner look like? This is your 48 to 52. In whatever area of your life that you choose your 48 to 52, identify your good and bad buckets. The truth of your value system and the way you prefer to work or show up will be found in the good buckets of the parents. Part of dethroning your parents is knowing what to keep. Don't throw the baby out with the bath water! Once you identify your 48 to 52, link it with your parents' values and your new value system. This way, when you dethrone your parents, you will make an offering, not a sacrifice.

In the movie *Practical Magic*, Sandra Bullock's character is believed to be cursed with losing every man she marries. She is tasked with writing her ideal mate's qualities, but to ensure that she never actually meets him (so he won't die), she writes one blue eye and one brown eye. It's classic self-sabotage out of fear, the child mode, the fight or flight response. We are so afraid of balance and growth, of being honest, of leaving others behind with our growth, that we stay small. Nelson Mandela stated, "Our deepest fear is that we are powerful beyond measure. It is our light, not our darkness, that most frightens us. We ask ourselves, who am I to be brilliant, gorgeous, talented, fabulous? Actually, who are you *not* to be? You are a child of God. Your playing small doesn't serve the world." It's a wonderful quote, though I don't agree with the "child of God" part. I think such a depiction can keep us small and waiting for a Savior. We are part of the Void—the childless void of the universe. A child of no one, but part of the universal consciousness.

The Principle of Mentalism, the idea of "the One," the belief that energy cannot be created or destroyed and that after death, we return to the same energy that created us, all confirm that we aren't children of God but one with our creator. The universe is not hierarchical; it is cyclical. Thinking you are a child may be comforting to your conscious mind, but it defies what your soul knows about its origins. All of your limitations come from your thoughts, the subconscious, the bad buckets, the lack of honesty with Self, the belief that you are flawed and must remain a child so as not lose a dysfunctional version of love. Your lack of hard edges. Fear of knowing yourself. Those are keeping you from owning the divine spark within and having the life you desire.

Sandra Bullock wanted a partner but interfered by trying to trick fate; however, what was hers, came. If you do your work, what is yours will appear. Get out of our own way! Stop sabotaging what is rightfully yours to honor an outdated script from conception and childhood. Get honest and clear about your values, the hard edges, the limitations, the negative thoughts—the internal forces that are dictating your life. Then be honest about where you want to be. Identify your 0 to 100, then the 48 to 52. Shift a little to the left or the right to find the balance—the "beyond 52." Voltaire said, "God is a circle whose center is everywhere and circumference nowhere." Find your center. Be the royal in your kingdom.

The last stage of grief is acceptance. Being truthful about who you are and what you want and then going after it despite who you leave behind is acceptance and surrender, all at once. Accept that your spiral will look the way you wish it to look. There are no right or wrong answers. It's about being okay with what you seek. You may only want to grow a little spiritually in this lifetime or you like the drama of not having enough money to pay your bills at the end of the month or suffering reminds you of your childhood. As long as you are completely aware and accepting of what you are doing and causing no harm, it's okay. Maybe the reason you don't want too much money in the bank is because you wish to honor a scarcity script where poverty is idealized. That's the self-mastery—owning that you are creating a situation because it's serving a need, usually linked to the bad buckets and unmet needs of the parents—based on having a solid rulebook, measurable values, and a philosophy of life. That is true growth. That's the Fibonacci spiral in your life. You are going to grow; it's up to you how much or how little. You are no longer a victim. When you own that you've created everything, the boss at work who challenges you is no longer a nemesis but a mirror to the truth that you *like* to be challenged at work because you enjoy the drama. However, you won't achieve anything close to self-mastery or a middle ground, even a little to the left or a little to the right, if you don't implement the hard edges (strong boundaries rooted in a value system) and soft corners (a space for listening and compassion).

Even though many spiritual texts correlate self-mastery with equanimity—when the pendulum swings aren't so wide—if you know yourself and your truth, your 48 to 52 can be a little bit "beyond." The point of life is to own what makes you feel alive. Own the exhilaration of not knowing where your next meal is coming from if that is what pleases you. Own the exhilaration of not knowing if your next paycheck will stretch to the next week. Own the exhilaration of not knowing if the guy you're dating is going to come home. Own it all! We create these psychological orgasms to feed the swings in life and to honor our parents and childhood programming and to satisfy unmet needs. This process is often subconscious, but once you make it conscious, you can decide to stay (or not) in that pattern without being a victim. Link these choices to your values, your buckets, and your judgements—be congruent! Pay attention to neutralizers. Become aware of the values that no longer serve you. Again, this is not about staying in the 0 to 100 but adding your truth to the 48 to 52: a little to the left or a little to the right. That's a good place to be.

The Kybalion says, "Upwards and onwards!" This is the direction of all growth. The spiral of your life never stops moving. Those darkest moments when you think you are furthest from the center is when you're closest to self-mastery, because in the metaphor of the labyrinth, the outer circuits appear furthest from the center—from Self—but you're actually closer. The Merriam-Webster dictionary defines upwards and onwards as "toward a better condition or higher level." How much do you really want to know about yourself? How much do you want to grow? How much do you want to change? How many hard edges do you want to put in your life? The answers to those questions will depend on the level of your self-knowledge.

CHAPTER THIRTEEN

The Height of Spiritual Adulting: 52–84

This next chapter will go through the stages of spiritual adulting *beyond 52*—from ages 52 to 84. There are additional cycles past 84: another Rahu-Ketu destiny change occurs at age 90, a Saturn cycle N-year occurs at 91, and a Jupiter cycle (or fat cow) occurs at 96. In astrology, *moksha*, which in Sanskrit means "the release from karma," is considered the domain of the planet Uranus, and a full revolution of Uranus takes 84 years, thus my focus on the first 84 years of a human life. Ken Wilber's last two stages of consciousness are found during these final 30 years past the 52: the *causal* and *non-dual* stages. In the causal stage, you are in utter transcendence; in the non-dual, you are united with the Void. In the appendices, I provide a space for you to write out key themes in your life during these stages. You will start to see a pattern with each cycle. These years are an alchemical process of fine-tuning the previous stages.

THE AGE OF 54

At 54 we have another switch in destiny. At this point, we are reorienting our outlook on life. This is our third karmic Rahu-Ketu cycle and, after returning home, identifying your primordial wound, and achieving a mystical marriage with Self, you leave on a journey to find your purpose. In this karmic turn, you are confronted with events and people that encourage you to follow your path. One of Joseph Campbell's most famous sayings was, "Follow your bliss." By this he was telling people to start on a path that has been there all the while, waiting for you—the life you were born to live. He spoke about sacred spaces for uninterrupted reflection and unrushed creative work. Creating such a space is the tenth step in the spiritual journey to help you find and manifest that purpose. As new people and situations enter your life, the doors to your bliss will open. This stage allows you to be comfortable with the gray areas.

I once asked myself, "What is your definition of life?" My response was, "Achieving spiritual growth and balance." I revisit this definition frequently because things change and evolve. If you can define something by putting some kind of measurement around it and then see if you're applying it, you are living according to *your* rules and not society's. You are spiritually adulting. At 54, you should be owning your spiritual adult and finally leaving child mode. Nietzsche, in defining his second stage of metamorphoses, called society and its rules "a dragon," adding that the purpose of youth is to kill the "Thou Shalt" rules of society. Joseph Campbell summarizes Nietzsche below in his book, *The Power of Myth*:

> "Nietzsche describes what he calls the three transformations of the spirit. The first is that of the camel . . . but when the camel is well loaded, it struggles to its feet and runs out into the desert, where it is transformed into a lion . . . now, the task of the lion is to kill a dragon, and the name of the dragon is 'Thou shalt.' On every scale of this scaly beast, a 'thou shalt' is imprinted: some from four thousand years ago; others from this morning's headlines. Whereas the camel, the child, had to submit to the 'thou shalts,' the lion, the youth, is to throw them off and come to his own realization. And so, when the dragon is thoroughly dead, with all its 'thou shalts' overcome, the lion is transformed. . . . No more rules to obey. No more rules derived from the historical needs and tasks of the local society, but the pure impulse to living of a life in flower. The rules are now to be used at will for life, not submitted to as compelling 'thou shalts.' It comes the time for using the rules in your own way and not being bound by them. You can actually forget the rules because they have been assimilated. You are an artist."

We don't know ourselves sufficiently; we are puppets to our programming. Socrates boldly stated, "The unexamined life is not worth living" when he chose death over other alternatives. When we embark on the path of spiritual adulting, we are choosing to examine our lives and a certain type of death: the death of our child, the unexamined mind, and eventually our conditional version of love. I often say you can live in the image of society, but you cannot *die* in the image of society. The "what will people think" or "people-pleasing" masks may help you navigate life, move ahead, and be accepted. However, when it's time to die, through Saturn cycles or grief cycles, you're asked to remove those masks and look at yourself honestly. You must die to these masks and images and rebirth into the truths of who you are. That resurrection is that of a spiritual adult living with his or her own philosophy of life and fulfilling his or her own dharma.

Socrates believed that philosophy—the love of wisdom—was the most important pursuit of all. I agree. I would add, however, that getting to know yourself through that wisdom is equally important. When we embark on the journey of self-knowing, we have to start by writing down our beliefs about how things work. Once we get these down on paper, we can determine whether or not these are rules we can—or want—to live by. This goes for the rules our parents told us as well. We need to question those beliefs and make room for new ones. Once you have your own rule book, you need to keep yourself accountable to them. Spiritual adulting truly starts here. Inversion is a practice of thinking things in reverse. To get more life, avoid death as Charlie Munger, the billionaire investor implied in his quote "All I want to know is where I'm going to die, so I'll never go there." The via negativa is the study of what not to do and has been studied by mystics like Meister Eckhart, describing what God is not. It is the philosophy focusing on what something is not. The old beliefs (0 to 100) are not our beliefs; we now know what we are not, to define in the 48 to 52 scale, what we are.

The Age of 56

This is the number of charisma and the stage of magnetism and finding your vocation. It's also about mastering your relationship. Five + six = 11: the master number in numerology. If at 28 you got married, you may be approaching the close of a 28-year cycle. If you are single or divorced, this is an appropriate time to do an inventory or your relationships and your responsibility in their failure. My book, *The Truth Is in the Triangle*, is a great resource for learning about healthy relationships, boundaries, and the renegotiation that generally happens every seven years. The renegotiation at the 28-year cycle is crucial, as you are building an entirely new foundation with this partner. Oftentimes, the children have left, leaving an empty nest. Loneliness can set in and a deep introspection. We may question our partnership and how it has served us.

When broken down, 11 is 1 + 1, which is a 2 in numerology associated with relationships, harmony, conflict, teamwork, and diplomacy. This is an opposition year—the fourth V-year—when valor relates to finding harmony within and finally achieving the *hieros gamos*: the mystical marriage within In mythology, Ares and Aphrodite are the masculine and feminine energy and represent the romantic couple. This does not have anything to do with gender or sexuality; this includes homosexual relationships as well. Everybody has a masculine and feminine energy which dictates sexual attraction. Ares and Aphrodite had three children: Deimos, Phobos, and Harmony. Deimos is demon, Phobos is phobia, and Harmony is harmony. As a result of the inevitable conflicts in a relationship, you get to choose what level of consciousness you show up with to re-establish the original snowglobe and creation story. If little changes, you may create the Deimos of two unsatisfied people or Phobos's fear of leaving the relationship despite being dissatisfied. However, if you work the model, you can birth Harmony from the re-negotiation process.

The first fight in a relationship is linked to Ares, the god of war. The fights that follow are about integrating what needs to be learned from that original conflict—which is also linked to your crack in the snowglobe. Conflict energy in relationships is also creator energy, which can birth something new when channeled as higher consciousness or remain stuck as conflict in lower consciousness. Your partner may be fighting your efforts to change because they are trying to prevent a "new life" from being birthed. They may also be fighting against a change in the power currency and don't want to give that up. Change is scary, hence the child Phobos in the marriage of Aphrodite and Ares. It's scary to have to start all over again and reacquaint ourselves with each other. What if we realize that we no longer like our partner? What if you lose weight or go back to school? All of a sudden, you've got new friends and a new Weight Watchers group and you're shopping at Whole Foods. Your partner may wonder whether they still have a place in this new paradigm, this new life.

Another child of the union between Aphrodite and Ares is Deimos. Working through our shadow while attempting to re-negotiate and re-birth a relationship brings up our demons, those we have tried to discard or pretend don't exist. Your partner may not want to expose those demons, to show their dirty laundry. It's about bringing to consciousness those unconscious issues that have affected the relationship. When you go through therapy, you make the unconscious conscious, and the truth about things like passive-aggressive behavior and codependence get revealed—the stuff that's contained in, and will inevitably shatter, the snowglobe.

Remember: a nemesis is someone who is at odds with you, for example, manifesting as your partner denying your wishes to start therapy. However, subconsciously, it's about overcoming your own Phobos about what you will discover about yourself and the relationship. Your Deimos will appear as well, those you've been hiding under the guise of love. These are scary things to confront in a relationship and in our own psyche. They are in the bad buckets. This process is hard work. But in order to have longevity in a relationship—for *hieros gamos* with self and our partner to occur—it must go through a process of renewal. Conflict is an opportunity to create something new, something harmonious.

In Greek mythology, Dionysus was a transgender god known as the "twice-born." He symbolizes the balance between the masculine and feminine energies we all possess. He is the complete version of Ares and Aphrodite. If you follow the accountability model I present in *The Truth Is in the Triangle*, you can achieve the Dionysian aspect of harmony in your relationship. Dionysus' birth was considered divine. Phthonus is envious of this divine birth. Our subconscious does not want to do things differently than our parents. We wish to stay in child so as to not lose the limited version of love we received from them. Rather than seeking unconditional love, the mystical marriage, the *hieros gamos*, we succumb to Phobos and Deimos and stay in our child script and fail to assimilate the un-integrated parent—usually mirrored by our partner. Phthonus represents the envy around the possibility of birthing our divine selves, first with Self and then hopefully with a partner. This envy also represents the tension that can emerge when you do your work and leave your partner behind.

Dionysus is killed by the Titans who burn and eat his body—leaving only his heart. Athena shoves Dionysus's heart into Zeus's thigh and he is re-born. The thigh is associated with the animal consciousness of the lower three chakras. The higher three chakras are associated with the human. Thus, the symbol of the centaur; half-animal/half-human. The symbolism of the heart in the thigh is the unification of the lower and higher consciousness. We need logic. We need the rational mind. We need ordinary consciousness. But we also need evolved consciousness. We need heart. We need wisdom. By combining our lower and higher natures, we rebirth our relationship and, more importantly, ourselves.

Athena represents the higher consciousness of Ares. She is the goddess of war, but the wisdom aspect of war, not the conflict. We need to transmute our own conflict into wisdom so we, too, can be reborn. The flesh (the body) represents the old story of a relationship; the heart represents the true essence—what remains after we confront our fears and demons. The love, represented by Aphrodite, is what brought two people together in the first place. Zeus is our highest Self, the mystical marriage, while the thigh represents our lower human nature. In our relationship, we can only experience a mystical marriage with ourselves *and* our partner after we change our level of consciousness. As Einstein said, you cannot change a problem from the same level of consciousness at which it was created. We first have to kill the lower-level consciousness of the child script to make room for the higher-level consciousness of the adult script: meeting our own needs. I am re-birthed in Harmony because I confronted the Phobos and the Daimos of the bad buckets that existed in my relationship during the integration process that happens while spiritually adulting. It is often through relationships that we make the subconscious (or the bad buckets) conscious and incorporate what the mistress/lover or un-integrated parent represents for us—a process described in *The Truth Is in the Triangle*. This is how we unify both of our parents and achieve wholeness. The fastest way to enlightenment is a relationship because our partner mirrors our shadow aspects to us daily; however, if you're not in a relationship with a romantic partner, you are in one with yourself. The entire cosmos is already in you.

Dionysius was re-born from his heart. If we really want to rebirth ourselves, if we really want to rebirth our relationship on the right foundation, it has to be from the heart: first from self-love and then from agape love—love for the other. The wisdom of the heart brings something new into our consciousness and our relationship—not through conflict but through wisdom. You can stop the power struggle in your relationship with kindness, love, compassion, and empathy while acknowledging that your partner is simply a mirror of yourself. He or she is also a little child who is too worried or scared to "do the work" for fear of losing something, of not belonging, of seeing their demons and their dark parts. Phthonus was jealous of Dionysus because he was self-tormenting, loveless, and stung with his own poison. Fighting, bringing up your partner's dirty laundry, bringing up fights from 20 years ago, is poison. You won't bring heart and love to a relationship when you're drinking poison, if you don't address the wounded alliance with your mother and your father. Instead, you will feel tormented. You will find yourself in a loveless relationship, first with yourself and then with your spouse. You must quiet down this inner power struggle through self-kindness, self-love, self-compassion, and self-empathy, while simultaneously owning your shadow, being reflected back to you by your partner.

Dionysus is the balance of the masculine and feminine, which makes us whole, which gives our partner permission to get whole, to shatter the snow globe. Love your partner as they want to be loved—not how *you* want to be loved. That's the whole concept of knowing your partner's love language. That's all heart.

Only through the soft corners within ourselves can we achieve the *hieros gamos* both within ourselves and then in our partnerships. Bring Athena's wisdom into your own competitive voice; transform your inner power struggle into a single, collaborative voice. Dionysus's rebirth was considered a divine birth: the unification of the masculine and feminine energies. When we unify our parents (egg and sperm) and our feminine and masculine energies (within) and achieve that mystical marriage, we birth ourselves and our relationship as divine. A new conception story begins at a new level of consciousness. Celebrate this new birth; sit happily in the snowglobe! Because after a time, the skinny-cow cycles will start again with your same partner or someone new.

Can you achieve the *hieros gamos*? Yes, but not every partner or couple wants to. Some relationships are meant to end, and that's okay. Some relationships will never shatter the foundation of their snow globe and will stay the same. Achieving the mystical marriage is for those who want to integrate their parents, who want to find a healthy partner. So yes, you *can* achieve the *hieros gamos*, but it takes work. Educate yourself and your partner that the individuation process is the only way to unite the conscious and the subconscious. It's the only way to integrate the light and the shadow. It's the only way to integrate the mother and the father. In order to birth something new—to birth the *hieros gamos*, the mystical marriage—you must birth something new in yourself. You have to allow your partner and/or yourself to marry themselves, to marry those energies of masculine and feminine of self-love. Only then, with heart and agape love, will you strengthen the relationship and with your partner, rebirth into Harmony.

The marriage of Themis and Zeus occurs at 60. This is where spirit meets matter and spiritual justice is served. This is the fifth cycle of Jupiter and the fat cows. The number five is an extremely important number; it's the number of proportional spiritual growth. There's a five-year difference between the seven-year skinny cows of Saturn and the subsequent fat cows of Jupiter. This difference correlates with the spiritual growth that occurs proportionately in our spiritual adulting process. Spiritual growth is spiral. We *will* grow, but it's not in a linear line. In this lifetime, you will work through many of the same issues, over and over again. Whether in your business, your relationships, or your family, we are always transforming. I think of it as a lovely chicken stock: you keep reducing the fluid until it becomes strong and hearty and a wonderful base for other recipes. The same thing happens with our spiritual lives. This life is about growth! Each of us will stumble and fall. Some will quickly get back up; others will take more time. Ultimately, it doesn't matter. At the end of your life, you will have dethroned some aspects of your parents and experienced some liberation. You will have gained some wisdom about your issues and your soul's purpose.

You don't tell your body to grow old. What makes you think you have to notify your soul? Good food, exercise, and a healthy lifestyle will help you live longer and cleaner, and the same goes for spiritual growth as you put more focus on that. Either way, growth is inevitable. The amount of growth you achieve in a lifetime will be based on how much you shift your level of consciousness. Nobody can determine that for you; that's free will.

The Kybalion states our spiritual growth is "upwards and onwards." This spiral begins at your moment of conception. Then, at seven, you have your neutralizer or first crisis. At 14, you experience the biggest expression of that crisis. This is also when children start opposing their parents and friends become more important as we seek to find our own value system and "think" about adulting. The way you handle this crisis at 14 will determine the rest of your cycles into adulthood. At 21, you face another neutralizer. At 28, you "leave home" in some way, probably physically but not yet subconsciously. At 28 to 30, we attempt to adult with a mortgage, a job, a family. The executive functions of the brain take over. You begin a new version of the creation myth from conception. At 42, you blow it up, thinking that's adulting. At 60, you do it right.

My 60-year-old client Nereida was overweight, overbearing, and a helicopter parent. She hadn't been sexually active in over 20 years, keeping herself hostage to her "good girl" story. When we broke it down, she was forced at 12 to take care of her "bad kid" younger sister, leaving her as the only "good girl" in the system. She lived up to this her entire life. When she began shadow work at 60, she realized that she hadn't ever honored her own "bad girl" which had impacted her sex life, her children's sex life, and her husband's sexual performance. The entire system was castrated—unable to perform because her prostitute archetype was never liberated. In realizing this, she was able to liberate herself and dethrone the story of "good girl." She owned her prostitute archetype and started living out her 48 to 52.

At 60, we come full circle with what started at 28—30. Self-love is critical at this stage, but you first have to know why you failed to love yourself in the first place! You cannot have self-love unless you forgive yourself, and you cannot forgive yourself until you know the story you've been holding yourself hostage to that keeps you in self-hatred. "Own your story, own your life!" not "Change your story, change your life." because you cannot change your parents, your moment of conception, low-level consciousness or your thread in this lifetime. However, you *can* transmute the vibration and level of consciousness that you were conceived into. This is how you own your story; change will follow. These cycles repeat throughout life: at 1, 7, 14, 21, 28, 35, 42, and so on.

This image is called the Fibonacci sequence or, by some, the "golden ratio." (They're not the exact same thing, but they are related.) This spiral is found in nature. It's nature's mathematical formula. There are no straight lines in nature. I remember going to Morocco many years ago and noticing that all of the artwork was spiral. There were no straight lines. This is important because in the image of The

Squared Circle, the inner circle (your "self" or third chakra) matches up with the outer world of your universe, your value system, and your beliefs. The connection between you and the Universe is interrupted by the thoughts (represented by the triangle)—the good and bad buckets—you inherit at conception from your parents. In this image of the Fibonacci spiral, notice that the only way to the inner circle is through a door. Similarly, to The Squared Circle image, the door is represented by the square. Straight lines and squares represent the body, the earth element and everything that must die to truly grow spiritually. However, they also represent structure, limits and the hard edges of consistency, stability and good order necessary to grow spiritually. That's the earthly door, what I call the "hard edges." That is the door of behavior change, of changing thoughts that lead to new beliefs and eventually a transformation and a transmutation of your vibration. Every single person has such a door or limitation in their life so they can access this inner circle, their inner self, their highest self. Limitations force you to leave your comfort zone. The earth element may be associated with limitation, but it's the doorway to your spiritual growth.

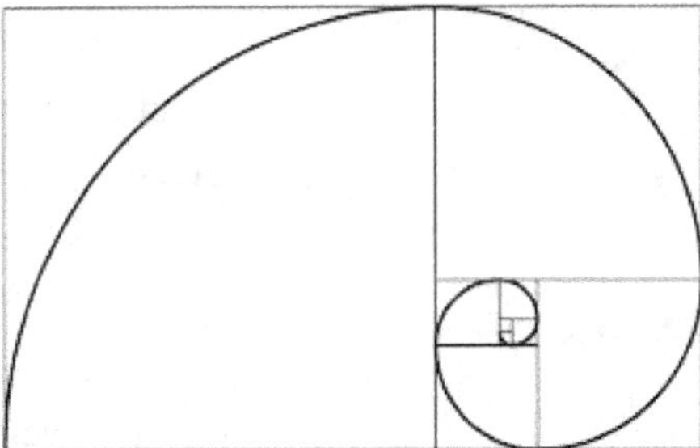

The Fibonacci Spiral: The golden spiral has a continuous curvature and represents the growth curve in nature, including our soul's growth. Spiritual growth is cyclical and spherical like the spiral.

In Matthew 7:13, the World English Bible states, "Enter in by the narrow gate, for the wide gate is broad and many are those who enter in by it." The Squared Circle is my favorite metaphysical symbol because in such a simplistic image, the entire universe is explained. It refers to setting limits and hard edges. The golden spiral shows the exact same thing. It is found in nature, on the earth. If you look at a pineapple, you will see the spirals. If you look at flower petals, you will see the spiral. But notice in the image the lines that make little squares, little doors. This is to explain that spiritual growth is mathematical. There is a pattern in nature for fruit and trees to grow, and a pattern of spiritual growth for humans that changes with age. The difference is that humans get to choose how big our growth spiral becomes depending on how much inner work we do. Many are concerned about their spiritual well-being, but opportunities for growth are already mathematically programmed. We endure through the skinny cow years and allow growth to happen during the fat cow years—if we've been taught to value being as much as doing.

Despite knowing these cycles and how they work, I still find myself rushing to gain even more spiritual insight. Again, it's the balance of both the feminine and masculine energies—the being and the doing—that leads to growth. For instance, you can pick a small piece of fruit from a tree but knowing that it will become much larger and juicier, you

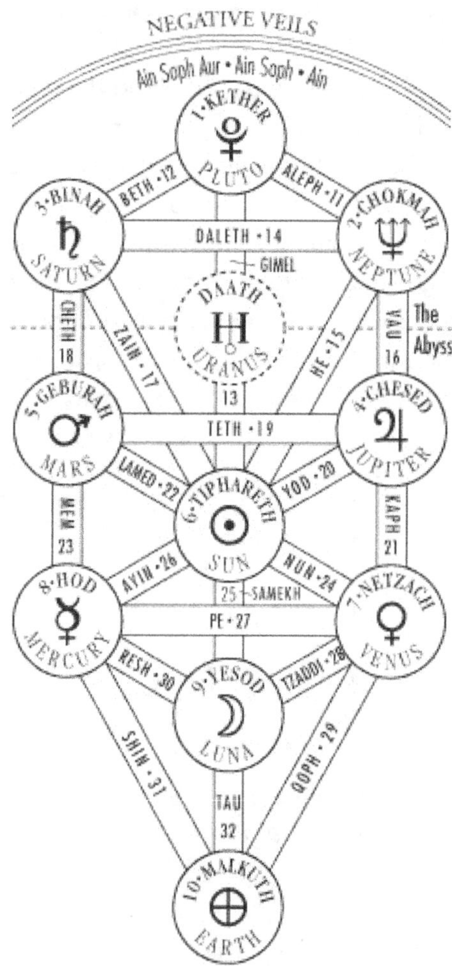

Kabballah Tree of Life

wait. Similarly, with deeper insight into knowing yourself, you can experience a much larger piece of *inner* fruit by being. Still, we have to do something as well; we have to honor the earth element. We have to put in the hard edges. We have to put in the structure. We have to put in the daily routine. We have to put in our hard work.

The Universe is circular and spherical; nothing is hierarchical. This is a difficult concept for most people to comprehend. All spiritual practices are associated with a circle: the medicine wheel, alchemy, astrology, the planets. The Fibonacci spiral begins with a dot—what I refer to as your origin story or creation myth. This is what happened at the moment of conception, during pregnancy, at birth, and then your zero to seven. That dot starts the story of your life. All other stories go back to that dot. That's all you have. You cannot change it. You can, however, change how you respond to it and, in the process, raise your vibration. Jupiter cycles every 12 years; 60 represents the fifth cycle, and by then you should really start to see the curvature of your spiritual growth. So, own your story. Own who you are and where you come from—your roots, your values—all of it. "Man. know thyself, and ye will know the wonders of the Universe." Your story will keep growing, hopefully in a healthy direction as you put in hard edges.

The Fibonacci sequence starts with 0 and 1 in a pattern that looks like this: 0, 1, 1, 2, 3, 5, 8, 13, 21, and so on. Each number after 0 and 1 is the result of adding the previous two: 0+1=1. 1+1=2. 1+2=3. 2+3=5. 3+5=8. This is the spiral of growth. Within the spiral are squares. These squares are the math calculations which speak to the symmetry. All beauty, whether in art, nature, or a human face, is built upon this sequence. People with "traditionally beautiful" faces follow this sequence. Find images on the internet and you'll see pictures of models with the Fibonacci sequence placed on their face and you can see the symmetry. So, you start at your creation myth and grow spirally as you get older. The spirals are the soft corners; the squares are the hard edges. You need both. Life will bring you hard edges (skinny cows every seven years) and soft corners (fat cows every 12 years) for an optimal chance of spiritual growth.

Notice that the first spiral occurs at the number five. The skinny cows occur every seven years, followed five years later by the spiritual progress gained from those previous seven years. The amount of growth is in direct proportion to the inner work you completed during that time. If you swept the hard work under the rug, squandered the chance with drink or drugs or other distractions during those skinny cows to avoid the pain of the experience, your spiritual spiral growth will be exponentially small. This is free will. The 12-7=5. Twelve correlates to spiritual growth as represented by the Jupiter cycles. Jupiter is also known as Zeus, the King of Olympus. (To find a shortcut to where you have permission to dethrone your parents, look for Jupiter in your birth chart. It's not that hard to dethrone your parents in the house where your Jupiter resides because it's inherent in the archetype. The Saturn cycles are much harder.) The Jupiter image has the same loop as the Fibonacci spiral—the soft corners that you need in your own life. Jupiter cycles tend to be easy, soft-corner types because you are reaping the rewards, the growth, from the previous hard edges, the Saturn seven-year cycles. This is a natural sequence. It does not change. It just goes on and on and on and on. At 60, you experience the fifth 12-year cycle of Jupiter. Jupiter cycles relate to compassion, empathy, vulnerability, love—the things we have to give ourselves first and foremost. What's interesting is that we often fail to do the work of the hard edges, the hard times. It is easy to love ourselves during the growth periods, but we need to honor the hard edges, like budgeting our money or learning a new and healthy habit.

Jupiter glyph: This glyph represents Zeus or Jupiter and the 12-year cycles representing the fat cows. If we concentrate on inner work, even during growth years

with Jupiter, when the skinny cows hit, the growth will be exponential.

In the Bible story, Joseph prophesied to the Pharaoh the skinny and fat cows as years of feast and famine. During the feast years, he placed hard edges on Egypt so there would be enough grain during the famine years. This process worked and Egypt never felt the hunger. If we feast during the growth years and starve during crisis years, we are simply succumbing to the 0 to 100 cycles. Take advantage of both the hard edges and soft corners so you can finally dethrone your parents.

From 63 to Death

Erickson stated that the "stage of maturity" was 65 to death; I am calling it 63 to death. These cycles are repetitive of what we have seen throughout life, and this final period is about fine-tuning. Erickson also described this stage as one of ego identity versus despair, characterized by a life review—looking back at life and determining if we are happy with our choices or regretting things we did or didn't do. Sixty-three is another N-year, an extension of the snowglobe crack at zero to seven and the neutralizers or nemesis that are part of our spiritual family, nudging us forward. At 63 and again at 77, we repeat these neutralizers, leading to another attempt at equanimity and slowing the pendulum swings. At 63, you identify if you're a little to the left or right of 48 to 52 scale. Perhaps you like a little drama and chaos so you're happiest at 35 or 65 pendulum swings. This final tweaking really starts to extract the essence of that crack in the snowglobe, reminding us that balance is individual and that we are enough.

At 70 and 84 years old we have our two final V-years: valor and value. Most of my clients realize that they value financial and professional success, but the roots of their value system are in family, friends and faith. We often see a return to religious practices or faith services to rekindle spiritual practices from childhood. These V years bring oppositions, and we sometimes confront death and loss in physical limitations through illness and disease. At 72, Rahu-Ketu nodes and Jupiter are once again open to the future. Edith is 72 years old. Widowed for three years, she now wants to date, and she has been working with me on her health issues. We realized her urinary incontinence reflected a loyalty to her mother. We identified that she was punishing herself because her mother had stayed single after she had widowed. Once we identified those loyalties, her incontinence improved. Her hip flexors were also quite tight. The hips are directly related to sexual relationships. She wondered why her hips couldn't carry her, and we discovered that the closer she got to a new sexual partner, the more she would sabotage the relationship. She was afraid of the gossip of neighbors who had known her previous partner. When we went further, we identified that nothing in her family was ever discussed directly; it was all gossip and murmurings. Her sister's abortion was a secret, and she felt guilty for not having helped her through it. The secrets in the family around sex, promiscuity, and loose women were being carried by Edith in her hips. Once we broke it all down, she met a partner and is enjoying a healthy, vibrant sex life. At 72, we often work the subconscious issues that are yet to be dethroned through our body.

At 77, we have our final neutralizer year—the final attempt to stop the 0 to 100 swings that have probably slowed down since age 63. It's the last return to the crack in the snowglobe to rewrite the story of our self-worth. At 84, we not only have a V year—a Saturn opposition—but a Jupiter cycle as well. Again, the years when Saturn and Jupiter cycles meet are auspicious periods of completion that can bring both death and liberation; they can be extremely enlightening years with a strong spiritual connection. Hospice physicians and nurses have written extensively about the spiritual lucidity they observe in people when they get close to death. Uranus also returns at 84, enhancing one's connection to the spirit world and those who have previously crossed. Uranus is the planet that asks us to wake-up and raise our consciousness.

In astrology, we achieve complete liberation at 84 whether or not we leave the body and close the cycle that started at 42. Martin Heidegger states, "Every man is born as many men and dies as a single one." If we indeed return to the cosmic womb and understand the twelfth truth, we will have attained unity in the human form—unity within a dual world. We will reminisce about how we tried seeking liberation at 42 and, for the last time, re-evaluate the priorities we set at 42. The Uranus opposition and the higher vibration of that cycle at 84 is ruled by The Tower card in the tarot: a tower being blown up by a lightning bolt. This bolt can represent flashes of intuition, sudden insights, epiphanies, and revelations. At 42, we sought the metaphorical Hephaestus to crack open our logical-rational mind. We embraced curiosity and imagination. At 84, we may suddenly make illuminating connections with our childhood.

In the *Mandukya Upanishad*, there are four states of consciousness: *visva* (waking state), *taijasa* (dream state), *prajna* (dreamless sleep), and *turiya* (pure consciousness). The waking state is described as being aware of our daily world. It is an "outward knowing." You are aware of the gross body, the gross elements, but nothing beyond ordinary reality. The dreaming state is an "inward knowing." Here you are aware of the subtle body. The third state of consciousness is deep sleep and connecting to the underlying ground of consciousness. Like Chiron or the pituitary gland ("lying under"), this state of consciousness directly relates to the Universal mind and the Principle of Mentalism and correlates to the causal body. It leads to the understanding that the Universe is the Creator of all things.

Lastly is pure consciousness or *turiya* in Hindu cosmology. This transcends all other states of consciousness. Here we understand that we are both absolute (unified) and relative (dual). In my opinion, this relates to the transmutation process where we own our changes and no longer think about old behaviors. The focus is on new thoughts and the state of consciousness that has transcended that moment of conception. This is enlightenment. We grasp what we've been and what we've created, transmuting our thoughts into a higher vibration and living at this new level of consciousness. Once we transmute one thought, we continue the process, repeating the stages of spiritual growth and raising our consciousness. The closer we get to the Uranus conjunction, the more apt we are to experience these higher states of consciousness.

These four states of consciousness correlate with the mantra A-U-M or OM. The *Mandukya Upanishad* opens by declaring, "Om! This syllable is the whole world." A-U-M is considered the master syllable or master mantra that activates all states of consciousness and all of the chakras. A in AUM refers to *apti*, which means obtaining or reaching. We are simply here attempting to identify that we indeed have a different throne than our parents—an awareness we first have at 14. The U in AUM comes from *utkarsa* or *ubhayatva*, which means exaltation and intermediateness. This refers to the 28-year Saturn transit when we have reached adulthood and attempt to do it differently than our parents, but don't. The M in AUM is for *miti*, which means erecting or constructing. At 42, with the Uranus transit, we attempt to destroy the foundation of our psyche in order to achieve freedom and independence, not realizing it is the subconscious liberation we seek. We re-establish ourselves sexually, professionally, and personally, maybe acquiring spiritual knowledge, developing intuition, or finding a guru. AUM itself means "without an element, without development, beyond the expanse of the Universe." At 48 to 52, you return home, dethrone your parents, stop making sacrifices and giving offerings, and own your throne. You are now transmuting the original thought at conception that you are separate from your parents, the Universe, and all other beings. This is our original state—our perfect state within the body. This is the Law of Gender: balancing the masculine and feminine energies and finding our 48 to 52 scale.

When we are first kicked out of Olympus and until the age of 7, we are in a waking state. Here we realize that we are separate from the original snowglobe and a crack in our psyche occurs. There is no unconditional love, we have unmet needs, and we must wear a mask to become loveable. We are distinctly aware of our gross body. Developmentally, children touch their bodies, play with their food, and identify the outside environment as different from themselves. They start school, sleep in their own beds, and learn that there is a separateness between them and their parents. This started at birth, but from 0 to seven, they get the story. The next state of consciousness, the dreaming mind, occurs between 14 and 28, when we start to dethrone our parents in our heads. We recognize that we have a different inward-knowing than they do. We discover that we are different from them and have different ideals, goals, and dreams. At 28 to 30, we leave home and attempt to dethrone our parents by taking on burdens that we think are different from theirs. At 38 to 42, we begin to understand the deep-sleep state, the third level of consciousness. A neutralizer shows up to make us aware that there is something beneath, something "lying under" how we think the world works. We may begin a spiritual journey. We may not know how or why, but we long for something beyond the logical and rational. In the myth of Athena being birthed from Zeus' head, I mentioned that Hephaestus helped crack open his helmet so Athena could be born. Hephaestus, representing the imagination or spiritual domain, rules this third stage of consciousness. We unknowingly confuse this stage with liberation from responsibility, but it's about freedom from the limiting thoughts from conception, the upper limits. We are seeking a higher state of consciousness, but we aren't yet aware of what that is or what that means.

The turiya, or fourth state of consciousness, rules transcendence. Here we return home, integrate our parents, understand that we have created our life based on faulty programming and low-level consciousness, we grieve what was. This state is not truly achieved until a new vibration and level of consciousness emerges. There is a key difference between behavior change rooted in belief change and mimicking behavior change. Behavior change that isn't linked to a new vibration or state of consciousness will lead to relapse. A transmuted thought is a form of enlightenment: the transmutation of low-level consciousness. Here, the low-level centaur turns into the high-vibration centaur, Chiron. What occurred at 42 is doubled at

84 because we have now come full circle with understanding the true nature of freedom and consciousness. One of the ultimate goals in life is learning how to die. At 84, in pure consciousness and aware of the purpose of our lives, we finally return home and prepare for physical death. The deeper the emotional and psychological deaths we've experienced, the better-prepared we'll be for the ultimate liberation from the body.

Transcendence while we are in the body is not a permenent state, in the sense that you cannot sustain the *energetic* levels of the experience. You cannot. Transmutation, or enlightenment, is a mental state where you have new thoughts and learned a new behavior and changed your state of mind, you've transmuted consciousness around your limiting beliefs and low-level consciousness from conception. A Zen koan states, "Before enlightenment, chop wood, carry water. After enlightenment, chop wood, carry water." This refers to the fact that while your state of mind—the level of your vibration—has changed, your external life will essentially remain the same. This is an eternal process. Spiritual growth is subtle. It's not a production; there are no bright lights and billboards. This is very different from the animal kingdom, such as when caterpillars metamorphosize into butterflies. Metamorphosis is simply a physical change in form and habits, usually after the embryonic phase in normal development.

On the Kabbalah's *Tree of Life, Da'at* is linked to knowledge, but *Binah* (understanding) and *Chochmah* (wisdom) are the only two that lead to *Keter*: the crown head, true ownership of our kingdom, and our spiritual adult. Together, the three are known as the "intellect triad." Knowledge (Da'at) is a rational, fact-based process linked to metamorphosis—changes in behavior—but not to wisdom and understanding. It is head-based, not heart-based. Binah refers to beliefs based on an intuitive understanding. It is the feminine principle related to the *yoni*, or womb, and The Priestess card in tarot. Chochman is an intellect that doesn't emanate from the rational process. This explains why Athena, goddess of wisdom, needed Hephaestus's intuition and imagination to be born. We cannot birth wisdom or understanding without spiritual guidance and spiritual adulting. In alchemy, transmutation occurred when base metals (low-level consciousness) were converted into gold (higher consciousness). Transmutation defines what happens when we own the original thought that we are separate from Self and replace it with the absolute wisdom that we are One.

The Hellenistic philosopher Plotinus wrote in the *Enneads* that there are three principles: the One, the intellect, and the soul. He believed in a supreme, transcendent "One" containing no division, multiplicity, or distinction, and that the soul and intellect were emanations of the One. This is represented in *The Principle of Mentalism*: the hermetic law that all is mind. He said that even the self-contemplating intelligence contains duality because anything other than the One introduces deficiency. The One is the Source or the Creator, unchangeable and immutable. All creation emanates from this One. In Greek mythology, this is related to Uranus, father sky, the cosmic consciousness and the cosmic womb. Buddha's teachings, known as *dharma*, taught wisdom, kindness, patience, generosity, and compassion as key virtues that lead to nirvana or enlightenment and the Buddha's third noble truth: *the truth of the end of suffering.* This is also the twelfth stage on the spiritual path. This level of transcendence, if achieved in a single lifetime, is related to the Void and nothingness. We are no longer "children of God" because we reunite with the One, without distinction or dogma. Despite what your religious beliefs are regarding an afterlife, the energy of your soul reemerges with the One upon physical death. Energy cannot be created or destroyed. In Ecclesiastes 12:7, it states, "Then shall the dust return to the earth as it was; and the spirit shall return to God who gave it."

British novelist Muriel Spark wrote, "It is difficult for people of advanced years to start remembering they must die; it is best to form the habit while young." This sounds a bit comical, but it isn't. We begin this process at age 14, while the Saturn cycles guide us to die every seven years in preparation for physical death. The Kybalion says, "All are on the path. All progress is a returning home. All is upward and onward." To be a "child" is to be in a hierarchy, and the Universe is non-hierarchical. There is no distinction between your divine spark and the Source that created all. And yet fear often sets in after age 52 because we begin to confront our mortality. However, if we have spiritually adulted and learned to die in smaller ways, we'll have an inner knowing that we return to universal consciousness—the physical world is simply an emanation of the One.

Most people transform; they don't transmute. **Transformation is a behavior change; transmutation is a belief change.** For instance, transformation is when you don't eat cake you normally used to because you realize it isn't good for you, but you still want it. You have the thought. Transmutation is a belief change; the thought of eating the cake doesn't even occur to you because you've transmuted it. Transmutation is associated with the third and fourth chakras. The fire element in the third chakra includes self-love, boundaries, owning your kingdom, and your 48 to– 52 scale. These are your hard edges. The only way you're going to sustain both an ordinary state of consciousness (chop wood) and a shamanic state of consciousness (enlightenment) is through transmutation. You have to be in the body and working in the earth while also connected to spirit. Binah, Shekinah, Shakti, Aphrodite Urania, and The Graces are all representations of the feminine principle. It is through the feminine principle that the One emanates on earth. You cannot clear your karma, dethrone your parents, do it differently, raise your consciousness from conception, and raise your vibration if you don't transmute the thoughts behind them. And that requires the use of free will.

DiClemente & Prochaska created the Transtheoretical Model of Behavior Change, a public health model that shows five stages for creating behavior change. These stages are precontemplation, contemplation, preparation, action, and maintenance. However, the model is cyclical, and maintenance can slip right back into precontemplation if the mind itself doesn't change. This happens through transmutation: the only way to ensure true behavior change and a shift in vibration. When a thought is transmuted, one's inner world changes. When you transmute the original impure thought from conception—the one that is linked with our shadow and unintegrated shadow parent—you become one with the Creator. There is no duality, no distinction. In general, if you don't fully own the thought that created a particular behavior, you may transform, but not transmute. Lasting change only happens when the thought that created the low-level consciousness is transmuted into higher-level consciousness. As stated above, transmutation is a voluntary action; it takes free will. You cannot transmute via coercion, bad news, a health scare, or even from a fear of dying. And once you've transmuted one thought, another pops up, and then another and another and so forth. Thoughts never cease. In meditation, you simply observe your thoughts so you can start to identify the quality and content of what you are thinking. Observe a thought, let it go, sit back in meditation, and do it again. This is Truth 10 on the spiritual path, Truth One is the awareness of the impure thoughts and their origin and questioning where they came from, realizing that impure thoughts materialize into pain in your life and engaging in a personal TED talk, to disperse the energy. I use a *Sphere of Consciousness* technique with clients when they're identifying their impure thoughts that arise during a personal TED talk. If something enters your sphere of consciousness, you must deconstruct the thought with the personal TED talk. The sphere of consciousness is acknowledgement that you create everything and the Law of Correspondence, "as within so without" is always at play. 1) Identify if the thought symbolically represents mother or father most; 2) Identify the judgement and what you don't like about the thought (linked to a person, place, thing or situation) and 3) Identify the emotion behind the thought and what it proves about you to have this thought and the emotion linked to the thought and where you hold that emotion in the body. Once you identify step two, the judgement, I will link the judgement to a vice and place it into one of the seven gates (linked to the vices and deadly sins). This impure thought is what you're trying to hide and it creates 0 to 100 swings to cover up the vice. For example, Jonathan was out to lunch and encountered a homeless man in his sphere of consciousness. The judgement was linked to the vice of greed and the emotion of hopelessness. In his subconscious he honored his mother's loyalty to hopelessness because she could not achieve financial success after deciding to be a stay-at-home mother. In order to transmute the belief around greed, he defined the 0 to 100 swings, greed and charity, and with measurable and objective criteria defined the 48 to 52 midpoint, which became his template for his new belief system around greed.

This is the cycle of our soul. A single thought can create a world of suffering. All thoughts link back to that moment of conception (rooted in desire), that bad bucket item, the one belief about getting kicked out of Olympus, your identification with the snowglobe being cracked or shattered. It doesn't matter. The snowglobe is no longer intact. This is the first state of consciousness, the waking state, your identification of being separate from everything else, your internalized belief of being flawed, imperfect, or broken. The rest of your lifetime—the Universal cycle, the skinny and fat cows—are all designed to guide your soul back to the snowglobe, realizing you are both intact and shattered, all at once.

Chapter Fourteen
Conclusion

"Spiritual adulting" is the path we all start at the moment of conception. Once we leave the universal consciousness, our snowglobe cracks. During pregnancy we inherit a shadow love language from our mother, during birth we learn the subconscious language linked to how we will transition through the "deaths" or skinny cows in life and from 0—7, we form a personal mythology—a "story"—that we live out every year to subconsciously remain in child so that our parents (and their representatives throughout life) can rescue us, meet our needs, and help us feel worthy. Nevertheless, age-by-age, we are guided in our spiritual growth. This is programmed into our soul and the cycles of our lifetime. Whether or not we take advantage of these opportunities is up to us.

When I work with clients, I share my *Twelve Truths to Spiritual Adulting* process to help guide their journey back to spiritual wholeness. Those truths are as follows:

Truth One: Truth of Thought

Truth Two: Truth of Desire

Truth Three: Truth of Emotion & Breath

Truth Four: Truth of Instinct, Intellect & Intuition

Truth Five: Truth of Ego, Personality & Soul

Truth Six: Truth of Purification & Health

Truth Seven: Truth of Balance & Fun

Truth Eight: Truth of the Shadow

Truth Nine: Truth of Wisdom

Truth Ten: Truth of Simplicity & Silence

Truth Eleven: Truth of Service

Truth Twelve: Truth of Unity

I've devised these twelve steps according to my understanding of how our spiritual growth gradually unfolds at each age. These twelve truths are further organized into my three-stage Band-AID model of spiritually adulting: Awareness, Integration, and Doing it differently. The first stage refers to becoming aware of what you've created in your life and owning your child script. This is usually linked to the first four truths: *The truth of your thoughts. Truth of your desires. The truth of your breath. The truth of your intuition.* The second stage, integration, refers to a realization that you are your parents—the good, the bad, and the ugly, that we willingly stay in child to get our needs met, and that while we aren't yet transmuting that pattern, we understand what we are doing and why. This stage includes mental awareness and knowledge, but not necessarily wisdom or heart awareness. The truths associated with integration include the following: *The truth of the personality and self-love. The truth of purification. The truth of balance. The truth of the shadow.* The third stage relates to transcending your parents. These truths are directly related to wisdom, the intelligence of love, and transmutation, and include the following: *The truth of wisdom. The truth of silence. The truth of service. The truth of unity.*

Owning Our Value System

The crux of the spiritual path is our value system, or rather, dethroning our parents' value system—given to us at conception—and finding our own high-vibration way of living. The flip side of values are judgements. Every value has a judgement. When we left the universal consciousness—the original and intact snowglobe—we inherited judgements and values. Our spirit understands we are all one and that all judgements and values link back to a dogma we must ultimately transcend. However, until we reach the twelfth truth of "unity," we will be unable to transcend the dogma, so we must get very clear on what we value and judge. All judgements are linked to bad bucket values, we don't want to admit, like greed or gluttony, but were inherent at the moment of our conception. We also develop good bucket values like integrity and honesty, that we will need to define in measurable and observable criteria, to hold ourselves accountable as spiritual adults.

From conception, pregnancy, and birth through age 7, we received the story—our personal mythology—with characters, protagonists, villains, and a storyline. We are ready for Netflix! This story is flawed, built on a value system you want to dethrone. Unfortunately, you don't have such permission and you don't know how anyway. At 12, you realize you have permission, but you still don't have knowledge of how to do this. At 14—16. we start building the spiritual infrastructure that will begin to crumble at 42 and totally dissolve at 84 should we reach the twelfth truth. This spiritual infrastructure is built on the value system from our parents' low-level consciousness. This is what we call *karma*, a manifestation of divine law, so it's vitally important to *mind your pleck*, to own your throne: knowing your strengths and weaknesses, your good and bad buckets, and having self-love while meeting your needs. Whatever you want to dethrone will revisit you at every age of the spiritual cycle as described throughout this book. It is the one thread: Pull on it and your entire story and child script will unravel, like a knit sweater. Until we give ourselves permission and learn how to dethrone this value system, we will swing from 0 to 100, pretending we are doing it the same as our parents or exactly the opposite. Both are still of a low-vibration child frequency.

When we clearly define our 0 to 100 bookend values in measurable terms, we can hold ourselves accountable for changing our thoughts and behaviors and start achieving the balance of 48 to 52 scale—the beginning of true spiritual adulting. Without this step, we cannot adult spiritually. Anything outside the 48 to 52 scale is still in child and keeps us honoring our inherited story and our parents' low-level consciousness. When you identify your value system, you can begin to see how you have woven it into every story and every age. Depending on your age, you will also see how you began deconstructing those values at 42 and eventually, at 84, dissolving them completely if you have done the work properly. Every value system has a judgement, and these judgements are confessions. They are directly related to the crack in the snowglobe and are projected onto others, especially our parents, when in truth, we are judging ourselves. If you know your judgements, you also know your values. They are directly related and tell us everything we need to know about our spiritual process and progress. Unfortunately, most people don't know their philosophy of life or their values.

When I was judging myself for being a bad mother, I stopped and asked, What value would I give my child to make me a good mother? The answer was obvious: spiritual growth. My main value system is spiritual growth (defined and in measurable terms); therefore, if I truly grow spiritually in my actions and not just in my thoughts or judgements, I am a good mother. So I started writing measurable ways on how to grow spiritually, which began my journey of creating work-books to help others *and* myself on the journey. I realized that most spiritual paths were very loose. I was still a child and I needed tools to help me hold myself accountable. When clients begin their journey, I invite them to tell me their top two values. They usually hem and haw, but eventually they get there. However, they don't define what those values are *in measurable terms*. I often hear words like honesty, goodness, teamwork, and leadership. These are vague ideals and are defined differently by everyone. The moment we define our values in measurable terms, we can actually hold ourselves accountable for doing or not doing them. We get out of child and the game of self-hatred and self-betrayal is over.

One thing that astrology has taught me is that children (grown or otherwise) want to have their minds read. Water signs in particular love for their partner to read their mind. This is childish. "He should know what I want and need." Uh, no, he shouldn't. How can he if *you* don't even know what you want?! This applies to men as well as women. Since we are all children, we are all guilty of this in some areas of our life. We want our minds read so we can stick to our story and our victimhood. Now, if we can define more specifically what we mean by love, peace, balance, honesty, and the other values we have, we can better hold ourselves and others accountable. (See my books *Truth Is in the Triangle*, a step-by-step guide to holding yourself and your partner accountable in relationship, and *Dethroning Olympus*, a step-by-step guide to holding yourself and your family members accountable.) What would happen if we actually held everyone accountable, like at work, for example, with an employee manual? I create manuals for those gray areas in life but it's an uncomfortable process.

Chapter 15 has a number of case studies. You will see how the values my clients said were priorities are directly linked to their 0 to 7 story. We don't leave the apple orchard of our parents; the apple doesn't fall far from the tree. However, you can take that value system, define it clearly, and plant your own tree. Stay in the orchard like an adult, but don't eat off the tree your parents planted for you. My mother instilled in me the value of metaphysics and my father gave me the values of spirituality and hard work. But until I clearly defined them in measurable terms, I could not transmute them to a higher vibration. If you don't know your judgments or value system or your philosophy of life, you won't know what to judge. So, figure it out and write them all down. Then find the 48 to 52 between the values and the judgements. That's your spiritual adulting.

If this book is reaching you later in life, track your values starting at age 14 and see how you've swung from 0 to 100, especially in those N years and V years, how you tried dethroning it at 42, and how you returned home to self at 48 to 52. If you still haven't defined a value in measurable terms, or you still have the judgement, or you still swing from 0 to 100, start with the first truth: the truth of thoughts. Without observing your thoughts, you cannot progress spiritually. I've noticed an interesting phenomenon in my clients when I ask them to name their top two values (and it can't be family): They often link to their sun and ascendant sign in their astrology chart. My two top values are spirituality and leadership. My Sun is in Pisces, which rules spirituality, and my ascendant in Sagittarius is the sign of a spiritual leader or teacher.

And finally, if you're starting young, lucky you! You can identify your values early and avoid a lifetime of destructive behavior. You still need to live your life and honor the stages of life; just don't become an ascetic, thinking this work can only be done in an ashram or a monastery. It is intended to be done while we are living here on Earth, enjoying life. During this journey, you will dethrone your parents and you will punish yourself for doing so. So get very clear on how you retreat to child by providing offerings to your parents. The best way I've found to watch out for this is to identify how your parents either pampered themselves or self-destructed and then linking those behaviors to your own. When a boyfriend of mine became passive-aggressive by not answering a text after I ended the relationship, I noticed myself slipping into sadness. It was a subtle shift, but I caught myself. The boyfriend's response was typical of my mom's bad bucket behavior—she was passive aggressive. To try to meet her needs, I would chase her. His response was my mother ignoring me (again). But instead of getting trapped in child and chasing him to meet my needs, I stayed on my throne and met my needs by feeling the feelings.

The closer you are to removing the seven veils as you progress closer to the twelfth truth, the self-sabotage becomes more subtle, and you have to pay even closer attention to your thoughts and judgements. In the example above, I remembered that my mother would give me the silent treatment and I was honoring that script. I caught myself within a few minutes and returned to adulting. This confirms that I haven't yet transmuted that particular thought, but that's okay. I'm in awareness and will keep working on integration and doing it differently as I go forward. The first truth ("the truth of thought") and the sixth truth ("the truth of purification") are steps that you must revisit daily. I've marked them with an asterisk when mentioned in the appendices because we cannot refrain from analyzing our thoughts or purifying the body throughout this entire process. If you do nothing but these two steps, you're well on your way to spiritually adulting!

Appendix A

Chapter 15

Case Studies

Below I feature several case studies from varied clients of different ages. I break down their initial snowglobe theme and track its influence throughout their life. The focus is on dethroning the parents, embracing values, and rewriting the original script at a higher level of consciousness.

Case One: Reginald

Reginald is a 60-year-old physician in Austin, TX, who is married and has two grown children. His pregnancy was planned and unremarkable. He lived in a row home in Pennsylvania and his childhood included a lot of people. His major themes include a big move during 0—7, his father's domestic violence toward his mother, caring for his mother who had a severe eating disorder, and the birth of a younger brother. He remembers a teacher hitting him with a ruler in grade school, having a lot of girlfriends in middle school, and his parents never being "tight" financially. **Keywords**: Abusive relationships, eating disorder/caretaker, moving

0-7 snowglobe crack / Saturn N year	Parents argued a lot, there was abuse I have blocked out, and my mother had a severe eating disorder. We moved to a rural area, but I had a TV in my room which was exciting. I fought with my brother a lot.

12 Jupiter re- turn	My mother broke her wrists and I helped take care of her. She would ask me to buy her enema kits because of her eating disorder.
14-16 Saturn oppo- sition V year	Parents got divorced. We moved to a small apartment; couldn't afford the bigger house. I helped my mother with the bills. I was the man of the house. Neither parent could handle me, so I switched back and forth living with mom and dad.
18 Rahu-Ketu	I went to college but needed a place to live. My parents had their own lives with their new partners. I found an estate that needed a caretaker and got a job on the premises that included room and board.
21 Saturn N year	Applied to medical school and started the following year. Moved to Florida.
24 Jupiter re- turn	Started my relationship with my now wife.

28 Saturn re- turn V year	Moved to New Jersey and got married. Bought a house in an old-fashioned neighborhood in a good community.
33-35 N year	Move to Florida. Working round the clock as a new physician. My wife is also a physician, and we never see each other because we are always working. I'm exhausted and out-of-shape.
36 Rahu-Ketu Jupiter re- turn	Had my first child. (My second was three years later.)
42 V year Uranus op- position	Working hard, changing hospitals. I'm lost, overworked, and burned out. I was having relationship problems and my life had no meaning. I went to India on a medical mission.
48-—52 Chiron return N year Jupiter re- turn	I separated from my wife. Part of me wanted to break out. I wasn't *living*. I needed to believe in myself. I started meditating like I had learned in India. I became more relaxed and started enjoying life. I was at the top of my career and I changed jobs.

54 Rahu-Ketu	My wife and I reconciled and rediscovered each other.
56 V year	The kids go away to college; mom comes to live with us.
60 Jupiter Return	I'm working out with an emphasis on myself and my self-development. My wife and I continue working on our relationship. I buy a boat and invest in real estate and stocks. I want to move to Asheville.

Commentary: Before the age of seven, Reginald moved to a rural area for a better life and a safer neighborhood. His parents never struggled financially, but they had an abusive relationship. His father beat his mother, and he identified that he could meet his mother's needs by taking care of her health. At 12, he realized he could dethrone his father by taking care of his mother. Since his father beat her, he attempted to do it differently, but taking care of her was simply the opposite, still in the 0 to 100. He continued this process by taking care of his wife but neglecting himself. Every major stage in Reginald's life includes a move and buying a house. When he attempted to do it differently at 18, he ended up living in a large house and taking care of the estate while in college. Only once, during the divorce, has he lived in an apartment. Real estate, buying homes, and renovating them are key themes in his life. His marriage has been a frequent source of pain. He wanted to dethrone his parents by making his marriage work, but he lost himself in the process.

At 42, he went to India to "find himself." He started to restructure his habit of taking care of others—especially his wife—and started focusing on his own personal development. At 48 to 52, he temporarily leaves the marriage. At 56, his mother re-enters the picture and moves to Florida. He is becoming balanced and no longer caretakes his wife or mother. He is meeting his own needs and is a better son and husband for it. At 60, he feels as if he is sitting on his throne with the perfect work-life balance. He is renovating his house again but bought a "moving house"—a boat.

When asked to name his two top values, he said "family" and "teamwork." Reginald saw his parents fail at teamwork, and he worked very hard to dethrone their bitter marriage and divorce and make his own work. He raised low-level consciousness around relationships that he inherited from conception. He also is a team leader at his medical practice. He honored the snowglobe crack around living in different locations by moving quite a bit throughout his adult life. He would travel for side jobs, buy real estate, interview at various cities around the world while job hunting, and, when he finally returned home to self, realized his dream of buying a boat. He stated that the boat is like a house because it has a cabin. This is integration. He honored the financial success he observed in childhood and re-experienced his mother's mental illness through a daughter with severe depression and anxiety. However, when I asked him about his first child, he responded that *his wife's* pregnancy was unremarkable—repeating a pattern of mothering his mother by not including himself in the conversation about his own first child.

CASE TWO: BEATRICE

Beatrice is a 79-year-old Cuban woman living in Miami. She was born Jewish, the youngest of four children. Her pregnancy was unplanned; she was an "Oops" baby. Her father was a salesman, and her mother was a homemaker who never in her life entered a grocery store. She had no control of the money or purchases and had no education. She didn't know about her own pregnancy or birth story. At 0 to 7, Beatrice left the local public school to attend the Presbyterian school near her house. She was the favorite pupil and won awards throughout her time there. **Keywords, themes**: School, religion, male and female roles

0-7 Snowglobe crack Saturn N year	I attended the local public school but didn't like it because the teacher made me teach the other children and I felt I wasn't learning anything. Even though I was born Jewish and my father was a devout Jew, I begged him to put me in a Presbyterian school near our house. The Jewish school that had recently opened up was too far away, and my father didn't want me to be on a bus for that long, so he let me attend the Presbyterian school.
12 Jupiter return	I received a special award for her academic achievement. The school created the award just for me with a $25 prize. I would secretly attend mass on Sundays without telling my parents.
14-16\ Saturn opposition V year	I graduated from the Presbyterian school and then attended the School of Commerce in the next city over. My father asked me why I wanted to go there, since women didn't study. No one in my family, especially the women, made it past 6th grade. I studied accounting because I saw my father manage the money and his books every night after work for his textile business. My mother never had a say in the finances. She woke up at 4:30 to cook a feast every morning and yet never stepped a foot in a grocery store.

18 Rahu-Ketu	I left Cuba to live in the United States. I started working in New York City and made a lot of money—more money than my husband.
21 Saturn N year	I had my first child, who was born mentally retarded. I was in a new country with a sick child. I lived surrounded by my family and the Sephardic Jewish community.
24 Jupiter return	I had my second child. She was advanced, an early walker.
28 Saturn return V year	My son was born. We were making good money. We opened a furniture store in New York and it was thriving. My two daughters were attending Yeshiva, the Jewish school.
33-35 N year	I joined a spiritual community. I needed help understanding why my daughter was mentally ill. My marriage wasn't healthy. I needed support. We moved to Florida and waited for my dream home to be built. While we were waiting, we lived in an apartment that flooded. The carpet was wet and disgusting. Unexpectedly, I got pregnant.

36 Rahu-Ketu Jupiter return	We finished building my dream home. It was perfect. It was my first home. Everything was great. I graduated college with my AA in Psychology.
42 Uranus opposition V year	When my son left for military school, I discovered Ayurvedic medicine and changed my entire diet and life. We had never been healthier. These were the two best years of my life. I had never cooked and so I started cooking and eating healthy. Then my first daughter died.
48—-52 Chiron return N year Jupiter return	I was at a dead-end job in Accounts Payable for 11 years. I retired and started taking care of my grandson full-time.
54 Rahu-Ketu	We bought a house in Miami to be near a spiritual community.
56 V year	My granddaughter was born.
60 Jupiter return	We bought a new house near my daughter. I took care of my grandchildren full-time and started a beautiful garden. It became my obsession and my project.

63 Saturn N year	I started crafting. I had always dreamed of going back to school and studying interior design and fashion.
70 Saturn V year	I left the spiritual community. I was very unhappy with the way the leader was behaving.
72 Jupiter Rahu-Ketu	I divorced my husband of 52 years and bought my own home. I own two rental properties. I have a wonderful garden.
77 Saturn N year	My granddaughter is studying fashion design in college, and I am helping on all of her school projects. I have been struggling to reconcile how I love Judaism and the Presbyterian religions equally. I miss Cuba. I get very emotional every time I see news reports about my country. I think I feel more for my country than most exiles. I want to help Cubans. I am learning a lot about saltwater therapy, and I want to find a way to educate the Cuban population about the ability of ocean water to heal illnesses. Cuba is a country surrounded by water, but they don't know that ocean water is medicine.

Commentary: Beatrice was her father's favorite child. All of his children had green eyes like his wife; she was the only brown-eyed child. He would peel grapes for her when she was little. She was the apple of his eye. Her snowglobe shattered when her father decided to send her to the Presbyterian school for convenience and not the new Jewish school. Even though that was her preference, she felt he didn't her love her enough to make the effort to support her learning the same teachings that he was studying. She dethroned her parents by attending mass on Sundays without them knowing. Over the years, she would continue trying to dethrone her parents by joining various religious and spiritual communities, but at 79, she is returning to the roots of her traditions from childhood, integrating herself and her father.

Leaving her home country at 18 to pursue financial gain and the chance to be free with her children, she still longed for her mother country. After arriving in New York, she tried dethroning her mother by working and making money. Beatrice never did any hard work because her husband took care of her, and even after her divorce, she dated another man who took care of her like her father did. In her new relationship, she decided to control the purse—the opposite swing on the 0 to 100 since her mother never handled the finances. Even at 79, Beatrice had a lot of pendulum swings with money and food, but her attempt to dethrone her father and integrate both Judaism and Presbyterian to find her 48 to 52 was at the forefront of her life.

She longs for her mother and her mother country. During her interview, she was crying. The ocean water represents the "toxic water" of the womb and her mother country represents her mother. She is still very much in child, even at her age. Her adulting occurs in the spirituality she seeks, although she is still struggling to find her way. One of the ways we can honor ourselves is through our grandchildren—what Erikson calls "generativity." In mythology, Jupiter avenged the unlived life of his grandfather, Uranus. Similarly, Beatrice's granddaughter is breathing life into her by asking for help on her fashion school projects. When asked her two top values, she said family and work, and then elaborated with progress and betterment, especially spiritual growth.

Jack is a successful business executive who, at 56, is on his second marriage. He has two children in college. He parents are Columbian-Chinese, and he grew up in a very traditional home where academic achievement was stressed. **Keywords**: Alcohol, freedom, academic achievement, moving, cultural assimilation

0-7 Snow-globe crack Saturn N year	We moved from Chicago to New Jersey. That was a culture shock because we used to live around a lot of family, and in NJ we were practically alone. My uncle did live with us, and he would smoke and drink when my parents weren't home. I would run away to the nearest park just to get out of the house at night without my parents knowing. I failed third grade and my parents were very angry.
12 Jupiter return	My parents didn't speak English, so I had to translate for them.

14-16 Saturn op- position V year	In my freshman year at high school, I started drinking beer. I didn't want to be associated with my culture, I wanted to be Americanized, and my parents weren't big drinkers. My uncle was a senior in high school who would bring me to parties. I played baseball and started chewing tobacco. My mother found out and I got in trouble. I fought with my father because I got a C in geometry; Bs or better were expected. They gave me incentives if I got straight As. I wanted a bike, I earned straight As, and my father bought me one. However, my mother was angry because she felt it was dangerous. They wanted me to go to medical school, but I didn't want to.
18 Rahu-Ketu	I got a brand-new Jeep. I felt free with my new wheels. I moved to Philadelphia for college.
21 Saturn N year	I married a Filipino woman.
24 Jupiter return	I got a great job in a medical supply company making a lot of money. I started graduate school.

| 28

Saturn
return

V year	I had my first child. I bought my first house.
33-35

N year | I self-medicated with alcohol. I have a lot of anxiety and I drink too much. I got divorced and drank to ease the pain. My mother died. |
| 36

Rahu-Ketu

Jupiter
return | I got a top executive position at a pharmaceutical company. I was a CFO and making more money than I ever thought possible. I bought a big house and started traveling the world. |
| 42

Uranus
opposition

V year | I was drinking too much and checked myself into rehab. I started AA and found my higher power. My girlfriend broke up with me. My son was getting bullied at school. |
| 48—-52

Chiron
return

N year

Jupiter
return | I learned to meditate and started seeing a therapist and a spiritual counselor. |

54 Rahu-Ketu	I married a woman who lives in Russia, and we are trying to bring her to the U.S. My son went away to college.
56 V year	I started seeing a nutritionist, I'm drinking again, but trying to limit it. My daughter comes home from school and doesn't even stop by and say hello. My wife still lives in Russia, and I am alone in a 6,000 square foot house. It's lonely.

Commentary: Jack is a successful professional. He has met the expectations that his parents set for him; however, he is now evaluating his life and wondering what does a big house, fancy cars, and a big paycheck mean? His wife lives in Russia because she can't get a visa, his daughter doesn't visit, and he self-medicates with alcohol. His snowglobe crack proved that academics are valued, so he excelled. His parents' inability to speak English, and growing up without a family, is honored by having had two foreign wives—the newest who is unable to live with him. Freedom has been a big theme in Jack's life, especially with all the movement and vehicles—he has several cars considered "collectibles." He is "free" while his wife is in Russia, but he's alone in a big house and reconnects with his "toxic water" through alcohol. He is at the point that academic and financial achievements are no longer fulfilling; it is time to dethrone his parents. His values include friends and family.

Spiritual Adulting
Worksheets

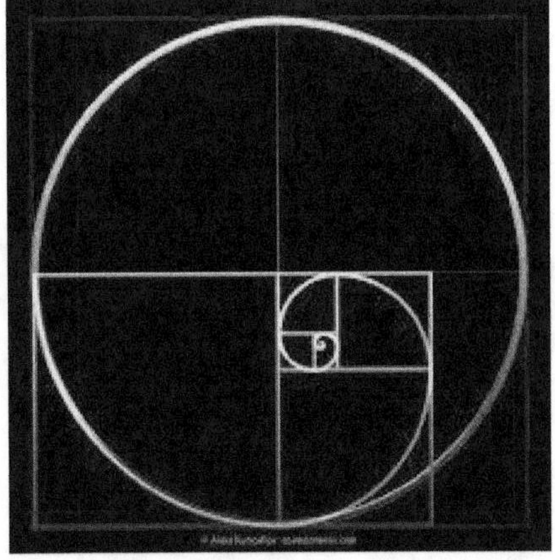

Appendix A

Spiritual Adulting Tracking Sheet (Example)

Age	Thread
0-7: Snowglobe crack Saturn N year	The wound you experienced in childhood—the "theme" of shame or blame or unworthiness—will repeat at ages 21, 35, 49, 63, and 77.
12: Jupiter return Here you identify that you can dethrone—and even surpass—your parents in some theme. But will you?	What you identify here is fully dethroned at 60. You will come full circle with the seven veils at 60 based on this theme.
14-16: Saturn opposition V year These are the most important "construction and destruction" years of the spiritual foundation. Pay very close attention to what happens at 14-16.	This theme will repeat at ages 28, 42, 56, 70 and 84. This is the story you've attached yourself to that creates the self-hatred and why you can't love yourself until you integrate, do it differently, and come full circle as you find your balance in the 48 to– 52.
18: Rahu-Ketu	This is the positive response to what happened from 7—9 years old.

21: Saturn N year	A revisit of what happened at 0—7. This is the first response to the snowglobe crack that occurred there.
24: Jupiter return	This is the next level after what you learned at 12.
28: Saturn return V year	A revisit of what happened at 14-16. This closes that cycle. You will want to do the same or the exact opposite of your parents in the area of your life that is most prominent now. Pay very close attention! Also, be sure to have a plan for your spiritual life in addition to the material and emotional. This cycle will last 28 years, and to avoid an existential crisis at 42 where you "blow up" your life, create a spiritual context.
33-35: N year	This is a collapsing year related to the snowglobe and the neutralizer at 21. If you didn't address the original wound at 21, it will be too heavy to carry. You will start to feel your structures begin to crumble.

36: Rahu-Ketu Jupiter return	This is the next level from what happened at 18. It's the most important cycle for restructuring your life to avoid a breakdown at 42.
42: V year, Uranus opposition	A time to seek liberation and the removal of limitations in order to embrace spirituality, social justice, and humanitarian pursuits. Be careful to not blow up your life to dethrone your parents. Check what happened at 14 and 28 to see what you're really trying to escape from. This is also related to the 21 N year.
48—-52: Chiron return N year Jupiter return	This is your return home. You will make yourself and your spirituality the priority. You may first go through grief or have an existential crisis because you realize your mortality and have no clear purpose or meaningful legacy. The Jupiter return at 24 should be directly related to this return home.

54: Rahu-Ketu	Check what happened at 18 and 36; this year is an extension of those cycles.
56: V year	This is the first response after the Uranus opposition, the freedom year, and the 48 to 52. At this point, you should have established a spiritual practice and perhaps chosen a spiritual teacher. See what themes from 14, 28, and 42 you still haven't dethroned. This is directly related to what you started at 28. Here you should find a midpoint between the responsibility you assumed at 28 and what you tried freeing yourself from at 42.

60: Jupiter Return	The start of leaving a legacy. Ask yourself, What are my two top values? See where you can leave a legacy linked to those values. Go back to 14-16 and see how those values differ from what you were taught in childhood and how you're raising consciousness around those values. This is coming full circle from age 12, a time to finally dethrone your parents and do it differently. This is the seventh gate, the removal of the seventh veil, and owning your prostitute. Meet your good-bad inner child (midpoint) here and get your F*** on! Prepare for the 11th truth and liberation from the body at 84.
63: Saturn N year	Review themes from the snow-globe, 21, 35, and 49.
70: Saturn V year	Review themes from 14, 28, 42, and 56. This should relate back to your 33—35: the Jesus years. Whatever you broke down there should be rebuilt on your truths and values.
72: Jupiter-Rahu-Ketu	Review themes from 18, 36, and 54—especially 36.

77: Saturn N year	Review themes from the snow-globe, 21, 35, 49, and 63.
84: Jupiter return Uranus Return	This should culminate your spiritual adulting. Beyond 84, enjoy the progress you've made and give back to humanity. Whatever you deconstructed at 42 is totally disintegrated here.

Appendix B:
List of Houses in Astrology

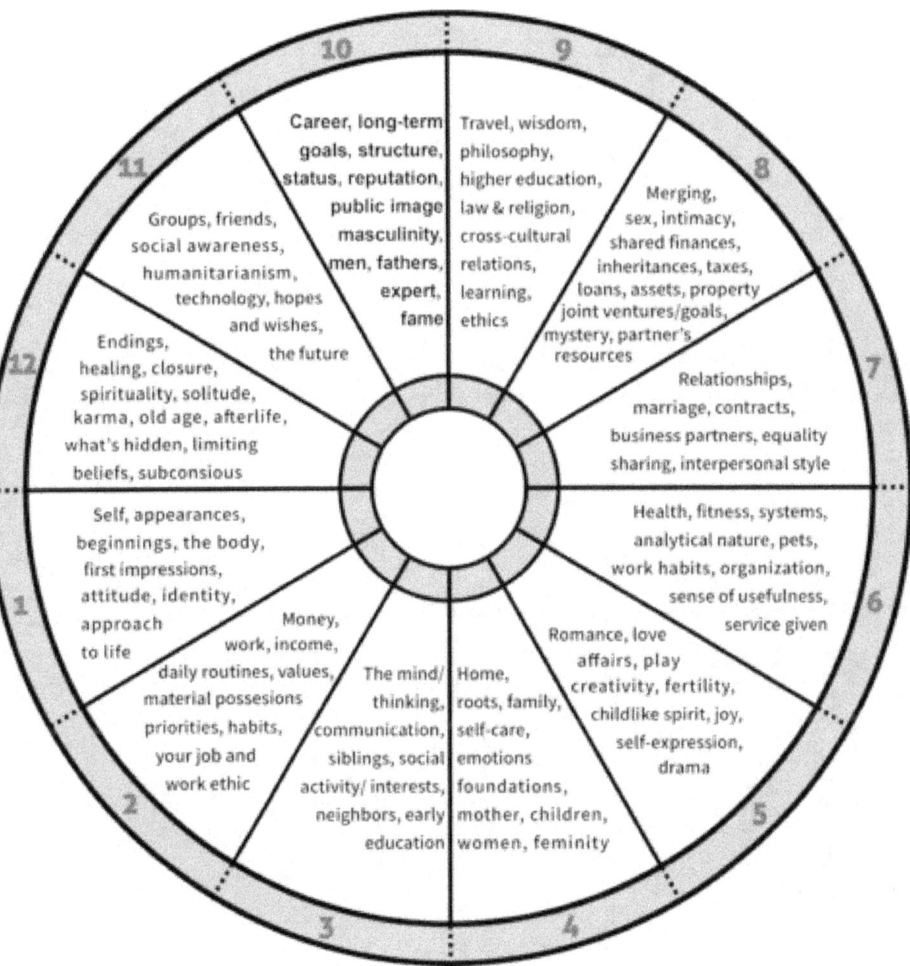

APPENDIX C:
Signs and the Decanates

Sign	0-10 degrees	10-20 degrees	20-30 degrees
Aries	Mars	Sun	Jupiter
Taurus	Venus	Mercury	Saturn
Gemini	Mercury	Venus	Uranus
Cancer	Moon	Pluto	Neptune
Leo	Sun	Jupiter	Mars
Virgo	Mercury	Saturn	Venus
Libra	Venus	Uranus	Mercury
Scorpio	Pluto	Neptune	Moon
Sagittarius	Jupiter	Mars	Sun
Capricorn	Saturn	Venus	Mercury
Aquarius	Uranus	Mercury	Venus
Pisces	Neptune	Moon	Pluto

APPENDIX D:
"I Like Thin Crust" Worksheet (Example)

Parental Values	The value you're trying to dethrone. (In the example below, the waste of eating out.)	What you learned around this issue. How you can do it differently in a 48 to 52.

What parental value bothered you at 14-16? Where did you differ or what did you fight about? Were you exposed to something new and liked that way of doing things—which was different from how your parents did it?	My parents didn't eat out, didn't throw food out, and had leftovers. The neighbors would get take-out and didn't eat the leftovers.	Mom: Good food is about giving yourself a chance to stay healthy when you're not eating out. Dad: Why waste money? You are simply paying for Convenience. Client: I need to be more financially responsible. I prefer to not be ordering out all the time. I see it as a treat, a reward. My 48 to 52 is once a week.
How did you repeat this story at 28-30?	I would eat fast food when I would drink.	

How did you repeat it at 42? This is an attempt to liberate yourself from your parents in your psyche, so you make an impulsive purchase, a drastic change, seek a new relationship, and so on, that's totally different than the norm. This is linked to the 14-16 value you tried to dethrone.	I am more like my mom now. I eat leftovers and go to the grocery store.	
How did you repeat it at 56?		
How did you repeat it at 70?		

How did you repeat it at 84?		

Neutralizers Worksheet (Example)

A neutralizer appears to help you dethrone your parents.	Example	What you learned around this issue. How you can do it differently in a 48 to 52.
Based on a value you observed at 14-16, what neutralizer showed up at 21-23 to help you do it differently?	I moved out on my own and didn't eat well.	I would wake up and feel bad. It started to affect my energy levels.
How did you repeat this story at 35-37?	I started traveling for work. I went back and forth eating well and poorly. I went through phases when I was fantastic and others when I was a disaster—which had to do with whether I was drinking. There was no balance.	I would beat myself up, but it didn't stop me from doing it again.

How did you repeat it at 49-51?		
How did you repeat it at 63?		

How did you repeat it at 77?		
How did you repeat it at 91?		

Spiritual Growth Worksheet: Jupiter Cycles (Example)

Dethroning Your Parents	Area to Dethrone	Your Jupiter Cycles
At 12, you realize that your parents aren't gods—they're imperfect—and you can dethrone them. Spiritual growth cycles show up to help you.	Name an example of that.	What did you learn every 12 years around this topic? How did you do it differently? What's the midpoint between mother and father? What does 48 to 52 look like?

At 12, what did you realize about your parents?	Annoyed with my dad for not being friendlier. If I had friends over, and they say, "Hey Coach," he wouldn't respond.	I'm friendly, I smile, I say "Hey there." I became my mom. My sister said I had to start saying "Hi" to people because I was shy. My 48 to 52 is to not go out of my way to say hello, but if someone tries to communicate with me, then respond.
How did you change around this theme at 24-26?	I was over-the-top friendly. I was the Mr. Nice Guy.	Because I was super insecure, scared to death of people not liking me. But I didn't like myself.
How did you change around this theme at 36-38?	I found a good middle-ground. I didn't go out of my way, but I wasn't a jerk.	
How did you change around this theme at 48—-50?		

How did you change around this theme at 60-62?		
How did you repeat it at 72-74?		
How did you repeat it at 84-86?		

Appendix G:
Twelve Truths to Spiritual Adulting

*You will repeat Truths One & Six
daily until your last breath.*

CATEGORY 1: AWARENESS

*TRUTH ONE: THE TRUTH OF THOUGHTS

Controlling of thoughts; observing thoughts

Use a personal TED Talk (Thoughts, Emotions, Desires) to observing
and control your thoughts. Anytime an upsetting thought enters your
consciousness ask yourself "what don't I like about it?" The answer
is a judgement you have about yourself. Identifying that you have in
the past, present or future been or are capable of being that thought
(judgement) returns the judgement back to you and off of the other
person or the situation. Processing the thought this way diffuses conflict and keeps the impure thoughts from materializing as illness or
conflict in your life. We equate the spiritual path with "leaving home,"
not physically but in our thoughts. Control your thoughts, observe
your thoughts. Keep a journal of what you say, when, and to whom.
For one full day, pay attention to your thoughts: the quality of your
thoughts and the vibration of your thoughts. Did you blame someone? Did you judge others? This is useful information about yourself.
Don't judge it. Write it all down so you can really start to observe your
inner dialogue. Inner dialogue speaks to your inner child and reflects
the quality of your life. You created it. The first step of any practice

is to restrain one's speech, otherwise we stay in child, justifying our actions and asking permission for who we can be. Name your inner child. Create an altar or space for him or her.

Know that you will need to revisit this first truth – as well as Truth Six – every day. Mastering these two truths will be an ongoing challenge until your last breath. You will self-sabotage to honor your low-level consciousness at all points of the spiritual adulting process until Truth Twelve. This first truth is also where you ask yourself, Where is my story serving me? We all have unmet needs, and we create stories around our cracked snowglobe to reaffirm that we are worthless – or whatever message you learned from 0 to 7.

Truth Two: The Truth of Desire

Create space for spirit and matter, equally

Identify judgements (from Truth 1 above) and link them to one of your vices. Every judgement is linked to a vice. When you identify a thought in step one, ask yourself could it be categorized as which of the following:In every culture, there is room for the Spirit. It may be a closet or a shelf, but the Spirit has importance in each person's life. In your own personal space, create a place for your Spirit. Decorate it or not – it's up to you. The point is to honor the Spirit as equal to matter. Make room in your day for the Spirit just as you do for food, sleep, sex, and work. Slowly build the amount of time you dedicate to your Spirit each day. This honors your Spirit as well as your inner child.

1. Pride/Vanity
2. Gluttony
3. Envy
4. Lust
5. Greed
6. Sloth

7.   Wrath

Once you identify which vice it is linked to you can link it back to an impure thought from conception, pregnancy, birth or 0-7. This step simply reminds you that you're human, conceived on desire and you can still have self-worth and self-love despite having vices and desires.

As Westerners, we value materialism, so stop negating it! That judgment doesn't serve you. It's a child script and false. You aren't bad because you want money, time, and resources. So, stop "pilfering" them and simply value them. Once you own your love of comfort and abundance, you no longer have to live in scarcity. But remember to balance that with spirit.

Truth Three: The Truth of Breath

Breathe, slow down, observe your judgements, find a spiritual teacher, mirror

After you process your thoughts with the personal TED talk above and then identify judgements, take a breath and see where you feel the emotion in the body. If you need extra help, write the emotion on a piece of paper and roll it on the body and see where you feel it. Expand the emotion and sensation and breath through the emotion fully, releasing the negative identification with the source of the emotion.Don't just observe your thoughts but stop to think about them. Pay attention to patterns you have, both from the past and those you are repeating in the present. If, for example, you have judgements about others, you have judgments about yourself. This is called "mirroring." Take a breath before saying something. Catch yourself when thinking negatively. Can you stop the negative self-talk and say it differently in a less negative way? Breathe and pay attention. Raise the vibration of your thoughts.

The lungs are represented by the child. We take our first breath as we leave our mother's body and become a separate entity. When we get anxious or scared or talk fast, we stop breathing and return to child.

The practice of learning to breathe and paying attention will influence the type of teacher you may seek on your journey. Be sure that the teacher you choose is living the truth he/she preaches and isn't making false promises. Look at their life. Does it resemble their teachings? Do they promise you easy techniques for spiritual awakening? There are no easy techniques.

Lastly, schedule a breath – a break – in your life. Don't ask for permission. The world will continue without you. If you don't schedule it yourself, the Universe will do it for you, and possibly through a physical or mental breakdown. Practice ho'oponopono – the Hawaiian practice of reconciliation and forgiveness. Taking responsibility for yourself and the world you live in is a great exercise in developing spiritual maturity.

Truth Four: The Truth of Intuition

Intuition development

Each day, set a timer for a specific time. When that timer goes off, whatever you're hearing, thinking, or saying in that moment is guidance. What is it telling you and where can you apply it? Intuition is a subtle art – but can become a roar once you know how to listen. Most of us react to a situation out of instinct, impulse, or fear. Instinct comes from the reptilian brain, previous trauma, and subconscious programming. Our subconscious gets stuck at a point of trauma, and we don't grow from there unless we first take a breath and objectively evaluate a situation. This is the intellect at work. It's the first step. I recommend contacting the Akashic records – the "peer-reviewed journal" of the intuitive arts. You can take a class or teach yourself how to access those records through books or online.

The next step is transmuting that intellect into intuition and then applying what we learn, which is wisdom. When you start listening to your inner voice, you start dialing down out the noise and discover what the Universe is really saying. I recommend getting a symbol dictionary and/or learning about myth and metaphor. This is the language of the Universe. Also, Intuitive or psychic development is not the same as high consciousness. Your intuition will only be as clear as your level of consciousness. If you are living in chaos and child, that's the quality of guidance you'll get. Raise your vibration and your guidance will get much clearer.

Category 2: INTEGRATION

Truth Five: The Truth of Ego, Personality & Self-Love

Identifying the masks you wear and why you created that personality. To compensate for…what?

Here we start paying attention to the personality we' have created – the masks we wear – as a false way ofto getting our needs met. We all wear masks, all the time. This may change your vibration, but your essence doesn't change. You may be acting falsely as learned behavior despite your essence being something else entirely.Initiate a spiritual STD (say, think, do). Start harmonizing what you Say, Think, and Do. When you do, you honor your soul and divine will, which leads to self-love, rather than the ego and personality which make you feel disconnected from your purpose and others..

I recommend identifying the distribution of air, earth, water, and fire in your astrology chart to see which element is lacking or in excess and how you may be overcompensating for that. (You can find this free online.) You can also take a personality test like the Myers-Briggs Type Indicator. Are you more of a thinker or feeler? How is your balance of masculine and feminine energies?

Upgrade your diet and exercise choices. Purify your body with a daily routine.

Pick one behavior related to your health to include in your life in a balanced way. Try to avoid all or nothing behavior. When overdoing a behavior you deem negative (i.e., sex, cake, drinking) ask yourself, how did my parents reward themselves? Punish themselves? We often choose our "purification" and "punishment" behaviors linked to what our parents did. We all castrate one parent – the one who has the power, the one who holds the gold. To honor Truth Six, you must inventory what you don't like about that parent, mourn the reality that you have those exact qualities, and start your shadow work. Your imbalance and strife come from not accepting that the qualities you dislike in that parent, which inevitably show up in your children, partners, and other people, are mirrored in yourself. This is an important time to take a break and grieve what you have created in your life – the suffering you've chosen to avoid rewriting the script, to pretend there is nothing going on.

This is also a time for shifting your diet and adding physical exercise to recharge your body and mind, support the changes you are making in your thoughts, and balance your elements. For instance, I lack Earth, so I eat root vegetables like beets and sweet potatoes. An Ayurvedic practitioner would be a great resource here.

We use our thoughts and our body to punish ourselves while honoring our parents' low vibration. For example, you will use food or another coping strategy to stay in child with your mother and honor the "feminine" at a low vibration. Instead, swap the low-vibration coping skill of your mother for a high-vibration "muse." Identify how your mother may have pampered herself or self-sabotaged; honor her at the midpoint between those two. Develop a pattern or behavior into a high-level consciousness "art form" around your mother and the feminine.

During your life, you will seek material pleasures – or other "masculine" pursuits – to honor your father. How did he show up to prove he was a "man"? This pattern will be repeated in your psyche in the way you get validation. For a high-vibration version of the father, set some limits and boundaries. Use your energy to create a new a structure around these patterns.

Truth Seven: The Truth of Balance & Fun

Stop the pendulum swings of your thoughts and behaviors. Track their cycles. Return home to the self.

In the third step of the TED talk, you Iidentify the ways you try to prove you are unworthy, unlovable, abandoned, broken, or not enough. Give that limiting belief a 0, find the exact opposite and name it 100, then find your 48 to 52 and name that. For instance, scarcity (0) / abundance (100) / efficiency (48 to 52). Inadequate (0) / perfect (100) / sufficient (48 to 52). Now define your 48 to 52 with three measurable and observable terms to show that you are living in balance. In these ways, you stop the pendulum swings of your thoughts and behaviors and return home to the self. Engage in at least one behavior that has no outcome other than creativity, fun and play. This truth is about working toward equanimity and the 48 to 52. We all have four basic needs: safety/security, emotional protection, validation, and love. Love is everyone's main unmet need, but be sure to focus on the other three. Are you constantly seeking validation? Are you in fight-flight to get your safety needs met?

Pick a word that describes your main theme in life and give that a 0. Then name the opposite extreme and assign it 100. Then find and name your 48 to 52. For example: scarcity (0), abundance (100), sufficient (48 to 52). Inadequate (0), perfection (100), enough (48 to 52). The main goal of your spiritual path is to use your thoughts, elements, personality, and intuition to find and live your 48 to 52.

Here's another exercise: List five qualities you like about yourself. Now list the opposite five. For instance, if you like to be calm, the opposite is anger. The five qualities you dislike represent the unhealthy measuring rod you are holding your inner child to. Name this child – the one with the five qualities you don't like. Anytime these qualities come out, slap her with a ruler, but then love her and listen to her. She will tell you what she feels and ask you why you don't let her come out to play.

Truth Eight: The Truth of the Shadow

Shadow Work – Bringing the bad buckets and aspects of yourself that you've repressed to conscious awareness and integrating them

Here you bring to conscious awareness the bad buckets and aspects of yourself that you've repressed and integrate them. This begins your return home to Self. This is the beginning of transmutation, when we you raise your vibration. It starts by listing all the things you didn't like about your mother and father. This is your shadow. If you've responded by doing the exact opposite in your life, you are still in child and not bringing light to the shadow. Truth Eight is oftentimes linked to Truth Two. Are you still hiding the vices? Pretending to be hardworking by excessive work to cover a sloth tendency? Shadow work is owning the darkest aspects of yourself, you deem unlovable. These are often projections onto other people as judgements and criticisms, when in reality they're about ourselves. If we think we can solve a problem at the same level of vibration it was created, we won't. To start, I invite you to ask your parents or family members about your moment of conception, your pregnancy, and your birth story. If that isn't possible, write down what happened to you between the ages of 0 to 7. Most of us have a few clear memories of that time in our life. Perhaps a sibling was born, a grandmother died, or you changed schools or where you lived. Write it all down.

Also, describe what you remember about yourself as a child as well as how others described you. The more information, the better. What you experienced from 0 and 7 will be the scenario you keep recreating in your life every seven years. For instance, I got in trouble for making a mess in our neighbor's pool and was kicked out of joining in on my family's Monday night ceremonies. And so every seven years I create some kind of mess that will get me kicked out of someplace. It could be a move, a divorce, a friendship, or a job. I may leave on my own accord or get dumped, but I created the situation to honor that story. This is the depth of subconscious programming. Without an awareness of such patterns, there can be no true change.

Truth Eight requires you to enter the swamp of the subconscious. NO TRUE SPIRITUAL GROWTH WILL OCCUR WITHOUT THIS STEP. I have free resources on my website as well as a YouTube channel and podcast to help you discover your subconscious patterns.

CATEGORY 3: DO IT DIFFERENTLY
(DETHRONE YOUR PARENTS)

TRUTH NINE: THE TRUTH OF WISDOM & MENTORSHIP

Identifying the external environment is giving you clues and guidance at all times.

Read one wisdom text for six weeks and see how the information influences different areas of your life. Seek to understand what you learn and apply it with heart to your life. Offer to mentor someone in an area of expertise you possess. This is the truth of synchronicity. Here you begin to see the connection between what is happening outside and inside of you and use it as guidance. A speeding motorcycle reflects racing thoughts or that you are going too fast. A messy environment reflects inner chaos. Everything is a mirror to your inner state. This step can profoundly change your life and elevate your intuitive skills to a new level.

There is a rule I share when teaching the Akashic Records: "Respond to all information given." Truth Nine is same concept. Pay attention! The Universe is talking to you at all times. Previous steps of listening to your thoughts, creating space for Spirit, knowing your subconscious patterns, and knowing that you've created everything in your life, culminate here. Pay attention and apply everything! The Universe doesn't waste a moment. It all has meaning.

Here you merge with universal consciousness and realize that everything is connected. Your brain synapses are firing. You are remembering details from your childhood and making connections. You soak up EVERYTHING as guidance; nothing escapes you. However, don't think that you are changing the world or can teach something to someone. Being the "teacher" or the "guru" by talking is not the point. This is merely the next step toward silence.

Truth Ten: The Truth of Silence

Silence, pilgrimage and contemplation

This is the step of silence and pilgrimage. You can make a small, silent pilgrimage in your hometown to your favorite temple or church or homeless shelter. You can also walk a labyrinth – my favorite way of contemplative practice. Here you clear your mind of all thoughts and how they relate to others. You will still have dogma, judgements, and criticisms, but you begin to merge with universal consciousness. You begin to see how you created your life and are trying to remain in child. You stop preaching; you live your truth, a truth that speaks for itself. When you find yourself talking or thinking, gently let it go. Eventually, in Truths Eleven and Twelve, you will transcend your thoughts. This is the step of silence and pilgrimage. In previous steps, you were preaching, teaching, perhaps talking about your spiritual growth, and having circles and ceremonies with friends. You've written the blogs or the books, you've offered the classes, people know what you believe. However, the changes up until now were to prepare you to vibrate at this higher level. Those who might be thinking of learning from or following you will make their decision by what you vibrate – whether you are living the teachings and not just teaching the teachings.

Teachings are taught in silence. Many spiritual aspirants think they are here to save the world, but they can't even save themselves. Prior to now, you've been learning about yourself. You have offered nothing to anyone other than maybe a word or advice that you your-self needed, but you are not a healer. That's the purpose of the first nine truths – to heal. Truth Ten states that it's time to start helping humanity because you have now transmuted into a higher-vibration being. Only when you return home and know your true self can you begin this step. Your external circumstances have changed, and you are living your truth. You are silent because no preaching is necessary. Everyone sees who and what you are. Here you begin the last three steps, each focused on helping others.

I have made many pilgrimages, such as to Fatima and Lourdes among others. You can do a pilgrimage in your hometown to your favorite temple or church or a homeless shelter. You can also walk a labyrinth, my favorite way of contemplative practice. Here, your thoughts and how they relate to others are clear. You will still have dogma, judgements, and criticisms, but you have merged with the universal consciousness. You that you have created it all and under-stand why something is showing up in your life. You stop preaching. You are living your truth, which speaks for itself. If you do find your-self talking, it is simply to state the certainty of your dogma and your theories and owning them as a boundary. But eventually, in Truths Eleven and Twelve, even this has to be transcended.

Truth Eleven: The Truth of Service

Serving humanity

It is now time to help humanity and be of service. You cannot get here unless you have observed and controlled your thoughts, grown your inner child, cultivated daily time to with your Spirit, balanced your energies, understood your subconscious, unified your consciousness with intellect and intuition, and transmuted your vibration to a higher state of being.

Your service to humanity can happen in three ways: unselfish service, self-sacrifice for others, and group work – but never at the expense of self. This is service that serves you and the other, equally. Your truth is your truth; you don't impose it on others. All dogma is transcended here. Everyone's No one's "truth" is validbetter than another's;. yours no longer supersedes anyone else's. This is the return to love.

Truth Twelve: The Truth of Unity & Universal Consciousness

Unity with universal consciousness; no separation between Self with others; an intact snowglobe despite being in the body

This is where Spirit rules matter. We've now come full circle. We left home, found balance, returned home, understood what our life has been and the role we've played in it, forgivenave ourselves and, forgave others, and learned compassion and empathy. In Truths 11 and 12, wWe begian to develop our Buddha or Christ consciousness and discovered who we truly are. We are ready to serve without expectations.

Here there are no judgements, criticisms, or beliefs that you are better than anyone or anyone is better than you. You don't need a parent because you understand that you are the Universe, and the Universe is you. This is a return to universal consciousness – the real womb and the real, un-cracked snowglobe. There is no hierarchy. This is true union with God or the Universe. This is your returning to the cosmic consciousness while still in the body. What started in Truth Two – the balance of spirit and matter – is now complete. There is full symbiosis.

Archetypal Spiritual Adulting Brain Map

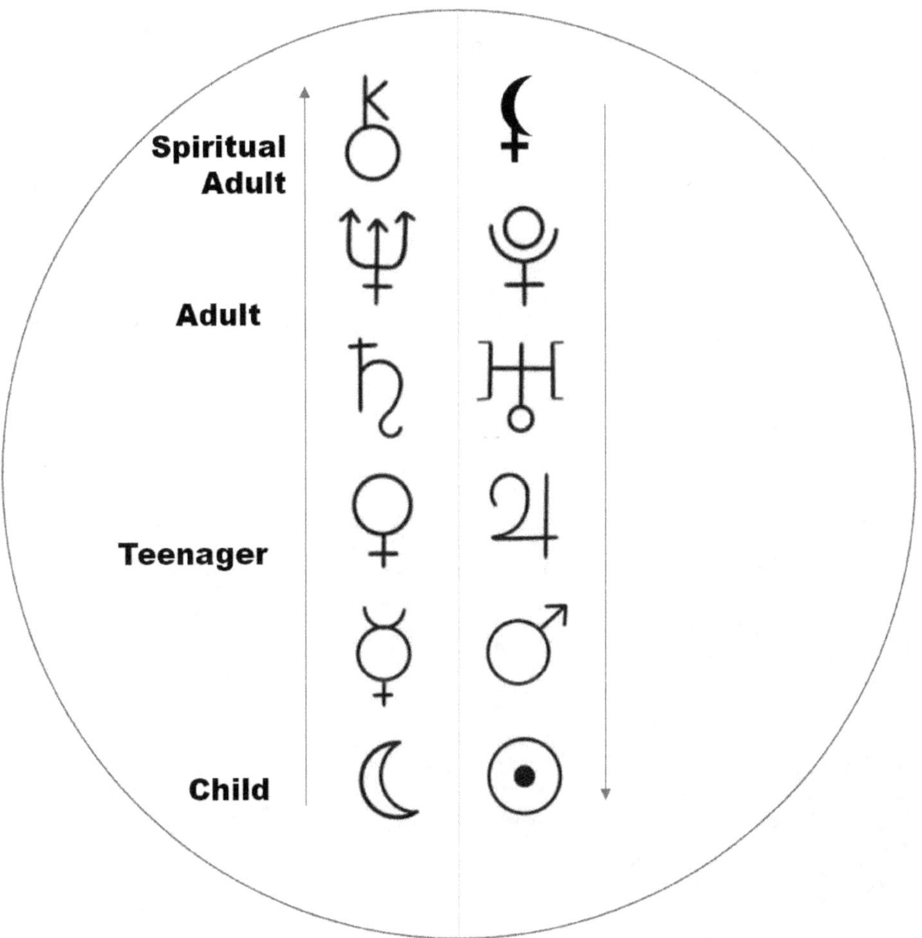

What Is a Spiritual Adult?

WHAT IS A SPIRITUAL ADULT?

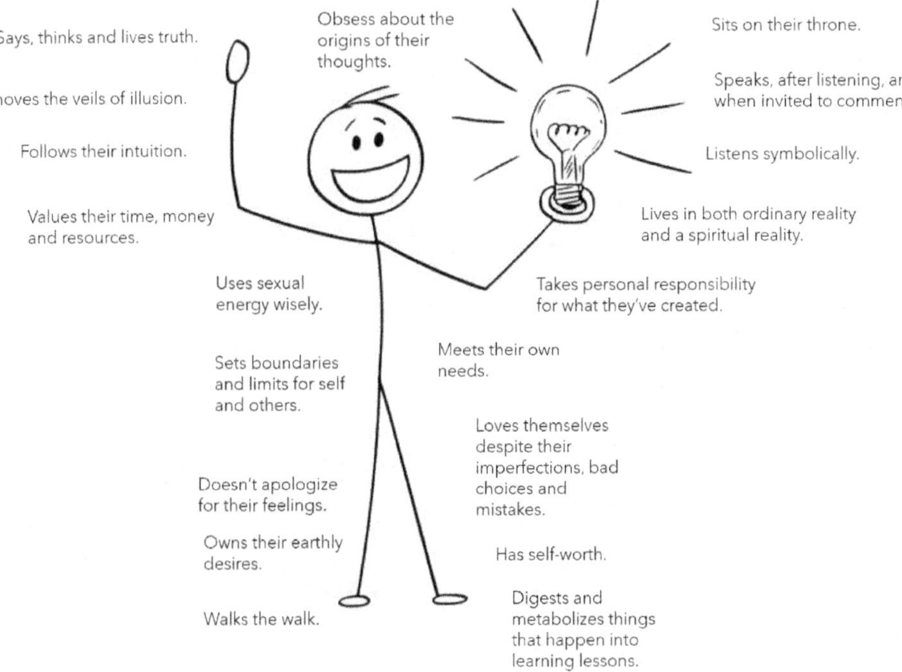

Chart of Brand Archetypes, Planetary Archetypes & Greek & Roman God Archetypes

Branding	Planetary	Greek & Roman Gods
Hero	Sun	Apollo
Creator	Mars	Mars/Athena
Seeker	Jupiter	Jupiter/Zeus
Rebel/Outlaw	Uranus	Uranus
Magician	Pluto	Pluto/Hades
Ruler	Black Moon	Hera
Caretaker/Nurturer	Moon	Artemis/Demeter
Trickster/Jester	Mercury	Mercury/Hermes
Lover	Venus	Venus/Aphrodite
Sage	Saturn	Saturn/Kronos
Innocent	Neptune	Neptune/Poseidon
Everyday Man	Chiron	Hephaestus/Hestia